KILLER

OXY

Donated by
Occidental Petroleum

MOB KILLER

Anthony M. DeStefano

PINNACLE BOOKS
Kensington Publishing Corp.

http://www.kensingtonbooks.com

Some names have been changed to protect the privacy of individuals connected to this story.

PINNACLE BOOKS are published by

Kensington Publishing Corp.
119 West 40th Street
New York, NY 10018

All Kensington titles, imprints and distributed lines are available at special quantity discounts for bulk purchases for sales promotions, premiums, fund-raising, and educational or institutional use. Special book excerpts or customized printings can also be created to fit specific needs. For details, write or phone the office of the Kensington Special Sales Manager: Kensington Publishing Corp., 119 West 40th Street, New York, NY 10018. Attn: Special Sales Department. Phone: 1-800-221-2647.

Pinnacle and the P logo Reg. U.S. Pat. & TM Off.

ISBN-13: 978-0-7860-2415-5
ISBN-10: 0-7860-2415-1

First Printing: June 2011

10 9 8 7 6 5 4 3 2 1

Printed in th

In memory of my parents:
Louise Jean and Michael William DeStefano

Contents

Introduction

"I made John Gotti dangerous."

Of all of the remarks attributed to Charles Carneglia, that has to rank as the one, made in passing to an acquaintance, that best sums up his reputation. It seems also close to the truth.

Charles—"Crazy Charles"—was one of the most feared Gambino crime family gangsters in the Gotti heyday of the 1990s. He had one of the biggest reputations for violence in the Howard Beach neighborhood, which was where much of the New York Mafia's bloody history had been spawned. Charles wasn't the only person close to the late crime boss who was feared. Salvatore "Sammy the Bull" Gravano chalked up a tally of well over a dozen murders committed for the crime family. But Gravano carried out his bloody business as just that: business. When it was done, he then could go on to be a charming gangster businessman. However, Charles impressed those who knew him in the Mob as being a volatile, scary man who carried a pent-up anger that could spill out unexpectedly. He was a man who, old friends said, was fascinated with death, something investigators said he caused in abundance.

Charles spent much of his life in East New York, a low-rent Brooklyn industrial backwater that lies along the border with Queens. The Carneglia family had a small two-story frame house on Hemlock Street. His mother, Jennie, was a seamstress; his father, William, was a blue-collar worker who was a reputed associate before his death of the late Lucchese crime boss Paul Vario. Travel west along Atlantic Avenue and Eastern Parkway and you will find predominately black communities, such as Brownsville, still struggling to emerge from decades of economic problems. Go east and the roads lead to largely white enclaves, such as Howard Beach and Ozone Park, where the homes have nicely manicured lawns and the property values always stay high.

East New York is a border zone, a buffer between two of New York City's largest and most populous areas. A place of auto salvage and junkyards, light industry and large bus terminals, it serves as a metaphor for the frightening journey Charles took in his life as a gangster. For Charles was a man caught between the old Mob and the new, the days when no one turned inform-ant and the more contemporary times when being a government witness seemed an acceptable career path.

While well-to-do brother John, who was only two years older, had the charisma that comes with being a high-ranked member of the Gambino crime family, Charles struggled. He struggled constantly to make ends meet, to gain the respect of other mobsters and acceptance into their way of life. He was weakened by chronic alcohol and drug use. Rather than try and astutely play the politics of the Mob, Charles was bedeviled by his volatile temper and found himself quarreling with friends, whom he alienated with paranoia and fear. But having a brother like John, who was respected on the street and who was close to men like John Gotti, eventually gave Charles an entrée to the Mob life he so much desired.

Mention the name Carneglia to an FBI agent or cop of a certain vintage and it will bring back memories of John, the imposing and businesslike gangster who rode the coattails of Gotti to prominence. Charles also became a member of the Gambino *borgata*, as the crime families are sometimes called, and earned his stripes with a reputation as a killer whom Gotti loved having around in his stable of criminals.

But as the younger of the two criminal siblings, Charles found himself in a different class as far as organized crime was concerned. John preceded him by over thirteen years in becoming a made man, and he was part of a group of men who came of age as criminals at a different time in the 1980s, when there was a kind of romance to the lifestyle.

Even in his personal life, Charles proved to be different. While brother John married Helene Forgione, had three kids, and lived in the Howard Beach equivalent of a house with a picket fence and a pool, Charles remained single. He bounced back and forth between sparsely furnished bachelor pads and a messy bedroom in his mother's home. Charles had some women in his life, but his erratic nature and lack of domesticity seemed to stifle his ability to relate to a woman in any sort of meaningful, committed relationship.

Instead, Charles consorted with a tough brand of girls barely out of their teenage years, but they could stick a man with a knife in a fight as well as they could slice a piece of veal. Such relationships were part of the wild, feral society a certain segment of Howard Beach typified. Pretty young women who found the gangster life attractive were plentiful in that neighborhood, and Mob men like Charles had only to show up at places like the Lindenwood Diner to find them. Most have gone on to quieter lives, working, trying to raise their children and move away from their past mistakes. Some have made it into this story, but at their request and to shield their children, I have chosen not to identify them by name.

Charles eventually was initiated into the Mafia around 1991, and while John "Senior" Gotti was still the boss, the younger Carneglia found himself under the control of Gotti's son, John A. Gotti, also known as "Junior." Nepotism was how Charles would later derisively refer to the younger Gotti's rise to power, and it no doubt made him feel like he was down a notch in the Mafia hierarchy to have to answer to the boss's son. Throughout this book, I will refer for clarity to the late crime boss as "Senior Gotti" and his son, also named John, as "Junior Gotti." I also reference to Charles by his first name to distinguish him from his brother John, who was often mixed up in his criminal life.

Straddling two generational worlds of *La Cosa Nostra,* Charles was a man who fulfilled his aspirations as a criminal with a younger crowd. While John Carneglia held himself above the more junior Mob associates, Charles seemed to gravitate toward the wild, immature, and impressionable young neighborhood men as a way of stepping out on his own. Often he would do business with them at the Lindenwood Diner, which he called the "Bat Cave," a takeoff on the secret lair of the comic character Batman. He seemed important to them in his own right, something that allowed Charles to come out from under the shadow of his older brother. "He was trying to find a place for himself," remarked one attorney who knew Charles.

The dysfunctional band of aspiring criminals who gravitated around Charles would kill when needed and cause all sorts of mayhem. But such allies held no loyalty to anyone but themselves. When the going got rough, those criminal associates of Charles would land him in some very big trouble. Some of those turncoats—"canaries," as Charles called them—would hurt not only Charles but also prove disastrous for gangsters such as Dominick "Skinny Dom" Pizzonia, and in late 2009, they would bring Junior Gotti close to spending the rest of his life in prison during his fourth, and final, trial for racketeering.

I first became familiar with the criminal career of Charles Carneglia after he was indicted, along with sixty-one other defendants, in February 2008 by a federal grand jury in Brooklyn. The pictures we saw of Charles during the roundup were those of an aging man who wore a beard that, at first glance, made him look like one of the Smith Brothers of cough drop fame. Look closer and you saw something more sinister in his eyes, as if Rasputin himself were staring back from the dark and final days of the old Russian Empire. This was a man, prosecutors charged, who killed five people, either for the most trivial of reasons or to enhance his stature with the Mob. The government intended to make this into a show trial, although most journalists quickly realized that a lot of the cases would result in guilty pleas. In fact, almost every defendant struck plea bargains—some to very good deals—as Judge Jack B. Weinstein cracked the whip and pushed the prosecution and defense attorneys

to agreements. But only one person—Charles—decided
to go to trial.

What emerged for me from the case and the evidence presented in court was a picture of a Mafia killer
who seemed to relish the art of murder and took a per-
verse delight in inflicting pain. Nineteenth-century
French theater had its Grand Guignol spectacle, where
plays about homicide and torture were regular fare.
Howard Beach had Charles as the modern-day equivalent. But unlike what Parisians had in the theater, there
were real bodies littering the streets and vacant lots
around Howard Beach. As his old homicidal associate
John Alite, often called "Johnny," would later tell the
FBI, Charles not only killed, he studied ways to do it.
There was even a book about murder that Charles kept
at his junkyard in East New York, said Alite.

Those who followed Charles's nearly two-month
trial in early 2009 heard tales of torture and slaughter that were graphic and intimate. Charles not only
stabbed some of his victims, but he also made a point
of twisting the knife to make quick work of things, witnesses said. It seemed that Charles suffered from emphysema and had to get the advantage during these
fights early, or else his victims might get the better of
him in hand-to-hand combat. One of the murders involved court officer Albert Gelb, gunned down one
night in 1976, about a year after he got Charles arrested after they both argued and fought at a Queens
diner. Another killing was that of armored-car guard
Jose Delgado Rivera, who died after a robbery at John
F. Kennedy International Airport (JFK) in December
1990. Mobster Louis DiBono was shot dead in the
World Trade Center garage in October 1990, while two

Mob associates, Salvatore "Sal" Puma and Michael Cotillo, died in knife fights, which investigators believed involved Charles.

But what really made the world take notice were stories of how Charles was the Mob's grisly mortician, using acid not only to torture his victims but also to dispose of human remains. That was what the FBI said happened to John Favara at the hands of Charles. Favara was the man who had the misfortune in 1980 of running over one of the elder John Gotti's children. Favara's murder and disappearance wasn't part of the case against Charles, but it was resurrected as prosecutors tried to show how he relished cruelty toward his victims and was prepared to carry out the most astonishing desecrations of the bodies of murder victims in his desire to please his Mob bosses.

Other stories surfaced of how Charles took the malodorous, biological slurry that resulted from the acid baths he gave a Mob murder victim's remains and dumped it into the sewers of East New York. For all of those reasons, many in Howard Beach, including those in the Mob, feared Charles and avoided him, preferring to stay away from the "Barn," a ramshackle building in East New York that had the reputation of being a local house of horrors. "If the walls could talk," Charles once said to Kevin McMahon, his younger sidekick.

Charles also drank and used drugs to such an extent that people said they could never be sure which personality would emerge. "If he was in a good mood, he was happy," said Charles's old criminal partner Peter "Bud" Zuccaro. "If he was in a bad mood, he would be in a bad mood, you know, he would be irritable." If he had a knife or a gun in his hands, there could be big trouble, some feared.

The trial covered a broad swath of time, from the early 1970s until the very day everybody was arrested in 2008. Howard Beach and its surrounding communities, like Ozone Park and Lindenwood, aren't very large in area, but they seemed from the testimony to be places that were as wild and as deadly as the worst blocks of Harlem or Washington Heights in the bloody crack-cocaine scourge of the 1980s. There was testimony about a mind-numbing series of stabbings, shootings, drug deals, hijackings, shakedowns, murders, and Mafia double crosses. A good Mob scorecard was needed to keep the players straight, since many of them weren't household names. The hit television show *Desperate Housewives* could have had a field day plumbing the trial for some fresh material. There were allusions to Mafia love affairs, domestic violence, and tales of a soccer mom who turned into the neighborhood's own mini version of Bernard Madoff, scamming her neighbors and friends to supplement the millions of dollars generated by her Mob associate husband in his own frauds.

In a very real sense, Charles's tale is the story that serves as the conclusion to the John Gotti era. Although Senior Gotti died in prison of cancer in June 2002, the hierarchy he assembled in the Gambino family persisted for some years afterward. But one by one, Senior Gotti's relatives and subordinates who were the power base of his Queens operation were picked off by prosecutors and consigned upon conviction to various terms of prison. Junior Gotti, who for a time was the direct supervisor of Charles, and knew many of the same criminals he did, insisted he dropped out of the Mob life by the time his father died in 2002. It was an argument that worked and appeared to have caused four juries to fail to agree on whether he was a racketeer—at least within the five years preceding his last indictment.

So it was Charles's 2009 trial that served as the coda, the final statement in the history of Gotti's flawed empire. Interwoven into this tale are the lives of so many who were part of Mafia lore and the Gambino family's last hurrah. Like the Bayeux Tapestry, the embroidered cloth that tells some of England's history through the Norman Conquest, Charles's story involved major points in modern Mafia history through the fall of Gotti and beyond. The story involved characters from the days of the Gallo Wars in the 1960s, the movie *Goodfellas*, and sensational crimes like the fabled Lufthansa heist of 1978. It encompassed the assassination of Paul Castellano in December 1985, as well as street slayings that hardly anyone noticed. Gotti's power and his murderous agenda all combined to push Charles further along in the Mafia and brought him into contact with the old men of the Gambino family.

Strange as it sounds, Charles actually had things about him that made him seem decent. There are those in Howard Beach today who strongly believe he would be the most loyal and caring of friends—provided he liked you, of course. One endearing trait was the way he adored his infirm mother, Jennie. Bedridden and with impaired memory later in life, Jennie became the main focus of her son's energy, at least when he wasn't in prison. He would dress Jennie, make her meals, arrange for her care, and kiss her before she went to bed. "He said it was the least he could do for her after putting up with him and his brother," said one woman who befriended Charles. It also seemed that Charles had a soft spot when it came to young children, particularly the toddlers. After a custody dispute arose about a child among some relatives, he tried to cool the heated arguments within the family and said, "This is a child here, not a piece of baloney." Spotting his friend Jodi Ryan in a park, Charles would stop his car and come and play with her kids.

The late John Gotti once bragged that there would be a *Cosa Nostra* not only till the day he died, but for the next one hundred years. Gotti died in June 2002, and, yes, the *Cosa Nostra* continues to this day. But it is hardly the *Cosa Nostra* that Gotti imagined when a surveillance bug caught him making that grand pronouncement about the Mob's longevity. Many of Senior Gotti's class of gangsters are either dead, incarcerated, or in the witness security and witness protection programs as cooperators with the U.S. government. One of the most promising career paths now in Howard Beach, one mobster's son wryly observed, was to become a confidential informant (CI).

The younger leaders of the *Cosa Nostra* have been for years trying to regroup and work with new members, who simply don't have the street smarts or experience to work effectively as criminals. This wasn't the Mob Charles or his brother, John, owed allegiance to for so many years. There was not loyalty among thieves. Sitting in federal court, Charles represented a link to the short-lived empire Senior Gotti tried to create and the modern band of aspiring wiseguys who were always struggling to keep one step ahead of the FBI. As this book was being written, federal prosecutors in Manhattan arrested a number of Gambino crime members in April 2010 on charges that were labeled as "sex trafficking" on the Internet, but the allegations really amounted to the pimping of prostitutes, some of whom were underage. We had not seen the Mob in this kind of sex business since the days of Charles "Lucky" Luciano, who in the 1930s reaped the profits of a widespread prostitution business and did it in style, living at the Waldorf-Astoria and dining at then-posh restaurants like Delmonico's.

Aging and laboring with his breathing problems, Charles Carneglia seemed to step back from the Mob life in his later years. After getting out of federal prison in 2006 for an extortion conviction, Charles tried to spend his time away from the Gambino crime family, his only luxury being occasional dinners at Carosello Restaurant, the family-style trattoria across the street from the palatial Russo's On The Bay catering hall, just a few blocks from where he lived with Jennie. He would try in vain to argue in court that, like Junior Gotti, he had abandoned the Mob life so far back that the racketeering law no longer covered what he allegedly did years ago.

But crimes as serious as murder are too significant for the government to let go by, particularly when they involve the Mob. The New York Police Department (NYPD) Cold Case Unit had too many gangland slayings to ignore that led them straight to Charles, no matter how quiet a life he lived. As decent as he was to those he knew and liked, the stories that emerged about murder, dismemberment, and the keeping of gruesome trophies made Charles seem like the Norman Bates character from Alfred Hitchcock's *Psycho*.

Charles Carneglia had a life that for long stretches of time seemed to be very domestic and even boring as he puttered around Jennie's house in Howard Beach, only to be interrupted by unexpected moments of wild fury and death. He seemed to have dueling personalities, with the dark side ultimately overpowering his humanity.

Anthony DeStefano
New York, June 2010

1

"What's with the Beard?"

Looking like oversized cigars, police battering rams are made of steel and weigh about thirty-five pounds. When swung by just one man, they can generate a shattering forty thousand pounds of force. They can punch a hole through concrete, crack a rib, or even shatter a skull.

The devices go by the trade names of Stinger and Thunderbolt—there is not a front door in Howard Beach that could stand up to them.

Bracing himself outside the front of the two-story residence on Eighty-fifth Street on the morning of February 7, 2008, FBI special agent Greg Hagarty wondered whether he could breach the entrance with just one slam of the battering ram he held in his hands. A one-shot entry with the ram was the gold standard for SWAT team members. Hagarty, a sandy-haired man who favored crew cuts, swung the ram backward and then, with a sharp forward movement, accelerated the stubby device into the front door.

Bam. Nothing. The door held up to the first of Hagarty's swings. It took another smash before the wood door frame splintered and the door swung open on its hinges in the predawn darkness. *I'll have to work on my swing,* a bemused Hagarty thought.

Early-morning breach entries of this sort were not common during law enforcement operations in this particular Queens, New York, neighborhood. True, Howard Beach, a white enclave near the Atlantic Ocean, had a reputation for being a Mafia haven. Known as Census Block 869, the neighborhood was almost entirely white. The well-manicured front lawns with the occasional religious sculptures and mini-mansions of Mediterranean style bespoke of its heavy Italian-American population. More residents here graduated high school than in many other city neighborhoods, but the same wasn't true of college. Most of those who worked had varied jobs of regular obscurity as teachers, construction workers, realtors, office administrators, lawyers, and accountants. Then there were those who made their living as wiseguys, the mobsters whom everybody knew.

Over the years, the FBI SWAT teams had arrested a number of gangsters here. But for the most part, takedowns were done with the agents knocking on the door in the early hours before dawn to announce their presence and taking their quarry away peacefully. All of the men in the Mob knew the value of a bad reputation, which was how they wielded power. Bosses like John Gotti and Joseph Massino mixed brutality and business in a balance that made them both feared and respected. Then there were those like Charles Carneglia whose value in life seemed to be measured solely by his bad reputation.

It was that reputation—there were allegations of at least five murders and claims that Charles was always armed to the teeth—that prompted Hagarty and the rest of the FBI team, which gathered at the Dunkin' Donuts on Cross Bay Boulevard in the hours when the coffee wasn't even warm, to don protective vests, ready their own weapons, and take along the battering ram for a surprise entry. After all, this was a man whose neighbors said he used to keep a life-sized poster of the Ayattolah Khomeini in his garage. It didn't seem prudent to the agents in this particular case to try and announce themselves with a polite knock.

After Hagarty made quick work in the breach entry of the door, other armed agents, who were stacked in line behind him, rushed inside. One of them stood among the splintered wood of the broken door to secure the foyer, while others scrambled up the stairs to the living area. Charles was said to have guns and knives stashed all over the house: in dresser drawers, in cupboards, and on windowsills. Informants said he even crafted silencers out of two-liter plastic soda bottles. But the agents saw nothing. It was safe. Gary Pontecourvo, the FBI team leader, went back outside.

"Clear," he said to the four men arrayed around the smashed door.

Detective Steve Kaplan, a burly man with a shaven head, took the lead and led the others up the stairway toward the living area and bedrooms. One of the agents from the team had already pulled a sleepy Charles, clad in a T-shirt and underwear, from his messy bedroom, where clothes littered the floor, and sat him down on a couch in the living room as Hagarty looked on.

With the last vestiges of sleep gone from his eyes, Charles glanced up at a familiar face. Eight years earlier, Hagarty had to arrest him on a different case. It was also one of those times when Charles was roused from a deep sleep in his bachelor pad near the airport. His ears plugged to ward off the noise of jetliners and his eyes covered with black eyeshades, Charles was oblivious that day to the agent's banging on the door. It was only after Hagarty climbed over a fire escape to rap on a window and yell out his name that Charles let him inside. This time, Hagarty didn't need to let the door stand in his way. Charles didn't like the unannounced approach.

"Hagarty, what are you doing that you had to break down my fucking door?" an irate Charles said. If he had known it was his old case agent, Charles said, he would have let him in without a fuss.

"Charles, this is not my case. I had to do it," replied Hagarty.

Faced with Charles's reputation as a stone-cold killer for the Gambino crime family, the FBI didn't want to take a chance that he might react violently to the approach of the agents. Any criminal in his right mind *wouldn't* try to battle it out with armed FBI agents carrying M-4 tactical assault rifles and protected by bulletproof vests. But Charles wasn't often in his right mind. He abused a lot of cocaine, became paranoid, and lived in a fantasy world in which he saw constant threats. If he wasn't doing drugs, Charles would drink to excess. His favorite libation was Cutty Sark whiskey. "Sinking the ship" was how friends described his binges when Charles polished off bottles of scotch. The drinking at times left him loud, obnoxious, and aggressive. Mix that type of personality with a gun, knife, or an ice pick, and there is no telling what would happen.

However, the commotion that soon erupted didn't come from Charles. Hagarty heard a woman's voice, crying out in fear.

"Oh, my God!" the woman yelled.

"Oh, my God!" she said over and over again.

The sudden, ferocious destruction of the door and the sight of the menacing armed men taking over the home stunned Elsie, the live-in aide whose job it was to take care of Jennie, the elderly mother of Charles. Once a vigorous woman, Jennie, a former seamstress, had become a frail ninety-four-year-old and needed Elsie to assure her everyday safety. From the way the house had been assaulted, and given what Elsie may have known about Charles's underworld friends, she could truly believe she and Jennie were in danger.

"Oh, my God!" the frightened woman kept screaming.

But Hagarty and the rest of the team never had any intention of harming the women. It was regrettable that the ladies would be scared by the forceful intrusion, but there really was no other option. A no-knock entry and show of force was the thing to do. Mercifully, one of the first things the agents did was go to the bedroom where Jennie was asleep and closed the door.

Striding quickly up the stairs and into the living area came Kaplan. He was a big bear of a man, with deep set dark eyes that seemed to be constantly sizing things up, watching for clues, any clues. Kaplan was an imposing figure who could have passed for one of the gangsters he hunted. But in truth, said his colleagues, Kaplan was a polite, shy teddy bear who had a knack for getting witnesses and suspects to feel comfortable and cooperate.

From the beginning, Kaplan had wanted to be a cop, and after spending his early New York Police Department (NYPD) years in the relatively staid rookie job as a neighborhood stabilization officer in South Jamaica, Kaplan went to a robbery task force and then on to the narcotics division of the Organized Crime Control Bureau (OCCB).

Promoted to detective, Kaplan then went to the career criminal apprehension unit, which arrested some of the worst criminals in New York City. Then, in 1996, Kaplan reached his final cop assignment: the cold case squad. If there is a plum, elite job in the NYPD for a detective, it is in the cold case unit (CCU). These are the cases that may languish for years as the regular detective squads, overworked and undermanned, have to place some of the difficult homicides on the back burner, where they can languish for years because of inattention. It then falls to the cold case detectives to fork over the old evidence, seek out new leads, reinterview witnesses, and turn up new ones in an effort to crack a case. CCU stories become legendary and fodder for television programs.

Kaplan's particular niche, and the reason why he had taken so much interest in Charles, was in the Mob hits that had remained fallow, their leads dried up. In a city with decades of Mafia involvement in the underworld, there were plenty of organized crime homicides that were unsolved. In the world of the Gambino crime family, there was a fair share of those killings, and Kaplan believed some of them lay at the feet of the strange man who sat in front of him in the Howard Beach living room.

Charles had, in fact, been expecting Hagarty, Kaplan, and the rest of the arrest team. There had been enough subpoenas flying around the neighborhood that Charles knew something big was coming his way. But what really led him to believe trouble was brewing was the news that Kevin McMahon, his old protégé known as "the Weasel," and the crazy Albanian gangster Johnny Alite had decided to cooperate with the FBI. Another Howard Beach denizen, Peter Zuccaro, had also decided to cooperate a couple of years earlier. Faced with life prison terms, the three of them had only one card they could play to have a chance to spend some of their remaining days outside of jail: talk about gangsters like Charles. They knew most things about him, and much of that wasn't good. For the FBI, that was just fine.

If the world of law enforcement viewed Charles Carneglia as some kind of heartless killer who like Norman Bates in the film *Psycho* only had affection for his mother, the man Kaplan gazed at before sunrise seemed more like some village eccentric who did nothing worse than scare children. His hair, once dark and trim, had grayed with age, leaving him with a thinning mane, which he had combed back over his head. His once ruggedly handsome face was hidden behind a dense bush of a beard that seemed thick enough to hide a canary. The edges were gray and the middle tinged with vestiges of his once darker hair color. He looked like some woodsman and quite out of place, considering the well-coiffed and neatly shaven appearance Mafiosi generally favored. In fact, it was very odd to Kaplan and the rest of the law enforcement team that Charles was so hirsute. John Gotti used to have a barber come every day to his social club in nearby Ozone Park to shampoo and cut his hair. From the looks of it, Charles had soured on barbers quite some time ago.

"Charles, what's with the beard?" Hagarty had to ask.

"You know, it's a Fort Dix thing," answered Charles, alluding to his days when he was serving a three-year prison sentence at what was once a military base but had become a federal correction facility. Growing beards became a pastime for the incarcerated, especially the mobsters, explained Charles.

For years, Charles had been something of a Mob recluse. He kept a shack at one of his properties in Brooklyn, which seemed forbidding to outsiders. But it was in such a place that he liked to stay for hours on end. When he needed to, Charles could cook his steaks and hamburgers on a grill. It reminded one lawyer who visited the premises of the kind of place, deep in some secluded woods, in which the infamous "Unabomber" Theodore Kaczynski dwelled when he was captured in the 1990s. In fact, the beard made Charles bear a resemblance to Kaczynski.

Unlike some seamless, cohesive organization, the New York Mob families were rife with cliques and factions. While they had the overall goal of making money, particularly for whoever was the boss, the various *borgatas* were in perpetual internal struggle. Sometimes the rivalries never surfaced or led to anything more dramatic than somebody being demoted—broken down—or ordered into retirement, an act that the mobsters called "being put on the shelf," as if the offending party was a can of corn in a grocery store. Other times, the struggles led to bloodshed, such as when John Gotti orchestrated the December 1985 slaying of Gambino boss Paul Castellano, one of the most seismic events in the history of the Mafia. Charles had been one of the group of men around Gotti and represented what Kaplan and the others believed was the last links to the violent group of Howard Beach men who became Gotti's source of power. Gotti's crew was known for its brutality, and it seemed to rely on loyal, vicious soldiers like Charles. His unkempt appearance seemed to symbolize the wild and brutal nature of what Gotti had spawned.

But it was the eyes that said it most about Charles. They weren't really wild. There was no fiery madness like Charles Manson had shown the world after he was caught for the Sharon Tate murders. Instead, what stared back at Kaplan and Hagarty were dark holes from which nothing—no trace of emotion, no spark of life, no joy—emanated. It was a face that offered no solace, no hope.

Hagarty told Charles to wash, brush his teeth, and dress for the winter cold. He preferred light-colored denim jeans and a patterned cotton sweater with a series of brown, black, and white rectangles.

After he was "hygiened," Charles had one request. "Can I kiss my mother good-bye?" he asked Kaplan.

Though she had lived long, Jennie was getting near the end, and even if Charles was able to beat the case, it wasn't clear if he would get out of jail in time for her. Her son had gone away for long stretches before, and Jennie always thought he was working in some faraway place, like California. In those times, Charles had made sure friends and neighbors took care of her, driving the increasingly frail woman to the store and to her doctor appointments. In her younger days, Jennie on paper was helping her sons own and run a junkyard and auto salvage operation in South Brooklyn. But those energetic days were over.

If she was able to do so, Jennie would visit her sons in prison, posing for family-style photographs as was the style on visiting days in the correctional institutions. But

Jennie spent what was left of her days watching television fare like the daily mass show. She could no longer go for walks to the local Waldbaum's supermarket or the Dollar Store, shopping visits that Charles would take her on. He doted over her as she crossed the street—the loyal bachelor son pushing the shopping cart ahead of Mother as he clasped her arm in the crosswalk. At times like that, they looked like just another close Italian family, one where the stay-at-home son who never married—though he said he had a fiancée—ministered to Momma.

Jennie had exceeded the actuarial tables, and Charles knew that time for Mother was growing short. Even with the morning commotion, the elderly woman seemed to lie in her bed oblivious to what was going on around her.

"This is probably the last time I will see her," Charles explained.

Kaplan had made a living as a cop arresting all sorts of hardened career criminals and he wasn't a soft touch. Kaplan's own steely resolve showed in his own eyes. He had a tough exterior that came in handy as he navigated the world of the Mob, whether it was in the search for information or to make an arrest. Yet, Kaplan was of a school of gumshoe who thought it best to treat his prisoners with some dignity and respect, even if they had not done as much for others: *Sure, go ahead. Kiss your mother.*

There was also another, more ulterior motive to be solicitous to Charles. There was hope among some in the FBI that he might want to cooperate. Perhaps if Charles saw that the agents were willing to accommodate him, maybe—just maybe—he would join "Team America" and spill what he knew about others in the crime family. Charles may have been the deadliest fish in the Mafia pond, but he wasn't the biggest. There was a large group of acting street bosses and important crime captains who were also considered large trophies.

Jennie was clothed in floral pajamas, and her son went over to the bed. Kissing her, Charles had a few parting words that Hagarty overheard.

"Mom, I am going on vacation," said Charles.

In Mob talk, "going on vacation" meant going away to jail. But in her current state, it was unclear if Jennie was even aware of what her son was telling her. She already had one son—her eldest boy, John—who was on a fifty-year "vacation," also courtesy of the federal government, for heroin trafficking. Turning to Elsie, Charles told the caregiver to make sure that she called someone to repair the front door. It was still serviceable, but the wood jamb and the lock had to be repaired.

As poignant as those moments were between mother and son before the team left the house that February morning, there was one thing that kept puzzling Kaplan. The prisoner continually glanced to the attic door. Like most modern homes, the upper level was accessed through a ceiling panel that when pulled down revealed a ladder. Surrounded by law enforcement agents, there was no way Charles would have gone into the attic. But Kaplan remained uneasy, and with Charles's reputation for gunplay, he began to suspect the worst. Lacking a search warrant for the attic, the agents couldn't go up without Charles allowing them.

"Is there anything up there that might hurt anybody?" Kaplan asked, motioning to the ceiling. "Can we go up there?"

"No fucking way," Charles answered.

With that, he was now ready to face whatever else the day would bring.

"Lets get the fuck out of here."

The black sedan was driven away by Detective John Reilly, a Port Authority of New York and New Jersey cop who was operating outside his normal law enforcement realm by taking part in a Mob takedown. FBI agent John Reynolds was seated in the front passenger seat, while Kaplan sat directly behind Reilly. Charles, handcuffed, sat to the right of Kaplan in the rear seat, a vantage point that allowed him an unobstructed view of the neighborhood that he knew, in his heart, he was looking at for the final time.

Similar scenes—an early-morning arrest and a handcuffed suspect bundled into a government car for a drive to Lower Manhattan—were taking place all over New York City that cold February morning. In a series of coordinated raids, the FBI, New York City police, and other law enforcement agencies were rounding up scores of people believed to be members and associates of the Gambino crime family. Italian authorities were also carrying out their own operations in Europe. A total of sixty-two people had been indicted by a federal grand jury in Brooklyn, and it was now time to get them all into custody and to court. In about an hour, by which time Charles and the other suspects would be at FBI headquarters, the first news reports would be giving sparse details of the massive operation.

This particular investigation had been under way for two years. While damaged by previous arrests, the penetration of its ranks by an undercover FBI agent and the dissipation of the power of the family of John Gotti, the Gambino *borgata* still retained clout in the world of organized crime. Old-time street bosses, such as Jackie "the Nose" D'Amico and the Corozzo brothers— Joseph and Nicholas—had remained active, consolidating the family's power and trying to do damage control. But the Mob wasn't like it used to be, and a number of associates had decided to cooperate in the investigation. Even Senior Gotti's old confidant, a garrulous Jewish garment executive named Lewis Kasman, had secretly been talking to the FBI for years, at times while the old Mob boss was being slowly killed by cancer at the federal prison medical facility.

Kasman seemed embittered by the way the mobsters had marginalized him after Gotti's death in 2002. But actually his betrayal of Gotti began before the Mob boss's death, as far back as March 1997. Plying his government handlers with stories about a secret stash of millions of dollars Senior Gotti supposedly had hidden away, Kasman went around taping the dead Mob boss's family, hoping to find the treasure trove he told the agents must still exist. Fishing for leads to the money, Kasman played up his role as confidant and friend as he taped Gotti's wife, Victoria, while she was recovering from a stroke. He even visited an Ozone Park funeral parlor to try and coax information from Gotti's celebrity daughter, Victoria, during the wake of her brother-in-law.

Though Kasman found nothing of value in the hunt for the reputed Gotti treasure, his recordings did give some heft to the FBI as it built a case against the Corozzo brothers—Joseph and Nicholas—who were now the top street bosses of the Gambino operation.

But Charles had never had much to do with Kasman. Driving away with Kaplan and the others toward the Belt Parkway, Charles knew that his trouble didn't come from the pudgy *garmento*. It was the short guy Kevin McMahon who posed the problem. Ever since Gotti had taken a liking to McMahon, the kid was a constant presence around the made men who hung out at the 101st Avenue social club known as Bergin Hunt and Fish. Senior Gotti, the compulsive gambler, thought McMahon brought him good luck. That seemed strange since it was a teenage McMahon who one day in 1980 loaned the minibike Gotti's son Frank rode to his death in a tragic accident. It was a tragedy not only for Frank Gotti but ultimately for John Favara, the man who accidentally drove his car over the mobster's son. Favara disappeared one day. They never found a body.

McMahon liked Charles and his brother, John, the most of all of the wiseguys who operated out of the Bergin. The Carneglias had become McMahon's surrogate family ever since his grandmother tossed him out of her Howard Beach house. McMahon never had the early breaks in life. His mother and father were junkies and he was born dependent on heroin. Family life for him was nonexistent, and McMahon was living in a foster home when his mother and her boyfriend killed his father. The grandmother won custody and did what she could with the child until he reached the age of around twelve or thirteen and then threw him out. She noticed her grandson was stealing cars and figured he would wind up like his father. His grandmother locked the door on him forever.

Turned out of the only real home he had known, McMahon found that the cabana at John Carneglia's place on 163rd Avenue seemed a good place to stay, so long as the weather was warm. The pool house had a toilet and a few comforts, so McMahon, like some homeless cat, could sneak in and sleep. John Carneglia found out later and rather than chase him away allowed McMahon to live in the main house. From that moment on, McMahon became like a member of the family, eating and vacationing with the Carneglias, who even gave him cash when he needed it.

Charles knew that Kevin McMahon had been talking to the government. But in the forty-five-minute ride, nothing was said about that. Reilly the driver was dying to ask the same question Hagarty had asked earlier.

"What's with the beard?"

Bad teeth was now the explanation that Charles proffered. Back in 2001, Charles said, he had been staying in a jail cell in Nassau County and needed some serious dental work that required implants. An infection set in, and Charles's mouth swelled like he had been in a brawl. He started growing the beard to hide the temporary disfigurement. The other inmates didn't like the new look of Charles and told him to shave it. No way, said Charles.

"It pissed them off so I kept it going," Charles told Reilly about the beard.

Small talk during these drives with a prisoner in tow ranged from food, to sports, to news. When Bonanno boss Joseph Massino had been arrested at home in 2004, he told the FBI agents that he thought his very own Maspeth restaurant, CasaBlanca, had the best pizza in town. Massino also said he made a very fine pasta sauce.

With Charles, a fan of the New York Mets—like any other guy from Queens—the talk was about baseball.

"What kind of fan are you, you should be a Mets fan," Charles said as he chided Kaplan for liking the Yankees.

There was also talk about the neighborhood tough guys. Being able to take care of yourself with your fists was something the men in Howard Beach prided themselves on. It was a mix of testosterone and honor. This was a place, one mobster's son once said, where the men weren't judged by how much money they made, who had the fanciest car or the hottest wife. You were judged, he said, by "how tough you were."

The men of Howard Beach fought each other, and when needed, to protect the cohesiveness of the neighborhood, they fought together. During the days when John Gotti was around, the teenagers, including at least one of his sons, honed their skills in boxing matches in a local park, complete with gloves and mouth guards as they pranced around a ring space demarcated by some string on the grass. Cops would sometimes show up and watch. Toughness—being able to take a beating and give the other guy worse than you got—meant status.

"Who was the toughest guy in the neighborhood?" Kaplan asked. That was easy for Charles to answer.

"My brother, John, was pretty tough, and so was John Gotti and his brother Genie. Those guys didn't smoke and didn't drink much. They stayed in shape," said Charles as the car continued west toward Brooklyn. There was also Oscar Ansourian, or "Big O," as he was known on the street. Dabbling in weapons and extortion, Ansourian, who was of Armenian ethnicity, earned his reputation as a tough guy, said Charles.

John Carneglia, the older brother of Charles, was certainly plenty tough. The story was that brother John was one of the men dressed in black fur Muscovite hats and white winter overcoats who stalked an unsuspecting

Paul Castellano as he drove up to Sparks Steak House on East Forty-sixth Street in Manhattan the night on December 16, 1985. As mobster Sammy Gravano remembered it, John Carneglia was the only made member of the Mafia involved in the hit crew. The other gun-toting men— Anthony "the Roach" Rampino, Joseph "the German" Watts, and John "Iggy" Alonga—were all Gambino associates at the time, said Gravano. Senior Gotti, the grand orchestrator of the Castellano hit, was about a block away in a car with Gravano when the slaying finally happened.

John Carneglia was in prison for fifty years for a heroin bust, along with Gene Gotti, another of Charles's vaunted tough guys who had played his role in a few Mob murders. But it was John Carneglia, Charles explained to Kaplan, who should have been the boss of the family. Both men went away to do their prison time and never turned on their fellow gangsters. They were stand-up guys. There was also Sal Puma, another tough guy, now dead. The irony of Charles bringing up Puma's name escaped him at that point in the drive to Manhattan. But he would learn soon enough how the story of what had happened to tough guy Puma would be his own problem.

Since Charles had brought up John Gotti's name, Steve Kaplan figured it would be a logical subject toward which the conversation could be steered as the car traveled west along Atlantic Avenue. What did he think of him?

"He was a great man, a true believer," answered Charles.

Senior Gotti had been dead just about six years, but at least for those who were part of the old Bergin crew, the legend of the old Gambino boss remained strong. Gotti loved being a gangster, loved the Mob life and the adulation it brought him. At the 101st Street club, he would not only hold court but also kept a stock of $2,000 suits, matching shirts and socks, as well as pocket handkerchiefs. The couture replaced the warm-up suit he often wore when leaving his house on Eighty-fifth Street, a few blocks north of where Charles's mother made her home. A Mob boss had an image to keep up and Gotti wouldn't leave the Bergin without being dressed for a man of his stature. The public demanded as much, Gotti would tell his men.

Gotti was nattily dressed the night he was finally arrested for the last time on December 10, 1990, at the Ravenite, the Mulberry Street club that became his Manhattan power base. The last photo taken of Gotti on the street showed him in his expensive overcoat, beaming for the news photographers, as he walked between FBI agents. Years later, ravaged by cancer, Gotti became a shell of his old self in prison. His jaw, the location of the deadly cancer, became puffy. Gone was the fleshy, smiling handsome face and the pompadour hair. To ward off a chill, an aging and dying Gotti wore a shawl when he sat in the visiting room to talk with his attorney.

The controversy about whether Gotti received adequate medical care in prison, indeed whether appropriate treatment was withheld, would rage on long after his death. Lewis Kasman once spoke, while he was secretly working as a turncoat, of filing a lawsuit for Gotti's family over the alleged mistreatment. Charles had also heard stories about what the government tried to do to his old boss, or *representante,* as the position was known in Italian.

"Did you know that he was offered medical treatment when he was dying if he just told them that he was in the

Mob?" said Charles to the men in the government car. "He refused, and they let him die like a dog," he insisted.

But others in the life weren't so strong, said Charles. *La Cosa Nostra* had become riddled with turncoats and informers. He called them "canaries." Even some of the big bosses, some of Charles's own neighbors, had lacked the backbone to stay with the blood oath of silence, *omertà*.

"Look at Joe Massino," he said, bringing up the biggest example, one Kaplan and the others in the car were very familiar with. As soon as Joseph "Big Joey" Massino had been convicted in July 2004 as head of the Bonanno crime family, he immediately, within minutes of the verdict being read out in court, approached the presiding trial judge and asked to talk with prosecutors. Facing life in prison for seven Mob murders, as well as the prospect of a death penalty case for another killing, Massino worked for months in secret while in jail to convince the FBI that he had good information to offer them. The agents initially greeted Massino's entreaties with skepticism. He was the convicted boss, the big fish, what else could he really offer the government?

But after Massino tape-recorded his trusted captain Vincent "Vinny Gorgeous" Basciano while they were together in jail, the FBI saw value to him. A handsome gangster from the Bronx, Basciano had long been a loyal protégé of Massino who had at one point made the captain his acting street boss. But loyalty aside, Basciano had seemed volatile, impulsive—a "mad hatter," Massino once called him. On the tapes, Basciano indicated that he might at one point have discussed with his boss the idea of assassinating the prosecutor who had convicted Massino. Basciano was also overheard talking about why it had been necessary to kill aspiring mobster Randolph Pizzolo in December 2004. As a result, Basciano found himself under indictment in a death penalty case.

Charles was confounded by what Massino had done, particularly to his own crime family and those who had been loyal to him.

"I don't get people like Joe Massino. He's in the life since he was a kid, and now he decides to cooperate. He hurt all his friends. Now's he's a canary," he said with a mix of contempt and resignation for his old Howard Beach neighbor. But that was to be expected from the Bonanno clan, Charles said, reminding Kaplan and other passengers about the duplicity of the whole hierarchy of the crime family.

"Look at Massino and those guys, Vitale and Lino, the guys at the top. They planned this, they are ratting on each other, and look none of them are getting hurt, they are ratting on dead guys," said Charles, a reference to mobsters who had died years ago.

Salvatore Vitale, Massino's own brother-in-law, testified against him in 2004, and Frank Lino, a captain, also became a cooperating witness in the Bonanno boss's trial. Lino had felt particularly vulnerable because it had been Vitale who had given some of the orders to commit the Mob murders that Lino had been involved in. When Vitale became a turncoat, guys like Lino, lower down in the hierarchy, also became government witnesses in the hopes of winning leniency when they were sentenced. But it was just that kind of reliance on cooperators, who had all kinds of incentives to lie, that Charles found offensive.

"You guys got to stop listening to those canaries," said Charles.

Though he hated the informers, Charles felt no reluctance to continue talking to his captive audience in the sedan as it traveled through the early morning along the stretch of road that would become the Flatbush Avenue extension and eventually lead to the Brooklyn Bridge.

Kaplan had been involved in the probe of the Gambino crime family since 2005 as part of the cold case squad investigating unsolved Mob murders. The indictment against Charles, which the prisoner hadn't seen yet, painted him as the Gambino family's homicidal maniac. If his brother, John, killed for business reasons, Charles seemed to be from what all the witnesses were saying a man who slaughtered people—some who were barely out of their teens—in personal fights. There would be time later for Kaplan to try and question Charles about the killings—if he let him. The FBI had hoped that by raiding Charles's home that morning in civilian clothes and not in heavy tactical gear that the mobster might feel more comfortable and might cooperate. He showed no signs of that. But during the drive, the detective wanted to satisfy his curiosity about the history of the Gambino *borgata,* stuff that Charles, who was appearing very talkative, wouldn't hesitate to discuss.

Before he died and during the nearly ten years of his imprisonment, John Gotti had remained the Gambino boss. But being in the tough confinement of federal prison meant that Senior Gotti's visitors were screened, his mail and telephone calls monitored. It was not easy for him to run the affairs of the Mob from his cell. Prosecutors claimed Gotti was doing so after a fashion by talking with certain lawyers and passing messages. At least, that was the communication method Lewis Kasman had been telling the FBI Gotti had used to run things.

But the daily dealings of the crime family on the street couldn't wait for lawyers to fly out to Marion, Illinois, or whatever place Gotti was held at and ferry messages back and forth. For that, Gotti relied on his street boss. It became an open secret that Gotti's own son, John A. Gotti, or Junior, had been the crime boss's designated go-to guy to serve as acting boss, at least in the early 1990s. The younger Gotti was born in 1964. He was married with six kids and lived on a large piece of property in the wealthy North Shore area of Long Island. At least on paper, Junior earned his money through real estate rentals. Informants said he ran the drug rackets in Ozone Park.

Beefy and menacing as a young man who bore a strong resemblance to his father, Junior Gotti's induction to the Mob life, and his anointment as his father's acting boss, was a subject of intense debate among mobsters. His mother, Victoria, also didn't like the situation. Some didn't appreciate the way the youngster rose quickly, so Kaplan brought up the issue with Charles. The problem, Charles explained to Detective Kaplan, was that all the other likely candidates were unavailable.

"My brother and Genie were in jail," said Charles, referring to John Carneglia and Eugene "Gene" Gotti, the crime boss's younger and much feared brother. Their lengthy federal terms effectively took them out of the picture. So Gotti resorted to old-fashioned nepotism, something Charles, for all his admiration of the old crime boss, indicated quite strongly that he didn't approve of.

"If your father was in charge of IBM, would he put

you in charge?" Charles asked Kaplan rhetorically. "No way. He'd give you a good position, but he would put people in charge that know what they are doing."

It was quite clear that Charles didn't think Junior Gotti was up to the job of running a crime family the way it should be run. Charles's feelings about the younger Gotti mirrored what one informant said was John Carneglia's strong dislike of the kid, someone he wasn't shy about expressing his contempt about. Junior Gotti didn't last very long as acting boss, and the position finally devolved to his uncle Peter Gotti. The shift wasn't strictly nepotism, but at least it kept the leadership of the Gambino family within the Gotti bloodline. It wasn't the best of picks, since Peter Gotti also eventually found himself saddled with a life term and unable to lead much of anything from a prison cell.

The government car made its way toward downtown Brooklyn and finally onto the fabled bridge, past the old wharves and docks that had been a part of a bustling waterfront. After World War II, an explosion of commerce made the docks cry out for longshoremen, and it was the Gambino family that infiltrated the unions. Mobsters, such as Anthony "Tough Tony" Anastasio and his brother, Albert Anastasia, became powers on the docks. The rackets and their exploitation of the honest workers would inspire the Oscar-winning film *On The Waterfront* and trigger decades of efforts by reformers and law enforcement to root out the crime families. On this particular day in February 2008, the Gambino family had very little left of the docks as a power base.

As the sedan traveled over the Brooklyn Bridge for

the final leg of the trip into Manhattan, Charles mused about other things than lost rackets. It was almost as if he was resigned to the fact that the Mob life was over. From the span, he could see through its steel lattice work Lower Manhattan and Little Italy, where Gotti held court and where the Gambino family had ruled. It had been a great life, but that was then. There had been fun in the life he had lived, Charles told Kaplan. It wasn't all bad. There had also been a lot of laughs. Take the time John Gotti Senior had wanted to take back a $100 bet he had placed at Aqueduct Racetrack on a horse that didn't run.

"He grabs this kid Jerry who was always hanging around. 'Go get my hundred clams' and gives the kid the ticket," explained Charles. So the youngster goes out and thinks he is doing the crime boss a big favor. Jerry, who had the nickname of "Piss Clams," came back with what he thought Gotti wanted.

"The kid came back to the club with fifty clams," explained Carneglia with a chuckle. He was referring to the edible shellfish, not dollar bills.

"John went crazy. Everyone in the club had a good time over that. Even John had a good laugh over it," remembered Charles.

Once over the bridge, the government car drove to 26 Federal Plaza, the federal office building that towered over Foley Square, just opposite the old federal courthouse. The FBI office was on the twenty-sixth floor and was the place where all of the prisoners who had been swept up in the morning's raids would be taken. As Reilly steered the car into the basement garage, Kaplan knew that the time of his bantering with Charles was now over.

"We won't disrespect you and we'll stop talking to

you," said Kaplan. He had worried that if Carneglia appeared to the other gangsters to be chatting with the agents that it might cause some problems for the old Mob soldier. But Charles couldn't care less about the other mobsters.

"We're allowed to talk. Fuck these guys."

Agent Reynolds, Reilly, and Kaplan took Charles into a room. The prisoner wanted to know what he had been charged with, but before any more talking took place, Kaplan wanted to be sure that Charles had received his Miranda warnings. Long the bane of law-and-order folks who thought the courts had given suspects too many rights, the legal cautions were rooted in settled U.S. Supreme Court precedent that required that prisoners be told of their right to remain silent. Defendants also had to be told of the right to have an attorney present before any questioning took place, and that a lawyer would be appointed if they couldn't afford one. Kaplan read out each of those rights from a form entitled "Advice of Rights"; and each time things were explained, Charles indicated he understood. To avoid any problems later on, Kaplan wanted him to acknowledge being "Mirandized" by signing the form.

"No autographs," responded Charles tersely. He refused to sign. Kaplan noted the refusal on the form, along with the time as being eight thirty-five in the morning.

Getting down to business, Kaplan told Charles that he had been charged with "RICO," which the detective meant as verbal shorthand for the crime of racketeering. Charles, a man who was no stranger to the criminal justice system, knew very well what RICO meant:

the Racketeer Influenced and Corrupt Organizations Act. A lot of the old crew out of the Bergin club had fallen victim to the statute, which carried maximum penalties of up to life. It's what had ensnared Senior Gotti and had made him spend his last days in prison. Still, Charles felt in the mood for some humor. The only RICO he knew was the character by that name played by Edward G. Robinson in the 1931 film *Little Caesar,* he told Kaplan.

Joke around if you want, thought Kaplan. The detective then spelled out exactly what the charges involved. There were five homicides, and Kaplan listed each one individually, waiting for Charles to react.

Albert Gelb, a state court officer, was killed in 1976. Gelb's body was found shot multiple times in a car in Brooklyn. He died from shots that punctured his torso.

"Don't know him," responded Charles.

Michael Cotillo, slain at the Blue Fountain diner in 1977. He had been stabbed in the chest, with the knife going directly into the heart and tearing into the left and right ventricles. There was so much bleeding that the coroner found over a quart of blood in the abdomen.

"Don't know him, either."

Sal Puma in Lindenwood in 1983. He was also stabbed in the chest, with the knife slicing into the left ventricle. The heart, damaged beyond repair, spilled about 40 percent of his blood into the left side of his chest.

Charles said he knew a "Sammy Puma" but not a "Sal Puma."

Louis DiBono, a Gambino captain, killed at the World Trade Center in 1990. An obese man at 310 pounds and barely five feet tall, DiBono was found with seven gunshot wounds, four of which struck his head, with one entering the brain. Another bullet damaged his subclavian artery, the one that supplied blood to his left arm.

"I know 'Louie,'" Charles admitted. But that was all he would say about that.

Then there was Jose Delgado Rivera, an armored car driver, killed during a heist. Delgado Rivera was shot twice in the torso with a shotgun.

"Never heard of him," answered Charles. "Your canaries said I killed a court officer, a guy at the Blue Fountain, Puma, Louie, and a guy at Kennedy Airport. You guys got to stop listening to those canaries. They're all rats."

There is an old adage among seasoned defense lawyers that anybody who gets arrested, even when a lawyer is present, shouldn't talk to the cops. It is not that a street-smart defendant, especially one like Charles, would confess. But it can be the little things—the small details, the offhand remark—that can raise the eyebrows of a careful cop.

Kaplan had been careful enough in his short remarks about each homicide never to mention to Charles the place where Rivera was shot, which just happened to be JFK Airport. But when Charles, unprompted, mentioned not having anything to do with the killing of the armored car guard at the "airport," Kaplan looked at Reilly, who smiled back. Both investigators then nodded to each other. It was a moment pregnant with meaning, one to remember for later.

Small talk followed. There was baseball. Food again. Maybe those small indulgences got Charles thinking about how delightfully uncomplicated life was for a free man. But in custody, it would be difficult for Charles to mount a defense. Sensing the impossibility of his circumstances, Charles started to think out loud, his mind going through a checklist of what had to be done to prepare for trial. Friends said he was compulsive about keeping lists and files, trying to be organized.

"I got to get out of here," he said.

Kaplan was slightly amused in that Charles was going nowhere without bail. The issue of bail would be brought up later in court. But prosecutors had long anticipated this day, and with Charles in custody, they had prepared a letter for the court aimed at denying him bail. The letter was actually a 169-page memo that dealt with many of the mobsters who had been swept up in the morning's raids. In connection with Charles, the memo pointed out to the court the fact that he faced five murder charges, and reminded everyone that over twenty years earlier he had fled, gone on the lam, when facing a different set of federal charges. Given the severity of the indictment and his proclivity to flee, prosecutors planned to ask the court to deny Charles bail later that day.

"That guy has a little bit of rabbit in him," one informant had told Kaplan about Charles.

But unaware of the surprise he faced, Charles told Kaplan what he needed to do.

"I have to mount a defense. I have to go with my investigator and we have to go and talk to these witnesses."

However, something finally made Charles seem resigned to his fate. "I am fucked." He sighed. "Is this a death penalty case?"

The question truly surprised Kaplan. The issue of capital punishment had never come up before; the detective had never even hinted at such a thing.

"What does it matter to you?" Kaplan inquired.

"Longevity runs in my family," Charles reminded Kaplan. "My mother is in her nineties and I don't want to live in prison for thirty years. I would rather get the needle."

Racketeering murder carried a life sentence upon conviction. Even if he was convicted of only one of the killings, a life term in a federal prison meant that Charles would die behind bars. It was a fate he considered worse than death, so capital punishment somehow seemed preferable.

One murder would be too much. But five murders to Charles seemed like prosecutors were piling on the charges, trying to make sure something would stick and make sure he never went home to Jennie. He got angry. Suddenly standing up and with his hands together in a supplicating gesture, Charles became defiant. His question seemed like a challenge to Kaplan.

"*Minga* (the word loosely translated to "wow"), why did you charge me with five murders?"

"There were others, but we couldn't prove it," answered Kaplan dryly.

At that point, Kaplan looked around and noticed that the room was filling up with some of the others who had been arrested in the citywide roundup. FBI teams had been steadily pulling into the federal building all morning with the suspects, and processing was going to take some time. A news release distributed by the Brooklyn U.S. Attorney's Office heralded the eighty-count indictment. While it stated that Gambino, Genovese, and Bonanno organized crime families were represented in the rogues' gallery of defendants, there was no mistaking that this was essentially a case that targeted the Gambino *borgata*. *The charged crimes span more than three decades and reflect the Gambino family's corrosive influence on the construction industry in New York City and beyond, and its willingness to resort to violence, even murder,*

*to resolve disputes in dozens of crimes dating from the 1970s
to the present,* trumpeted the press release.

Charles had asked Kaplan if any of his people were in
the room. But all he had to do was look around to get
the answer. Right there, directly behind Charles, was
Vincent Dragonetti, a reputed crime family soldier.
Although not charged with murders, Dragonetti faced
major racketeering charges involving extortion, illegal
gambling, money laundering, and securities fraud.
Meeting in the room as they did, the only thing Charles
and Dragonetti could do was nod at each other.

The door opened and coming in with his FBI escort
was Joseph Corozzo. A stocky, dour man with a full
head of graying hair, Corozzo knew Charles from the
days when they both visited Gotti at his club on 101st
Avenue. Spending his time between Florida and Queens,
Corozzo was the *consigliere,* or counselor, of the crime
family, the advisor to whoever held the title of boss,
which at this particular point in time was an incarcerated Peter Gotti, brother of the late crime boss.
Corozzo never much cracked a smile and seemed to
complain constantly, a trait that earned him the moniker
of "Miserable" among his associates, although that
wasn't spoken in his presence.

From the looks of him, Corozzo seemed pretty miserable. After entering the room, he didn't glance at
anyone but just looked straight ahead. Corozzo took a
seat and did nothing else.

"Is Joseph in trouble like me?" Charles inquired.

"Worry about yourself, you have enough problems,"
Kaplan replied.

* * *

In reality, Joseph Corozzo had very big problems. The indictment accused him of extortion in the construction industry involving the Staten Island cement company that the informant Joseph Vollaro had been running, all the while making incriminating audiotapes for the FBI. But it was Corozzo who also faced, along with Gotti's other brother Vincent, a conspiracy charge that accused him of plotting to distribute cocaine. The narcotics charge galled Corozzo, prompting him to blurt out in court days later that he didn't want to sit together with any codefendant who was accused of drug dealing.

As mobbed up as he was, Corozzo had two sons who were attorneys and seemed to be doing well in their chosen professions. Richard Corozzo had an office on Cross Bay Boulevard in a building that sported a big sign. He specialized mostly in civil work. His brother, also named Joseph, or "Little Joe," had chosen the field of criminal law. Little Joe Corozzo, a former high-school football coach, was known as a tenacious defense attorney who managed to snare his share of mobsters as clients. Prosecutors had haunted Joseph Corozzo, the lawyer, for years in the hopes of catching him in illegal activity. Prosecutors continually filed papers with the courts alleging that Joseph Corozzo, as a lawyer, functioned as nothing more than a house counsel to the Gambino family, giving mobsters advice. At times, prosecutors said, citing what informants had told them, the attorney served as a messenger who carried all sorts of messages from jailed mobsters to their friends outside. At one point, Kasman said, young Joseph would take a list from an imprisoned John Gotti saying what new members of the Gambino family were to be inducted. Kasman also said Corozzo was among a group of lawyers he sometimes paid in cash, an action that wasn't necessarily a crime but which Kasman tried to make into something sinister.

But try as they might, prosecutors never made a case against Corozzo the lawyer and grudgingly had to admit that he was a good trial opponent. The only tactic the government could use that sometimes worked against Corozzo was to show the court he had a conflict of interest and get him recused from representing some mobster.

Looking at Corozzo, the reticent *consigliere*, staring out into space, Kaplan couldn't help but wonder why he had his son become a criminal lawyer. He asked Charles that very question.

"It was not his choice," answered Charles. "His son 'Rocco' is a civil lawyer, and he is very successful. Young Joseph wanted to be a criminal lawyer."

Finished with Charles, Kaplan beckoned to Reilly and Reynolds, who escorted the prisoner so he could get fingerprinted and have his photo taken for the mug shot collection. By that time, a gaggle of news photographers, tipped off to the arrests, had gathered outside and waited for the ritual walking of the Mob suspects from the south side of the federal building to vans that would take them to the Brooklyn federal courthouse. When it came to Charles's turn to exit the building, his countenance as the bearded, freaky guy would catch everyone's attention and give the news photographers a field day.

As Charles Carneglia left the room, Detective Steve Kaplan's eyes followed him to the door. *He is done, finished, headed for the scrap heap, a busted valise,* thought Kaplan as he watched Charles leave. That old Mob life didn't leave him much to show for it now.

2

"Alby Is Dead."

"Everybody in my neighborhood was a gangster."

That is what Peter Zuccaro would always remember foremost about growing up in Brooklyn.

With a voice laden with a slow, tough-guy cadence, Zuccaro was a character who seemed to chew over his words and speak them slow and sullenly. He did it for effect. He was hard to the bone.

"Everybody in my neighborhood aspired to be that, and that's the way it was in the neighborhood I come from," he said.

The power, the money, the lifestyle—all appealed to Zuccaro, whose uncle was a member of the Bonanno crime family. Because he idolized his uncle, Zuccaro's early forays into crime as a teenager in the mid-1970s was as an associate with the Bonanno *borgata*. Zuccaro's early years committing crimes involved car theft. Whenever he got his hands on a vehicle, Zuccaro said, he was able to drop it off at the auto and junkyards run by his friends John and Charles Carneglia in East New York. There the cars would be tagged or chopped. Good cars, which had high resale potential, would have their vehicle identification numbers (VIN) changed, with the bribed cooperation of the Department of Motor Vehicles (DMV), in a process known in the underworld as "tagging." The other cars that weren't in high demand or were in poor shape would be chopped up for parts. Chopped autos often fetched more through their various individual components than they could as a complete vehicle.

Zuccaro was an inveterate gangster, but one with principles. Though he would commit any crime when asked by the made men of the Mob, he wouldn't do anything near a church, especially kill someone. That would be a despicable act, said Zuccaro. Houses of worship, such as St. Helen Roman Catholic Church in Howard Beach, shouldn't be disrespected by the bloody business of *La Cosa Nostra*.

But Zuccaro's principles didn't extend to treating women well. The act he would later admit to was that he had a fight in which he not only struck his wife but her mother, both of whom then went running to the house of John Gotti to seek refuge. For that ungentlemanly display of hubris against the women Gotti demeaned Zuccaro by giving him a dressing-down.

Everything Zuccaro was doing in his life was geared to being a made man. But the strange thing about Zuccaro was that while he aspired to be a gangster, he would pass up the opportunity to be inducted formally into *La Cosa Nostra* when it was offered to him. He didn't want the headaches and instead remained an associate for all of his active life as a criminal.

But that was well off into the future. On a February night in 1975, it was a somewhat depressed nineteen-year-old Zuccaro who decided with a couple of close friends to seek out a diner in which to find some peace and think about what had happened to his younger brother. Zuccaro was in mourning following the death of Robert, who had died suddenly a few days earlier in his apartment in East New York. It wasn't clear what had happened to the seventeen-year-old kid. Robert was a drug abuser and might have overdosed. There was also an abscess on his back that may have become septic and caused him to go into shock. In any case, Zuccaro's younger brother was dead, just the same.

"I was looking for a place where I could be basically alone," Zuccaro remembered about the night. "Just my two friends that were with me."

The best and worst of life sometimes takes place in a diner. These peculiarly American institutions—the French have their cafés and the British the ubiquitous pubs—become places that patrons gravitate toward for all sorts of reasons. Be it starry-eyed lovers gazing at each other over a late-night meal, businesspeople trying to squeeze in a quick meeting, or the forlorn looking for a place to be in the presence of other people, but without the need to have much social interaction, the chrome-and-glass eateries fit the bill.

In Howard Beach, diners serve all of these purposes. But like Rick's Café in the film *Casablanca*, they also are meeting places where mobsters did business outside of the usual social club venues. It was also said that gang-sters provided protection to the businesses. Usually cen-trally located on a main road, such as Cross Bay or Northern boulevards, diners are convenient neutral meeting grounds where members of various *La Cosa Nostra* families can come together. There are also times, particularly late at night, when mobsters just want to sit down and while away the time and deal with whatever source of depression or angst is ailing them. Espresso may not help one sleep, but sitting in a corner booth in the presence of those who are friends for the moment, while a cute waitress takes care of you, is sometimes the best kind of solace.

Zuccaro drove to the Esquire on Cross Bay Boulevard in Ozone Park with Malcolm Settle and Andrew Curro. Settle, a close friend of Zuccaro's, was behind the wheel of his mother's station wagon. The three of them had been cruising for an open diner and came upon the Esquire, the only diner in the area that was open beyond midnight. Located near a busy intersection of Cross Bay and Rockaway boulevards, as well as a subway stop, the Esquire was a place where those who haunted the night could settle.

Though Zuccaro was an aspiring Mob wannabe, Settle wasn't part of the Mob world. However, Curro was a right-hand man to Charles Carneglia, one of the neighborhood toughs at the time. Charles wasn't a member of *La Cosa Nostra,* either. But his brother, John, was on the verge of becoming a wiseguy. John Carneglia was tight with John Gotti, who had made his mark about two years earlier doing a big favor for Carlo Gambino— *that* Carlo Gambino, the cagey immigrant who had skillfully negotiated the dangerous world of Mob power struggles decades earlier to lead the crime family that bore his name.

The favor for Gambino involved the slaying of James McBratney, a brash Irish thug who was suspected of being foolish enough to have kidnapped the crime boss's nephew and demanded ransom. In January 1973, Emmanuel Gambino's body was found by police buried in New Jersey, and Carlo Gambino wanted McBratney held accountable. Which meant *dead*. So in 1973, in a Staten Island bar known as Snoope's, Gotti, his close friend Angelo Ruggiero, and the hijacker Ralph Galione posed as cops and confronted McBratney. A serious barroom brawl erupted and finally, as Gotti and Ruggiero pinned McBratney against a wall, Galione fired three times into the Irishman, killing him. For the McBratney slaying, Gotti got a two-year manslaughter sentence, but his stature in the Mob life in Howard Beach, where he lived in a two-story frame house, grew tremendously. He became a made member of the Gambino *borgata* soon after his release from prison in 1975.

Zuccaro and his two friends settled into a corner booth, facing the entrance and ordered. They were not at the table long before Charles Carneglia entered. Among the Howard Beach crowd, Charles seemed raucous and a little strange. Though he was nearly thirty years old, Charles seemed like a man who didn't want to grow up. He consorted with a younger crowd of men and women—people, like Zuccaro, who were still in their teens. His arrest record showed a series of cases of increasing severity over the years: 1966, receiving stolen property; 1967, petit larceny; 1968, possession of stolen property and conspiracy; 1970, a federal rap for theft of an interstate shipment. All had resulted in dismissals. Until he was convicted in Brooklyn on a felony grand larceny charge and sentenced to a year in jail, Charles had led a charmed life as a criminal.

Though not known as the most snappy dresser around, on this particular night Charles had on a long winter overcoat, tuxedo, matching tie, and a dress shirt and shoes. He had actually been at the wedding of an associate of the Lucchese crime family known as Thomas DeSimone and the daughter of an associate of the Gambino family. It wasn't uncommon for people linked in various ways to different crime families to wed. But in this particular case, the situation was laden with potential trouble.

In the strange links that developed in the Mob life, DeSimone had become a major player in the crime crew of James Burke, which would later in 1978 pull off the fabled Lufthansa heist at JFK, a crime that became fodder for the film *Goodfellas*. If people thought Charles was strange and violent, DeSimone was in a class by himself. He is said to have shot a man dead on the street just for sport and, as informer Henry Hill related, shot and killed a teenage bartender at one of the Mob social clubs because the kid told him to go "fuck himself."

DeSimone was a brutal guy, a true psychopath among Mob killers. What had particularly stirred things up at the time of his wedding was that it was DeSimone who had about two months earlier shot and killed Ronald Jerothe, another member of the Bergin crew on 101st Avenue. Though little known in Mafia history, Jerothe was close to Gotti and his brother Gene. Around the Gotti household, Jerothe was known as "Uncle Foxy" or just plain "Foxy." Living as he did in the Lindenwood area of South Queens, Foxy worked the East Brooklyn neighborhood where Charles and his brother had their junkyard. Over a period of time, said a person familiar with the Howard Beach Mob scene, Foxy and the Carneglia brothers gravitated together toward Gotti.

Foxy was not only a hijacker but also reputed to be a drug dealer. He also had a reputation of being a ladies' man and a prankster. He and DeSimone were said to have gone streaking along Cross Bay Boulevard when it became the rage in the early 1970s. But in the Mob, friendships are transient and ephemeral, destroyed by egos that often go out of control. The trouble between DeSimone and Foxy stemmed from the fact that DeSimone began dating his friend's sister behind his back. This was a serious breach of Mob etiquette. But what also added to the problem was that DeSimone was said to have assaulted the young woman after the breakup. Fearing retaliation, DeSimone made a preemptive strike and shot Foxy three times at point-blank range on December 18, 1974, as the two fought at the front door of the victim's apartment.

When Gotti learned of the killing of Jerothe, he was stunned, returning home the night he learned of the murder in a state of depression. But it didn't take long before Gotti's shock turned to anger. The Gambino family was outraged by the homicide, and some years later would extract its revenge. But with Foxy's death in late 1974 as a backdrop, Charles suspected trouble at the wedding and was said to have armed himself with not one but two guns.

Charles didn't sit down at Peter Zuccaro's table but leaned against it as he related how he had just come from the wedding. As he tilted forward, Charles's suit jacket opened around the side vent, revealing two hand-guns stuck in the waistband of the trousers.

"Hide the guns, those guns are showing," an alarmed

Zuccaro said in a low voice, so as not to be heard over at the next tables.

Charles stood up and fixed the suit jacket to conceal the weapons. Since he needed to visit the bathroom, he then turned and went down the stairs where the lavatories were, next to the pay telephone.

Lynn Baranello had arrived at the diner a few minutes after Zuccaro and his small entourage. She was accompanied by her good friend Albert Gelb, who was a prematurely bald man of twenty-four. Gelb, Baranello, and her husband had become the best of friends as neighbors in Howard Beach. It had actually been Lynn who as a seventeen-year-old first met the jocular Gelb while he was walking his retriever in the neighborhood. He impressed her as being a good-hearted, generous soul.

"He was kind of funny," Lynn remembered. "Because he was bald, he would like to wear different kinds of hats. He came over with a large hat on that looked like a cowboy hat. It was white, looked like a hat that Hoss Cartwright would wear."

Gelb lived across the street from Lynn with his grandmother, and when the old woman died, he had given Lynn some of her furniture and a cookbook. Lynn had a boyfriend at the time, and when she married, Gelb remained friendly with the newlyweds.

Gelb tried a number of different jobs and became an emergency medical technician (EMT) before settling on a career as a court officer with the New York State court system. Court officers are considered peace officers under state law and are permitted to carry guns, both in their official duties and on private time. If necessary, they can make arrests. Some say the court system is the employer of last resort for those who just can't decide on a career. But it's a steady job, although it can get physically demanding if there happens to be trouble in the courtrooms. But if a guy doesn't screw up, the job of court officer offers good indoor work and a full pension.

Lacking a car to get to his courthouse in downtown Brooklyn, Gelb would sometimes borrow the one Lynn's husband used. The young woman's spouse worked as a school bus driver and retired early in the evenings so that he didn't need a car to get to work until the morning. Gelb was then able to take the Baranello vehicle and would return it.

When Gelb brought the car back around midnight, Lynn would sometimes prepare him something to eat. But on this one particular night, Lynn didn't feel like cooking and so she and Gelb—her husband was already in bed at that hour—drove to the Esquire. It was their second choice. Their usual destination was the Lindenwood Diner, but that was closed. Arriving sometime around 3:00 A.M. at the Esquire, Gelb and Baranello sat in a corner booth, just like the group of men they noticed were already inside. The couple sat close to the stairway that went to the lower level, where the pay telephone and bathroom were.

Baranello glanced over to the men in the other booth and noticed that they seemed very intent on their conversation. They also were hassling the waitress, a neighborhood woman named Debbie, who at that hour wasn't very happy about the suggestive comments she was getting. Gelb also noticed the woman's plight and went over and told the men to stop giving her grief. Thankful for Gelb's intercession, the young woman came over and took the couple's order. Gelb wanted a hamburger.

A few moments later was when Charles actually came

in. After leaning against the table to talk with Zuccaro, he squeezed into the booth. As he did so, Baranello saw his overcoat move enough so that one of the handguns became visible to Zuccaro and to her. One looked like a .357 Magnum and was visible on Charles's belt. He also had a five-shot Smith & Wesson revolver, which she couldn't see. In need of a visit to the downstairs bathroom, Charles got up and walked to the stairs, never bothering to adjust his coat. The gun was clearly visible now to Baranello.

Surprised at what she saw, Baranello nudged Gelb as Charles walked by, and the court officer checked him out.

"I think I'm going to find out if he has a permit for that gun," said Gelb.

Baranello tried to stop him, but Gelb insisted, getting up from the table and following Charles down the stairs. To carry a gun in New York City requires a police permit. Gangsters rarely get permission to pack a weapon, always risking a minimum one-year jail sentence if they were caught. Gelb didn't know with whom he was dealing, but his sense of public duty impelled him to go after Charles and find out what was going on. He followed Charles into the bathroom.

"Do you have a tin?" asked Gelb, which was his way of inquiring if Charles was a cop.

Charles looked at Gelb like he had two heads. *This guy is no cop,* thought Gelb.

"Please put your hands up against the wall and don't move," commanded Gelb.

That served only to anger Charles, who allegedly went for his gun. Gelb reacted by going for his sidearm.

Upstairs, the customers and the diner staff heard sounds that didn't bode well. There was clearly a struggle going on. Zuccaro, Settle, and Curro were alerted to the noise. Panicking, Baranelllo ran over to the waitress. Both women went into the kitchen, where they hid, along with the short-order cook and dishwasher.

This was the era before cell phones, and the only pay telephone that anybody could use to call police was right down the stairs by the bathrooms, where everything was happening. Baranello and the waitress then both rushed down the stairs and got a call into the 911 operator.

"Ten-thirteen, ten-thirteen," Baranello shouted into the receiver, saying a court officer was in distress. The waitress had told her to repeat the code, which every emergency operator knew indicated a law enforcement officer was in trouble. Of course, Gelb was part of law enforcement. That would definitely speed up the arrival of police. The women weren't on the telephone that long because Zuccaro reached over and yanked the telephone from Baranello and hung it up.

Peter Zuccaro knew he had heard the sound of Charles's voice crying out for help downstairs, so he rushed down the stairs. He saw Charles and Gelb in a furious struggle, and one of them—it wasn't clear who—held a gun in the air.

"Help!" cried Charles.

"I'm a peace officer! I'm a court officer!" Gelb exclaimed.

Gelb's announcement about who he was only served to inflame Zuccaro, who was determined to stick up for Charles. He punched the court officer in the head. Gelb fell to the ground as Charles ran up the stairs. Zuccaro gave Gelb a few kicks while he was down.

Upstairs in the diner, it was an angry Charles who jumped on a tabletop, yelling that he was going to get Gelb arrested. The telephone call by the waitress and

Baranello, though truncated, managed to get through to the police dispatcher, and the sounds of police sirens could be heard as Charles bayed on the tabletop. Zuccaro walked out of the diner, and one of the other men was seen taking the guns and hiding them under his sweatshirt. Baranello watched as the man—she wasn't certain if it was Settle or Curro—put the guns in the car. She made a mental note of where the guns went.

When the cops came into the diner, Gelb described what had happened. Seeing that he was a fellow peace officer, the officers asked him who he wanted arrested. He told them to take Charles into custody. Meanwhile, Baranello told the officers about the guns in the car, which were easy to locate. With Charles in handcuffs, Zuccaro, Settle, and Curro were told they could leave. But the car they came in was confiscated by the cops. It was to be evidence.

After leaving the diner, Zuccaro and his two friends took a cab to the Howard Beach home of John Carneglia, waking him to tell him about what had happened at the diner and that his brother had been arrested. John Carneglia had always been protective of his younger brother, but there were times he screwed up—and tonight was one such time. This could bring unnecessary attention, particularly on the Gotti crew, from law enforcement. That Zuccaro didn't keep Charles out of trouble, didn't prevent the situation from escalating, also displeased John Carneglia.

Gelb had played to his sense of civic duty, and though he got a bit of a beating, he had managed to get credit for the arrest of Charles. But the situation made things rather inconvenient for Lynn Baranello, who not only was a witness to a felony but also had to spend more time out late at night, since Gelb, who had driven her to the diner, had to go to the precinct to assist the cops in processing the arrest. How, she thought, could he put them in this situation? Sensing Baranello's anger, Gelb thought that maybe his heroics hadn't been the smartest thing to do. Maybe if he could talk to Charles, the whole thing could be smoothed over with no hard feelings.

But the belief that Charles—a man with a short fuse— could be talked down from his own anger was another misjudgment by Gelb. Charles would have nothing to do with Gelb. There couldn't be any peace between the two. Returning from his brief conversation, Gelb seemed distraught. He told Baranello that Charles had labeled him "a dead man." Charles had said he was going to kill him, said Gelb.

Had Gelb done nothing that night and stayed put in the diner booth, he would never have had to confront Charles again. But in criminal cases, the arresting officer usually had to show up at the arraignment or a preliminary hearing, which in this case turned out to be the next day. There was no getting around the fact that Gelb would have to face Charles again.

Baranello tried to lessen Gelb's distress. The suspect was probably just blowing off steam, she said. There wasn't any need to worry.

Dennis Quirk, head of the court officers union, learned that night that there was reason—if not to worry—to at least be concerned about the man Gelb had arrested. As in all incidents involving a member of his organization, Quirk showed up at the precinct, where an angry Charles Carneglia was being processed for arrest. A few other cops, not assigned to the precinct, also showed up as part of the Organized Crime Control Bureau detail. Pulling Quirk aside, the OCCB cops let him in on a little secret: the suspect seemed to be mobbed up.

Bridge men in the New York City criminal courts rule the roost. As the court officers in charge of the courtrooms, the bridge men call out the cases, distribute papers to incoming defense attorneys, and keep order in the room. They are the main liaison between the judges and the attorneys. The evening of March 11, 1976, Albert Gelb was the bridge man on the 6:00 P.M. to 1:00 A.M. shift at the Kings County Criminal Court Building on Schermerhorn Street. Since he was only a court officer for three years, Gelb had to put in some time on the undesirable late-night shifts. Gradually, with seniority, he would avoid the late-night tours.

Only twenty-five years old, Gelb had shown an unusual flair for making arrests, quite apart from the episode a year earlier at the Esquire. There had been a total of eight arrests to Gelb's credit, four made on duty and four, like the case in the diner, done off duty. The bust at the Esquire and another gun case led to two excellent-service medals for Gelb. An arrest of a purse snatcher got Gelb a citation for meritorious service. While regular cops receive lots of awards, Gelb's various citations made him the most decorated of the city's 450 uniformed court officers. He seemed to relish keeping the peace and didn't shirk from going the extra mile to apprehend a criminal.

But the day at criminal court had been fairly routine. He ended his official work tour by escorting criminal court judge Richard Brown to his car near the Schermerhorn Street building. Short in stature, but with a large reputation in the city criminal justice system, Brown had

only recently been appointed to the bench. He had earned
the moniker "Duck Down Brown" when after his first day
in court, a crazed defendant took out a guy, forcing the
newly minted jurist to duck down under the bench.
Brown liked Gelb, calling him "Alby," as everybody else
did. Court officers would escort the night court judge
to his or her vehicle, just as a precaution, in case any
angry defendants or their families were lurking around.

Done with work, Gelb started his drive from downtown Brooklyn to his home on 109th Street in Rich-
mond Hill, a trip that was about a half hour without
traffic. He could take Atlantic Avenue most of the way
to his home, which was about six blocks north of Aqueduct Racetrack. The neighborhood was on the fringe of
Ozone Park, which was becoming more ethnic with an
influx of Guyanese; among other things, Ozone Park
was a traditional bastion of the Mob.

Following Gelb as he drove home was another court
officer, David Vartian. Both men had planned to meet
at Gelb's home and do a little personal Bible study together. Gelb was Jewish by birth, although his family
wasn't devoutly religious. In the Gelb household, the
key Jewish holidays were observed, and the family observed the week of Passover each spring. His father,
Louis, was president of a local Brooklyn synagogue.
But his old friend Lynn Baranello was a Jehovah's Witness, and it was under her influence that Gelb had
become interested in that faith. He found that religious study had given him another focus in life, a
philosophical base in a world where the daily grind of
work exposed him to so much strife, depravity, and violence. He had also been troubled by telephone calls
from the angry man he got arrested at the Esquire. He
had confided that to Lynn Baranello, and she would

later tell investigators that it had been Charles who said
Gelb was a dead man, marked for death.

Those calls had increased as the months went on,
and Baranello had told Gelb to call police. But he just
shrugged. At times, he tried to reason with the angry
man, telling him to find peace in the Scriptures, as Gelb
said he had through the Bible and his meetings with
the Jehovah's Witnesses. It was almost as though Gelb
had become resigned to something happening to him.
His fate, Gelb believed, could not be altered.

The street where Gelb lived was one-way, and he was
about two hundred feet from his house when he came
up alongside a vehicle that appeared to be waiting in
the street. Meanwhile, Vartian's car had stopped on Atlantic Avenue for a traffic light about two blocks away
from Gelb's home. It was then he heard what sounded
liked firecrackers, about five of them. The sharp cracks
that sliced through the night were followed by the squeal
of tires. Then it was quiet again. The light changed and
Vartian continued onto Gelb's block.

Turning onto 109th Street, Vartian saw Gelb's car
double-parked on the right side. He didn't see his friend
and figured he might be making a quick visit to a neighbor. Vartian drove by the car and went a short distance
to Gelb's address and waited.

Five minutes passed. Ten minutes. Gelb didn't appear.
That didn't seem right to Vartian and he walked back to
Gelb's vehicle. The driver's-side window was rolled
down, so he peered in. There was Gelb, slumped over
on his right side in the front seat, unresponsive as
Vartian shook him. There was also some blood around
his mouth.

Seven shots had hit Albert Gelb in what was obviously
an ambush. The assailant knew the court officer's move-

ments, knew where he lived, knew his work schedule and habits. Gelb knew what was happening in those last moments of his life and had tried to defend himself by reflexively raising his left forearm, the one nearest the shooter. Two shots hit his left arm—one on the forearm; another higher up near the armpit. But it was the other shots that did the most damage. The chest was struck twice. Another round hit his left cheek. Two more bullets entered Gelb's back, an indication that he was shot either falling forward into the seat or else was already lying down when the rounds struck.

What was likely the coup de grace was one bullet that entered the left lung, struck the heart, piercing the left ventricle and right atrium, as well as the aorta, before winding up in the tissue around the right lung. The mangling of the heart muscle had led to instant death.

It was an assassination, but it wasn't done cleanly. The killer seemed to be in a frenzied hunt for the unsuspecting quarry. The frequency of the shots, the hits to the back and face, indicated this murder was done to punish, to destroy, to send a message. *You had done something we didn't like, Albert Gelb. You had to pay the price.*

Emily Gelb was older than her brother by a few years. She lived out of state, and while Emily and Albert were close as siblings, he didn't confide in her about some things. A few things he kept to himself, and didn't share with Emily, were the threats he had been receiving since the incident at the Esquire a year earlier. So when a girlfriend of Emily's who took a message from her mother, Muriel, and told her that she should call her parents right away, Emily at first didn't suspect anything dire. But the friend told her it had something to do with her brother, Albert, and then wouldn't respond when asked if he was okay. Emily braced for bad news.

"Alby is dead," Muriel Gelb told her daughter, who to this day remembered little else about that traumatic telephone call.

The funeral for Albert Gelb took place on March 14 at Westminster Chapel in Brooklyn. The crowd of cops, court officers, and corrections officers was so large that the hundreds of mourners spilled out onto Coney Island Avenue. The newspaper reported that Gelb's murder remained a mystery, and a $5,000 reward was offered by the Uniformed Court Officers Association, the union.

Dennis Quirk, however, had not been mincing his words. Immediately after Gelb was gunned down, he told a television reporter that he believed the killer was either Charles Carneglia or someone close to him. The motive was the incident some eleven months earlier when Gelb had made one of his fabled off-duty arrests of the man with underworld connections, said Quirk. The newspapers didn't mention the name, but it just so happened Charles's case was scheduled to go to trial just six days after Gelb's death.

Since the casket was closed at the funeral home, Lynn Baranello never had a final look at her friend before he was buried. The memory she was left with was both poignant and disturbing. Gelb had visited her at the office she was working at and said he had a premonition about death. He wanted her to know he really valued her as a friend. Gelb also knew that her marriage wasn't in great shape, but he told her she should try again and have a lot of kids.

Baranello was game to try marriage again. She just didn't know with whom.

Gelb had asked, did she believe in the resurrection?

Yes, Baranello replied with conviction as she was looking at him.

The two friends then hugged one last time.

Emily Gelb and her parents sat the traditional Jewish mourning period of shiva at the home of a relative in Canarsie. Jews don't have wakes, so the shiva period, which can last for as long as a week, is the time when relatives and friends visit the mourning family, talk about the deceased, bring food, and try to lessen the burden of death.

There were lots of people making condolence calls on the Gelb family. But two men stood out in particular because they were unexpected. They didn't appear to be Jewish. Emily thought they looked Italian, and no one in the family knew who they were. Their appearance at the home created a sudden charge in the otherwise subdued setting. It was like electricity had jolted the mourners. They asked to see Louis Gelb in private, and the grieving father stepped outside the home to hear what they had to say.

"A mistake had been made," said one of the mystery callers.

Albert's death, they said, was something no one had received any approval for. *Whatever happened shouldn't have happened,* the men explained cryptically. Their message delivered, the mystery men disappeared into the streets of Canarsie.

3

The Bergin Crew

There is nothing that galvanizes law enforcement in New York City more than the killing of a cop or someone else in law enforcement. The tabloids and television stations cover the story incessantly. The funerals become massive state occasions of camaraderie and public mourning. Hundreds, if not thousands, of uniformed officers line the streets. Sometimes even the mayor speaks.

Then there is the hunt for justice for the deceased as detectives press on with the investigation. In modern times, a cop killer is usually caught and swiftly prosecuted. While New York State had the modern death penalty for a brief time from 1995 to 2004, the state has effectively been without it since a 1972 U.S. Supreme Court ruling. The one exception involved the murder of two narcotics detectives on Staten Island in 2003. That case was prosecuted in federal court, where there is capital punishment. The defendant

Ronell Wilson was given the death penalty in 2006 by a Brooklyn federal court jury for murdering Detectives James Nemorin and Rodney Andrews. An appeals court overturned the death penalty in 2010.)

While there wouldn't be any death penalty for the killer or killers of Albert Gelb, if and when they were caught, the incident caused a lot of concern in the Mob world of Ozone Park. John Carneglia knew that the fight his brother Charles had in the diner made him a key subject of the homicide investigation. Though no witness got a good look at the killer who fired at Gelb, police learned that a Chevy car had sped away from the scene after the court officer was gunned down. That was a slim lead. Who knew, it might lead to something.

Then, of course, there were the public suspicions about Charles Carneglia voiced by union official Dennis Quirk. A labor advocate out of the old school of Irish leaders who spoke their minds without filtering through public relations experts or spokesman, Quirk took just about every opportunity he could to link not only Charles but also Charles's brother, John, to the slaying. In truth, Quirk didn't have any direct evidence about the murder, but he had heard from Gelb himself about the threatening telephone calls the young court officer had received for months to make him suspect Charles. The incentive for Charles to try to coerce Albert Gelb into not testifying against him, said Quirk later, was that even if it was only a gun charge, the testimony would stiffen his sentence. Detectives might never connect the dots and implicate Charles, but John Carneglia knew that investigative attention would focus on their criminal world at a time when things were going very well for them and their street boss, John J. Gotti.

Almost immediately, the Gambino crew out at the Bergin began to feel heat from the cops. It wasn't anything major, but gambling operations were raided, which disrupted some of the flow of illegal earnings. Surveillance remained at a high level. On top of that, the publicity generated by Quirk just didn't sit well with the Mob. For a time, Gotti is said to have barred Charles Carneglia from coming around his social club in Ozone Park.

Just how much the higher-ups in the Gambino family tried to distance themselves from the Gelb slaying and those who did it became evident one night on Staten Island. Quirk, who lives in that borough, was attending a function at a local restaurant near the Todt Hill section. A lawyer who knew the union official walked over to Quirk, who noticed the attorney was accompanied by another man.

Union officials like Quirk, particularly those who garner a lot of publicity, are often sought out at such events. But the stocky gentleman who was with the lawyer was somebody Quirk immediately recognized: Thomas Bilotti, the driver and close associate of Gambino boss Paul Castellano. A cousin of the crime family patriarch Carlo Gambino, who had died recently, Castellano was the new leader of the *borgata*. A resident of Staten Island, Castellano portrayed himself as something of a respected businessman who ran a poultry and meatpacking operation. Bilotti served as his close confidant and driver, positions that merited his promotion to the rank of captain.

To Quirk's surprise, Bilotti had sought him out not only to express condolences about the killing of Gelb, but also to deliver a message from Castellano.

"I want you to know that my boss didn't authorize

this," said Bilotti about the murder, Quirk recalled in an interview with the author years later.

Bilotti's remarks, a tacit admission that Castellano was a power in the underworld, was significant because it was designed to distance the upper echelon of the crime family from the murder of the court officer. That Bilotti was allowed by his own boss to approach Quirk and say that was also an indication that whoever carried out the slaying had acted without authorization of the crime family leadership. The killer—or killers—had gone off the reservation, so to speak, to carry out the shooting. In the world of *La Cosa Nostra,* they were at risk themselves for retribution from the Mob. That the victim was a cop made matters worse.

The restaurant incident was the second time that someone who was linked to the Mob made it known that the Gelb killing wasn't an act done to further the interests of the Mafia. Gelb's father had been similarly approached by two men while he was sitting shiva. Castellano's apparent disgust with what had happened to Gelb was also an early indication of the suspicion he began to have about his own control over the crew of gangsters operating under Gotti out in Ozone Park. It was a rift that years later would lead to Castellano's own murder in December 1985 at the hands of Gotti and his crew from the 101st Avenue club. But Castellano was new to the job and had to consolidate his own power in the crime family. Besides, Gotti had some power allies in the Gambino leadership

Charles and John Carneglia wouldn't be anywhere in the Mob without the likes of Gotti. The product of the tumultuous marriage of John and Fannie Gotti, John was the fifth of thirteen children. As might be expected of an Italian household where the main breadwinner had a spotty work history, Gotti and his siblings were mired in a working-class environment. Mob historians said Gotti would go to school with unmatched shoes and ragged clothing. Bullies picked fights with him incessantly, but Gotti didn't back down. At an early age, he gained respect by fighting back.

There was a point where Gotti was trying to make it legitimately in life. But as his daughter Victoria would later relate in her own book, Gotti's father and his gambling addiction caused the old man to show up at his son's job, demanding money. The humiliating confrontations caused Gotti to lose whatever straight job he had, his daughter recalled. With no professional role models to guide him into the legitimate world, and lacking the right education, Gotti gravitated to the streets of East Brooklyn. School was a dead end for him: he dropped out of Franklin K. Lane High School in Queens and started making his mark on the street.

Gotti, along with his brothers Peter and Gene, as well as old friend Angelo Ruggiero, came together into what became known as the Fulton-Rockaway Boys. A street crew of young toughs, the gang was named after a major street intersection. Eventually the Gotti crew of young men who were quick to use their fists came to the attention of the local Mafia street bosses who used the Fulton-Rockaway Boys for errands and numbers running.

This area of East New York was also the turf of two mobsters in particular: Carmine and Daniel Fatico. Both were brothers and they each acquired the nickname of "Wagons." Carmine was the older of the two and was a captain in what was then the crime family of

Albert Anastasia. Known as the high lord executioner of *La Cosa Nostra*, Anastasia was a ruthless killer who took over the old Mangano Mob family after the boss Vincent Mangano disappeared in 1951.

The Fatico brothers came to the attention of law enforcement early on. Daniel got a nine-month sentence in 1960 for being involved in the operation of illegal stills in the city. The operation, federal officials reported, was run by John Livigno, of Brooklyn, who pleaded guilty and was given a two-year prison sentence. Officials said the operation cost the government $25 million in unpaid alcohol taxes over a two-year period.

At the age of fifty-six, Carmine Fatico in 1966 was arrested, along with other Gambino mobsters such as Castellano, at the Ravenite, then known as Raven Knights, on Mulberry Street, on state charges of consorting with criminals for unlawful purposes. Eleven gangsters were arrested in the haul, including an up-and-coming Gambino crime family leader named Aniello Dellacroce. But since none of the arresting officers were able to show that the men at the club were doing anything illegal, the case was dismissed and everyone was freed.

Back in the 1960s, it wasn't unheard of for prosecutors to bring charges against bar and club owners who opened places that catered to the gay crowd. While such cases would be laughable now, Daniel Fatico and three other reputed mobsters, including Genovese member Edward "Eddie Toy" DeCurtis, were convicted in Nassau County for operating a disorderly house known as The Magic Touch, which, as the newspapers stated, "catered to homosexuals." Odd as it might sound, reputed mobsters opened a number of clubs that catered to gay men and women to hook up. While gay mobsters are ostracized within the *Cosa Nostra*, the Mob saw a niche that it could fill, almost a vanguard of the gay rights movement.

Back in East New York, Gotti and his gang of toughs were taking care of some business for the Fatico crew. Both Faticos looked upon Gotti as a reliable young man and it didn't hurt that Ruggiero's uncle happened to be Dellacroce, who had been arrested with the elder Carmine Fatico at the ill-fated Raven Knights club raid by police in November 1966. By the late 1960s, Gotti and his band of brigands had gravitated into hijacking, a staple activity of the Fatico crew, and were regulars at the Fulton Avenue Social Club run by the brothers. In fact, Gotti, according to his daughter Victoria, began using the club as a refuge, since his own home was filled with the abuse of his father.

It was under the Fatico brothers that Gotti became a full-fledged gangster. The brothers had grown weary of the gritty East New York location of their club and transferred to new digs in Ozone Park on 101st Avenue, a location much closer to John F. Kennedy International Airport, and also Gotti's home in Howard Beach. The social club was christened Bergin Hunt and Fish, and the name "Bergin" seems to be a misspelling of Bergen Beach, an area of Brooklyn. The new storefront location was ideal for a band of hijackers because of its proximity to the airport and major highways. It was because of hijacking that Gotti suffered his first significant arrest in 1968, along with brother Gene and Ruggiero for committing three truck thefts at John F. Kennedy International Airport. They pleaded guilty and received short prison sentences. Meanwhile, the Faticos started having their own more substantial legal troubles.

The main problem for Carmine Fatico was his involvement not only in New York City hijacking but also loan-sharking out on Long Island. First, in May 1972, he was indicted by a Suffolk County grand jury on charges he was part of a usury ring that charged 250-percent-a-year interest. While freed on $25,000, Carmine was a year later again arrested and charged with another loan-sharking and conspiracy charge by Suffolk County prosecutors.

The Suffolk County cases were serious matters, and Carmine was distracted by the need to prepare for trial. While on bail, he also had to steer clear of the Bergin club and delegated the leadership of the crew temporarily to Gotti, whom Carmine made acting captain. This put Gotti in closer contact with Dellacroce, who by this time was the Gambino *borgata*'s underboss. Hijacking and gambling remained staples of the Fatico operation, now under the command of Gotti.

It was also by 1972 that the Carneglia brothers—John and Charles—became close to the Fatico operation and, of course, to Gotti. The East New York siblings had become components of the Bergin crew and its major hijacking operation, which federal investigators believed notched up several significant rip-offs from 1971 to 1972. Court records show that John Caneglia was indicted in Brooklyn federal court in 1970 for theft of goods from interstate commerce. But the indictment was dismissed in 1971 on motion by the government. Overall, the gang seemed to target any kind of commodity, from leather coats and fur pelts to zinc-alloy bars. If the score looked easy and profitable, the crew would take a crack at stealing it.

Already hobbled by his loan-sharking case in Suffolk County, Carmine Fatico, brother Daniel, and eleven others, including John and Charles Carneglia, were indicted by a Brooklyn federal grand jury for five truck hijackings. This appears to be the first major case against the Carneglias and the allegations documented for the first time their ties to the Fatico hijacking operation. As it turned out, Gotti wasn't charged in the case, although he had done a little bit of prison time for a hijacking rap in 1968.

The main hijacking caper involved the theft of ninety-eight mailbags delivered to New York on an Air France flight and on their way by truck to a U.S. mail facility at John F. Kennedy International Airport. The driver was stopped by four armed men and forced to lie on the floor of his vehicle while it was driven to Springfield Gardens, Queens. There the mailbags were transferred to a bakery truck.

But the suspects—and the Carneglia brothers were in that category—apparently didn't know the importance of what they had in their hands. Secreted within the bags was $3 million in cash, or its equivalent in negotiable instruments. Inexplicably, the Fatico gang left the $3 million in mail unopened in the bakery truck in Brooklyn. The gang didn't bother to open the packets, apparently thinking it was ordinary mail, when the envelopes, in fact, contained cash and negotiable securities. Instead, they settled on about $100,000 in proceeds taken from what they did open.

The key to the case was a cooperating witness named Salvatore Montello, who said that it had been Carmine Fatico who had made it known as far back as the 1960s that he was in the market for truckloads of stolen goods. Montello began working with the Fatico crew in 1971, which is around the time that most of the truckloads were stolen by the Bergin crew from the JFK airport area. Montello revealed to investigators the stature of the Fatico brothers in the Gambino family and told about visiting them at the Bergin club to talk about stolen goods. When a dispute arose over a truckload of fur pelts stolen in February 1971 while bound for London, it was the Faticos who arranged for a sit-down at the Ravenite club with underboss Dellacroce, said Montello. Dellacroce arbitrated the disagreement and ruled that gang member Manuel "Tutti" Llauget should be paid for the furs, as agreed, by a disgruntled buyer, Montello told investigators.

The Fatico hijacking case went to trial in 1976, but the jury was deadlocked, resulting in a mistrial. To wrap up their legal problems, the Fatico brothers finally decided to plead guilty to one count of conspiracy to possess the stolen furs, which Montello had told the FBI about. Faced with five years of imprisonment and a $10,000 fine, Carmine and Daniel Fatico should have received their sentence routinely. But the case set a precedent that would ultimately affect Mob cases for years to come. When Judge Jack B. Weinstein refused to let prosecutors submit evidence at sentencing from an unnamed confidential informant about the Fatico brothers' stature in the Gambino family, the government appealed. In reversing Weinstein, the Second Circuit Court of Appeals held that such evidence can be used at sentencing if the information is subject to corroboration by other means, such as the testimony of an FBI agent. As a result, U.S. courts now often hold what are called "Fatico hearings" before sentencing mobsters and even white-collar criminals. This legal procedural for sentencing is the brothers' singular, unique contribution to American jurisprudence.

When it finally came time for sentencing, the Fatico brothers received different results. The elder Carmine got a five-year term; Daniel also got five years, but had the sentence suspended with the condition that he stay away from the Begin club and the likes of Gotti and the Carneglia brothers. Carmine died in 1992.

The Carneglias were tried separately from the Faticos for the robbery of the mail and the use of guns in the various heists. They fared better than the older crime bosses. After three days of deliberation, the Brooklyn federal court jury couldn't agree on a verdict. The government considered a retrial but dragged its feet in getting things ready for a second shot at the Carneglias and a few of their codefendants. As a result, defense attorneys moved for a dismissal of the indictment. Seeing the case now on shaky legal grounds, the government moved to dismiss the charges, which Judge Weinstein did on March 21, 1977. Charles and John Carneglia were off the hook—at least for now.

Even though the key witness against him, Albert Gelb, was dead, Charles didn't escape problems over the fracas at the Esquire in 1975. State prosecutors pressed their case of gun possession and resisting arrest. At first, Charles Carneglia, through his attorneys, tried to get the indictment thrown out on the basis that the grand jury in Queens was empaneled under a state law that in New York State in 1975 allowed women an automatic excuse not to serve as jurors. In fact, the U.S. Supreme Court had ruled on a similar issue just before the diner fight that a Louisiana ordinance that effectively barred women from regular jury service tainted an indictment. It was a shot worth taking, and in Charles's case, the trial court held a full-blown hearing. But Queens County Supreme Court judge Arthur Lonschein ruled against Charles.

However, when the case finally went to trial in mid-1977, the legal situation continued to get complicated. On June 1, 1977, the trial court acquitted Charles of the weapons possession charge and convicted him of resisting arrest. It seems that the weapons weren't actually found on Charles but rather confiscated from the vehicle Peter Zuccaro had driven in when he arrived earlier at the Esquire diner. Charles appealed and argued that he couldn't be convicted of resisting arrest, because the arrest wasn't authorized and he didn't know that Gelb was a peace officer when he began fighting with him. The appeals court was sympathetic to Charles and indicated that Gelb may have committed an unprovoked attack on him in making the arrest, and Charles could have been justified in using self-defense at the time. The diner cashier, the court noted, also indicated that Albert Gelb may have been reacting to a disparaging remark uttered by someone else—not Charles. Since the trial judge didn't give the jury the right instruction on the law of self-defense, the appeals court overturned Charles's conviction.

Around 1977, the books of *La Cosa Nostra*, long closed in part because of Carlo Gambino's concern about heavy drug dealers being admitted to membership, were opened up for new entrants. It turned out to be a land rush. The same year John Carneglia beat the federal hijacking rap, he became a made member of *La Cosa Nostra*. Also inducted as members of the honored society were John Gotti and his talkative friend Angelo Ruggiero, both who had been paroled out of state prison for the McBratney homicide in the Staten Island bar. Another Howard Beach up-and-coming mobster, Joseph Massino, was similarly inducted into the Bonanno crime family around the same time. But others, like Charles Carneglia, weren't proposed for membership or were too problematic, which in Charles's case seemed to be the fallout from the Gelb incident a couple of years earlier. There were some in the Mob, notably Gotti himself, who thought Charles was just too unpredictable and impulsive, something that would be borne out later.

John Carneglia also seemed to harbor concerns about his brother and didn't keep them to himself. During a federal hijacking case he had in the early 1970s, John commented to Special Agent Steve Morrill that Charles was all but driving him to drink. "Charlie is driving me crazy," he told Morrill. Though John Carneglia didn't elaborate, Morrill remembered later that just by looking at Charles, when he showed up in court, he sensed he was uncontrollable.

"You could look in his eyes and you could tell he was nuts," said Morrill in an interview some years later.

While John Carneglia seemed to be a gentleman who could be ruthless when it came to Mob business, Charles impressed Morrill as being uncontrollable, with a personality that was cut from a different cloth than his older sibling.

The rumors and information John Carneglia was hearing from the street also would have led him to believe that his brother needed some watching. Such was the case in November 1977 with another incident at a Howard Beach diner, the Blue Fountain. Joy Girard remembered that day because it happened to be the same weekend of her birthday and she was out late when she pulled her car into the parking lot of the Blue Fountain to talk with a male friend and smoke a bit of marijuana. The hits of pot made her doze off for a short while. Once awake, Girard went into the diner and sat by the counter to get something to eat. She noticed a lot of neighborhood men in the Blue Fountain, among them Michael Cotillo, Charles Amato, and Charles Carneglia.

While waiting for her order, Girard noticed the decibel level inside the diner kept rising, as if an argument among the patrons was getting out of control. The men who were arguing numbered in the dozens and moved their business outside the diner, but the situation was so tense that the owner of the Blue Fountain wouldn't let any patrons, including Girard, go outside to get a closer look. When she finally got outside, Girard was stunned by what she saw. On the sidewalk lay Cotillo.

"Help me, I'm dying," the twenty-five-year-old Cotillo cried out as onlookers screamed in horror.

Although Girard didn't see any cuts or wounds on Cotillo, the handsome young man had sustained a wound to both his left and right ventricles of the heart. While blood was still being pumped by the damaged organ, there was also enormous leakage of blood into his chest cavity with every beat. Cotillo died a short while later at the old Interboro Hospital.

The entire incident at the Blue Fountain set off tremors in the Gambino crime family. Cotillo, it turned out, had been an associate of the *borgata* and was under the crew led by soldier Nicholas Corozzo. Gambino mobster Anthony Ruggiano, who became a federal witness, would later testify in court that the diner was affiliated with the crime family, a situation that required a number of immediate meetings or sit-downs following the killing. The result of one of the sit-downs was that Charles Amato and Robert Engel, two friends who were with Cotillo the night he was stabbed, were barred from the Blue Fountain. But in another meeting, it was life or death that hung in the balance.

The word on the street was that Charles Carneglia had been involved in the Cotillo stabbing and a number of mobsters were angered, including one whose daughter witnessed the slaying. Robert Engel, an old friend of Cotillo's, was so upset by Cotillo's death that outside the funeral parlor he ruminated over how much he wanted to get even with Charles.

"We were smoking and he just said, 'That fucking Charlie, I'm going to kill him, that scumbag, I'm going to shoot him in the fucking head,'" Ruggiano later related in federal court.

Ruggiano remembered some words of advice he gave Engel, should he try to go after Charles: "Whatever you are going to do, make sure you do it right, and be careful, because Charles is no fucking joke."

Since Charles was under John Gotti's Bergin crew and Cotillo under the Corozzo faction, both sides had representatives at the sit-down. In the arcane protocol of the Mafia, it was actually Gambino captain Anthony "Fat Andy" Ruggiano, the father of Anthony, who was supposed to be at the meeting, but since Corozzo was newly minted as a crime family member he wanted to get his feet wet by handling the meeting for his faction.

The meeting was actually a Mob version of a grievance procedure. But there were no administrative niceties.

Engel wanted Charles dead in return for the killing of Cotillo. It was up to the Gotti camp to try and save Charles's life. Gene Gotti, the younger brother of the crime family captain, sat down with Corozzo to decide what would happen. Engel, who pressed the case that Charles should die, finally got permission to get even with him for Cotillo's death, Anthony Ruggiano later told federal officials. But for a reason that was never clear, Engel never took a crack at Charles. A law enforcement source later told the author that Ruggiano's testimony was incorrect, and that as a result of the sit-down, Engel was told that retaliation could be meted out against a man who was at the diner but didn't do anything. It seemed to be that Charles was deemed too valuable to the crime family and thus received dispensation from being the object of any retaliation for the death of Cotillo. Better to sacrifice someone who wasn't important, seemed to be the Mob's idea of justice. In any case, no one died as a result of the slaying of Cotillo—neither Charles nor the low-level Mob associate who was offered up for retribution.

The Blue Fountain episode took place around the time that Gotti was made an acting captain by his mentor Dellacroce, with the approval of Castellano, and the Bergin crew began to become bolder. Law enforcement picked up rumors that some of the men around Gotti were flouting *La Cosa Nostra* rule against narcotics and was dealing in drugs. But the main source of income for Gotti seemed to be loan-sharking and gambling. It was because of Gotti's gambling addiction that he lost tens of thousands of dollars in bad wagers in a week.

* * *

Both the Carneglia brothers had a somewhat legitimate source of income at the Fountain Avenue junkyard. Their operation was becoming more extensive as
time went on. City records show that along with their
mother, Jennie, John and Charles Carneglia took out
a mortgage of $30,000 and secured it with several
pieces of property in and around Fountain Avenue.
In 1976, the Carneglia clan, including Jennie, acquired
the property on Fountain Avenue outright for $14,000,
with monthly mortgage payments amounting to $173,
city records show. The conglomeration of land was
extensive—junkyards need a lot of real estate—and the
Carneglias were proving to be land barons after a fashion. By 1984, they began leasing the premises on Fountain Avenue to Citiwide Auto Parts, Inc., another auto
junkyard and dismantling business for $5,000 a month.

The Carneglia junkyard was in an area of Brooklyn
immediately south of East New York known as the Mill
Basin section. The place got its name from working
grain mills that used to operate from the power of tidal
waters that flowed into the area from the seventeenth
century until the nineteenth century. The incoming
tidal waters flowed into a pond, which then emptied as
the tide went out, powering the waterwheels for as long
as six hours, twice a day. The mills are no longer in ex-
istence and the area is one of those out-of-the-way
places in the city that is easily overlooked. To the south
are some wetlands, which are filthy and used as dump-
ing grounds. The city has neglected the neighborhood
for decades, making it a perfect place for the Mob to do
its business.

The Carneglia brothers used the sprawling junkyard
complex as a place to collect more than just scrap autos.
According to Peter Zuccaro, from about the middle of

the 1970s to the late 1970s, the "Barn" building on Pine Street, about two hundred feet from the junkyard, was where a major marijuana distribution operation was carried out by both John and Charles. The brothers would get bales of marijuana in Winnebago RV vehicles, numbered them, and then put them in the barn, said Zuccaro in later testimony in federal court. Zuccaro said he would then get a couple of hundred pounds of the marijuana and sell it in about two weeks on credit, meaning he would split the money with the Carneglias.

Be it loan-sharking, gambling, hijacking, or extortion, the Bergin crew of Gotti had a number of niches in the Mob. But those rackets were the bread-and-butter operations of *La Cosa Nostra*. The big money could be found in drugs, and as Zuccaro's testimony indicated, the crew was trafficking early on in the drug trade, despite a professed ban of drug dealing among Mafia bosses reaching back into at least the 1950s. It was an open secret that all the crime families were involved in narcotics trafficking to some extent.

The suspected involvement of hundreds of Mob members and associates in drugs and other rackets was documented by the Federal Bureau of Narcotics (FBN), a unit of the U.S. Treasury Department, in a large dossier compiled from the 1950s through the early 1960s and publically released in 2007. Big bosses like Carlo Gambino and Paul Castellano in the Gambino *borgata* were against it in particular. Still, big-time Mafiosi were implicated and sometimes sent to prison for moving heroin or cocaine. Among them were boss Vito Genovese and one of his top lieutenants, John "Big John" Ormento. In the Lucchese family, Vincenzo "Vincent" Rao, an old-timer from Yonkers who earned the nickname "the Attorney General," was sentenced to five years in prison for lying to a federal grand jury probing narcotics, while Carmine "Mr. Gribbs" Tramunti, who became boss of the Lucchese *borgata* for a short time in 1967, was also sent to prison for narcotics trafficking and died behind bars. The Bonanno family had major drug dealers like the late Carmine Galante, and that family earned the distinction of setting the *Cosa Nostra* benchmark for drug dealing when a number of its captains, soldiers, and associates were convicted in the federal Pizza Connection Trial of 1987.

If Carlo Gambino kept steadfast to his own ban on drugs, the same wasn't true for Gotti's brigands at the Bergin. While Zuccaro told the FBI that the Carneglia brothers were big marijuana purveyors, others at the 101st Avenue club were into more serious drugs. Some of those who were part of the crew, such as Anthony "the Roach" Rampino, a gaunt, tall man who looked like something out of *The Phantom of the Opera,* not only dealt in heroin but abused it. Then there was Salvatore Ruggiero. The younger brother of Angelo, Salvatore had been turning big-time profits from heroin, and according to some Mob historians, he didn't need the cache of becoming a made member of the Mob. However, the problem for Salvatore was that the large income he acquired easily attracted the attention of the federal government. Rather than fight a tax case, Salvatore became a fugitive, dealing heroin when he could while on the lam.

According to Jerry Capeci and Gene Mustain in their biography *Gotti,* an informant in the Gambino family reported his suspicions to investigators that Salvatore Ruggiero kept in touch with his brother Angelo and Gotti Senior through calls to a series of ever-changing

pay telephone locations. That raised a suspicion, never
confirmed by the FBI, that Gotti pretended to adhere
to the Mafia ban on drugs but tolerated it among his
crew members such as Ruggiero, Charles's brother,
John, and others.

Sensing that the garrulous Angelo Ruggiero was talkative enough to leak information on the telephone, a
special FBI squad that had formed to probe the Gambino family got authorization in 1981 to bug the chatty
gangster's telephones. Ruggiero made it easy at one
point when he confided to an informant that he never
talked business on his own line but instead used a
Princess telephone in his daughter's room. The FBI
promptly got a tap for the Princess line as well. The
fruits of the Ruggiero wiretaps were bountiful. The FBI
spotted Angelo Ruggiero and John Carneglia meeting
with heroin dealers from Canada. Other mobsters, notably Massino, then a major Bonanno family captain,
were also overheard talking about their pending legal
problems. The wire really heated up when Salvatore
Ruggiero, in May 1982, having hired a private plane to
fly from a hideout in New Jersey to Florida, was killed
along with his wife when the aircraft crashed into the
sea on descent into Orlando International Airport.
After some frantic telephone calls, Angelo Ruggiero
and John Carneglia went to Salvatore's New Jersey
hideout to gather the dead man's documents, money,
and drugs. More telephone conversations implicated
Angelo and a lawyer, Michael Coiro, in a plan to hide
money Angelo might receive from the sale of his dead
brother's heroin stash.

If Gambino boss Paul Castellano had any illusion
that Gotti's Bergin crew wasn't dealing in drugs, his
mind was changed when on August 8, 1983, Angelo

Ruggiero, John Carneglia, Gene Gotti, and others were indicted by a Brooklyn federal grand jury for heroin trafficking. It was a monumental case, the first major one from the reinvigorated FBI offensive against the Gambino family. It would also intensify the problems that Castellano had with the Queens branch of the crime family led by Gotti. Castellano was preparing to break up the Bergin crew and bust Gotti in rank when the wily captain engineered the infamous preemptive strike that led to the murder on December 16, 1985, of Castellano and his driver, Thomas Bilotti. While he couldn't see it coming at the time, the indictment would also have consequences for Charles and would put him in a position of playing a greater and more deadly role in the Mob.

No sooner had prosecutors indicted Gene Gotti, Angelo Ruggiero, and John Carneglia on the drug charges than another investigation zeroed in on John Gotti himself and the rest of the Bergin crew, including Charles. This investigation was shepherded by Assistant U.S. Attorney Diane Giacalone in Brooklyn. Despite the fact that she had been handling the probe for about four years, many in the New York FBI office, as well as other prosecutors, thought Giacalone's case was premature and risked failing. The squad investigating Gotti's Bergin crew, led by supervisory agent Bruce Mouw, tried to dissuade her from pursuing the case and at one point reportedly declined to share transcripts of the Ruggiero wiretaps. One prosecutor went so far as to write his superiors in Washington, D.C., to say that Giacalone's case was extremely weak and that an acquittal risked immunizing the Gotti crew from further prosecutions because of double jeopardy.

But Giacalone stubbornly persisted, thinking she had a strong enough case for conviction and in March 1985 secured an indictment against Gambino underboss Aniello Dellacroce, John and Gene Gotti, Charles and John Carneglia, captains Leonard DiMaria and Nicholas Corozzo, and others. The racketeering indictment had the usual charges of gambling and loan-sharking. But it also included two acts of murder, including the slaying of court officer Albert Gelb, a killing that, one way or the other, had been precipitated by actions a hot-headed Charles had become involved in ten years earlier in the diner incident. The government's case dragged John Carneglia into the Gelb homicide, even though it had been Charles who had the fistfight with the court officer.

When they are indicted, most men stand and fight the charges. In Charles's case, he decided to run. Faced with the prospect of a lengthy prison sentence, Charles became a fugitive, abandoning his brother, the Gottis, and the rest of the Bergin crew to face the music. Informants later said that Charles went to hide in upstate New York, making occasional forays back to the city to take care of his mother and business.

Giacalone's case went to trial with initial jury selection in April 1986 and became the center of a media frenzy because Gotti had cemented his role as head of the Gambino family after the assassination of Paul Castellano in December. His flashy persona and flip comments were the dream of reporters who wanted an exciting Mob character to write about. Events at the trial, including a bomb scare, only fueled the spectacle. There was so much publicity that Judge Eugene

Nickerson, a mild-mannered patrician jurist, postponed jury selection until August.

What prosecutors hoped to do with the Gelb killing was to tie John Carneglia into the slaying based on some very circumstantial evidence. This proved to be one of the weak elements in the case. It was well known that Albert Gelb had complained to people, including Dennis Quirk and Lynn Baranello, that Charles Carneglia and his friends had threatened him if he testified against Charles in the state weapons case. Giacalone's indictment had alleged that Charles's brother, John, had a motive to slay Gelb and that the threats the court officer received were evidence of that.

To Judge Nickerson, the problem with the government's case was that Albert Gelb didn't say the associates of Charles who threatened him were part of the Gambino family. In fact, it seemed that Gelb didn't know the identities of Charles's associates who made the threats, said Nickerson. The court was reluctant to allow that evidence in but indicated that other evidence, including remarks by John that he had committed the Gelb murder to keep Charles from going to jail, might be more useful.

Diane Giacalone's decision to call Dennis Quirk to support the case against John Carneglia (Charles was on the lam and not standing trial) on the Gelb murder sparked another bit of menacing theatrics. The union official reported to prosecutors that two men in a black Mercedes approached as he was driving down Todt Hill Road in Staten Island to get on the highway. The men in the car motioned for him to open his window and said they wanted to talk with him about his testimony on the Gelb slaying. Hearing that, Quirk pulled his car off the road and drew his licensed handgun. The Mercedes sped away, going in the direction of New Jersey.

"For a long period of time, I carried my gun in my pocket," recalled Quirk.

Giacalone seized upon the appearance of the Mercedes as evidence that Gotti—who drove around in such a car—was one of the men who approached Quirk. The defense suggested that the whole incident was a government ploy to discredit Gotti. In court, Nickerson warned Gotti to stay away from witnesses after Giacalone said she would ask that bail be revoked for the Mob boss if he tried to contact witnesses in the future.

Although Gotti avoided problems with the Quirk incident, his luck ran out and he had his bail revoked after he was accused by local prosecutors in Queens with getting into a fight with Romual Piecyk, thirty-five-year-old refrigerator mechanic, outside a bar in Maspeth. By the time the federal trial resumed in earnest in August 1986, Gotti was in a federal detention center and had to be driven each day by federal marshals to court.

The trial was contentious. Defense attorneys—notably Bruce Cutler, who defended Gotti, and Barry Slotnick, who represented John Carneglia—sparred often with Giacalone and her co-counsel, John Gleeson. Some of the government witnesses didn't hold up well on cross-examination, and some government officials privately expressed doubts about whether Giacalone could win a conviction. There were also some sinister things going on with the defendants outside the courtroom.

Cadman Plaza Park is right outside the Brooklyn federal courthouse. The grassy, tree-lined expanse of land was named after Samuel Parkes Cadman, a twentieth-century Methodist minister who pioneered an ecumenical movement. During the Mob trial, John Carneglia would sometimes walk across the parkland with Kevin McMahon, the onetime Howard Beach street urchin whom the Carneglia family adopted, to go to a parking lot convenient to the courthouse. At the end of court proceedings one day, McMahon noticed in the lot one of the jurors in his car.

"Oh, there is one of your jurors," McMahon said to Carneglia.

McMahon jotted down the license plate number of the juror's car and passed it on to an associate of the Gambino family who was hanging around the courthouse. McMahon did that a few times with other jurors, and it didn't take long, he recalled, for things to start happening. The Gambino associate, known as "the Frog," had an insurance agent run the plate numbers through the state Department of Motor Vehicles in an effort to locate the jurors, McMahon later said. That was done, he explained, to try and get the jury rigged.

McMahon never learned if his license plate sleuthing amounted to anything. But in the end, Gotti's crew was able to get to the jury through an interesting coincidence. One of the anonymous jurors, an ex-marine named George Pape just so happened to be an old acquaintance of a Bosko Radonjich, a Yugoslavian thug who was friendly with Gotti. As soon as the trial got under way, Pape, who was having money troubles, reached out to Radonjich and said he could hold out for a price: $120,000. Sammy Gravano, then deemed Gotti's underboss, negotiated a price of $60,000 and passed the money through Radonjich to the juror.

The bribe would have at least assured a hung jury, since all Pape had to do was stand his ground and be the one vote for an acquittal. But instead, Pape, who was the jury foreman, convinced all the other jurors, many who initially had voted for conviction, that the government's case was wanting. A select few in law enforcement, including FBI supervisory agent Bruce Mouw, whose agents had developed a female informant who had learned through some Mob pillow talk of the jury-tampering bribe, reportedly knew that the case had been compromised. But to protect his informant, Mouw and the others kept silent and watched as on March 13, 1987, the jury came back with a verdict of acquittal for all of the defendants. Out the door as free men walked Gotti, his brother Gene, John Carneglia, and the others. Gotti's comment after the verdict was an angry "Shame on them," referring to Diane Giacalone and the rest of the prosecution team. Of course, that remark was just for show, since he knew the case was in the bag from the start.

Once Gotti and everyone else was acquitted, Charles Carneglia felt free to come back from his upstate hideout and take his chances. There wasn't much he was risking. After the disaster with Giacalone's prosecution, the government asked that the case against Charles be dismissed, which Nickerson granted.

Once they were back in Ozone Park, the victory in the racketeering trial, as rigged as it had been, gave Gotti and his crew an air of invincibility and added to his folk hero stature. As usual, the Bergin crew held its annual Fourth of July fireworks display for the neighborhood on 101st Avenue, an event that cops seemed to turn a blind eye to and let happen. No sooner had the racketeering case acquittal come down, but there was more trouble as Charles's brother, John, had to go on trial in the heroin case in June.

The talkative and imprudent Angelo Ruggiero had given the government plenty of incriminating surveillance tapes to work with in the drug case. But it still wasn't a cakewalk for the government. The first trial, which went on for nine months, ended when the government alleged that there had been an attempt to tamper with the jury. The 1988 retrial also resulted in a mistrial when the jury became deadlocked over whether prosecutors had tampered with some of the surveillance tapes. The defense first raised that allegation, and jurors insisted on listening to the originals of the tapes, not the enhanced copies, and also declined to use transcripts of the recordings.

John Carneglia wasn't that happy with the mistrial, since the government planned to do the case again for a third time.

"This case was over downstairs and it's over here," said John Carneglia, referring to the two different courtrooms used. "If Denver plays Washington enough times, Denver might win."

The government presented the drug conspiracy again, and as in the previous cases, there were problems with the jury. At one point during deliberations, one of the anonymous jurors said he had been threatened in his driveway. The juror had kept the incident to himself until, unable to remain composed during deliberations, he broke down in the jury room. Judge John Bartels then removed him and ordered the remaining eleven jurors, who had already said they were ready to announce a verdict, back to the jury room for more deliberations. Hours later, the panel came back and announced that it had found John Carneglia and Gene Gotti guilty of racketeering and a conspiracy to distribute heroin. Ironically, Angelo Ruggiero, whose chatter caught on the FBI bugs had caused so much trouble for himself and the Bergin crew, didn't stand trial for a third time because he was ill with cancer.

So the third time was the charm for prosecutors, who were desperately seeking a high-profile conviction against the key members of the Gambino crime family after the debacle in the earlier case with John Gotti. It also was the strongest evidence yet that a significant part of the Gambino family—in this case Gotti's own special crew—had been involved in narcotics trafficking. The Mob's prohibition against drugs was really nothing more than a hollow resolution of the old crime bosses of yesteryear.

Charles Carneglia would later take his own chances in further exploiting the permissive atmosphere that surrounded *La Cosa Nostra* when it came to drugs.

4

Father's Day

Anyone walking along the Hampton Bays beach on Long Island one weekend in June 1989 would not have been surprised to see the long speedboats pulling to the oceanfront of the house on Dune Road. The area east of Westhampton and bordering Shinnecock Bay was a popular summer spot for city folk who could afford to buy or rent the spacious homes as getaways. Expensive boats were one way guests announced their arrivals.

The crowd that gathered at the beach house seemed like any other family group enjoying the brilliant sunshine and calm waters. The men were a bit thick in the middle and exuded a kind of prosperousness. Their women were well coiffed, tan, and had a fleshiness that came from having to put up with years of child rearing.

There was plenty of food to go around: a barbecue grill was turning out chicken and Italian sausages. Desserts for this particular weekend, which just so happened to be Father's Day, included chocolate layer cake and cheesecake. There was also a birthday cake on the table. The coffeepot was working overtime, and the sauces were simmering on the indoor stove. Though it was still early in the season, a few revelers waded into the somewhat chilly waters of the Atlantic Ocean.

But this was not the typical Hamptons weekend bash of a young crowd of Manhattan professionals on the make. Nor was it a gathering of the wealthy crowd who would later spend the early evening at one of the charity spectacles that regularly attracted coverage from glossy magazines. What made this particular party different was its host, Gambino crime family soldier John Carneglia, and the fact that it would turn out to be the last time he, his family, and their close friends would ever party like this in their lifetimes.

Instead of a summer house, Carneglia was destined to be heading to the *big house,* a federal correctional institution somewhere in the United States, where the best sun he would catch was from walks around the exercise yard. Though free on $1 million bail, John Carneglia had been convicted a month earlier for heroin trafficking, along with Gene Gotti. Carneglia was on a short leash, restricted in his travels to the local jurisdiction of the Brooklyn federal court, where he fully expected in a few days to receive a very stiff sentence.

Still, there would be one more good time. John decided that it was best to assemble his closest family and friends for one big final fete, a long good-bye spread out over three days. The guest list included some wives and girlfriends, but for John it was the men who accompanied the ladies that attested to his stature in the world of organized crime, and the respect he still commanded. It was something he earned over a long, tough road in the world of the Mob. It had helped that he and the new crime boss, his old friend John Gotti, had pulled off one of the biggest putsches in Mafia history: the December 16, 1985, assassination of ruling Gambino boss Paul Castellano.

Carneglia's brother, Charles, and their mother, Jennie, who by this time was still relatively spry and active at the age of seventy-five, were among the guests. The gathering was a signal to those who showed up that Charles would be the anointed caretaker of his brother's interests and rackets. John Carneglia might be going away for a long time, but he needed someone he could trust to carry out his orders, follow simple directions, and be his point of contact with the outside world. Charles didn't make a lot of money for the Gambino family—his payoffs sometimes amounted to a measly $300—and his brother didn't hide his feeling that he didn't believe he had much of a head for the rackets. But both men were brothers, and John knew his sibling was often just a telephone call away. It also helped that the boss, John Gotti, valued Charles's ability to do the Mob's dirty work, although at times he questioned Charles's ability to maintain control of his violent instincts.

Charles sometimes would even get into arguments and fights with women, according to some from his old Howard Beach neighborhood. Events like that didn't escape Gotti's notice and became the subject of serious meetings in the social clubs, so-called sit-downs, according to people interviewed. A number of young, pulchritudinous women had gravitated to the area diners, enamored with the gangster life. One particularly beautiful friend of Charles's, nearly twenty years his junior, would go on car chases with Mob associates and even got wounded by gunfire. Another was handy with a knife and could hold her own in a street fight. Life was like that in Howard Beach, which had a Wild West element.

But it wasn't the women who attracted the attention of the cops so much as the men they fixated on. The word on the street was that Charles had a tendency to get involved in deadly street fights and use a knife with fatal results. Then there was the murder of court officer Albert Gelb, a crime that had brought a lot of attention to the Gambino *borgata,* as well as on Charles and his brother.

John Gotti had plenty of reason to stay away from the party. Narcotics trafficking was supposed to be forbidden in *La Cosa Nostra,* at least that was the official story given lip service by the crime bosses. But like the Catholic Church's view of masturbation as a sin, Mafia drug dealing—while officially banned—was done by just about every crime family. It was the Mob's big charade: even Gotti's own son John Junior was reputed to have been a big marijuana distributor. Still, if only for appearances, Gotti needed to keep a distance from the Carneglia bash.

Gotti's absence was conspicuous, and in a moment of irreverent humor, John Carneglia joked how the party crowd should call up Gotti to rib him and to remind him of what a good time he was missing.

"You should call up, you should call up John and sing 'Let Old Acquaintance Be Forgot,'" the host told the guests with a chuckle.

"I am with Johnny. He'd go crazy," one of the guests, Carlo Vaccarezza, said, laughing.

Carneglia said it was his party and Gotti should lighten up.

"I am over here with my friends. What are you (Gotti) getting hot about? It is Father's Day" was how Carneglia said he would razz the crime boss. That was a make-believe conversation. Nobody made the call to Howard Beach and risked disturbing Gotti, much less reminding him of the good time.

But while Gotti was nowhere near the Dune Road house, he was present symbolically at the gathering in so many ways. The most visible way was in the arrival of the first of the powerboats. The brilliant red Fountain boat—so named because its creator was North Carolina speedboat star Reggie Fountain—motored close to the shore. Looking like a giant dagger bobbing in the surf, the craft had been christened *Not Guilty* to commemorate Gotti's 1986 acquittal on a federal rap. It was about forty feet long and could hit speeds of close to one hundred miles per hour. Easing its way toward the beach, *Not Guilty* was steadied by three men who waded out into the gentle surf. The crowd on the beach tried to coax one of the hesitant passengers, a heavyset guy known as "Fat Richie," to jump into the water.

"He ain't getting off that boat," one of the women said with exasperation as she watched the portly man sit on the stern. The promise of food at the beach house finally lured Fat Richie into the water and up to the house, where he planted himself inside at the kitchen table.

Vaccarezza owned the boat and used it to ferry Gotti now and again on joyrides to the Hamptons and Fire Island. Gotti didn't like boats much but tolerated his trips on the *Not Guilty* because he thought Kevin McMahon brought him good luck and insisted that the young man sit beside him on the open water. Vaccarezza, owner of the Manhattan restaurant Da Noi, had become very close to Gotti. Well tailored and with a trace of an Italian accent, Vaccarezza sometimes functioned as a public face for the crime boss, speaking to the press on his behalf. Being close to Gotti, Vaccarezza had no trouble wrangling an invitation to the party. In one way, Vaccarezza and his speedboat served as Gotti's proxies, his representatives to the gathering.

The next boat, a white Baha speedboat that was smaller than the *Not Guilty*, edged its way to the shoreline. It was piloted by Hunter Adams, a small-time gambler and semi-legitimate businessman from Queens who was only twenty-two years old. Not being Italian, Adams, a Jew, had no chance of becoming a member of *La Cosa Nostra*. But he did eventually do a lot of work for the Mob: money laundering and stock fraud, the latter was becoming a very hot moneymaker for organized crime, once the gangsters figured out how easy it was to pump up the price of penny stocks and then cash out.

In the attenuated world of connections in the Mob, Adams got invited to the beach party because his main contact to the Carneglia crowd happened to be Michael Reiter, a man two years younger to whom he gave a ride on the boat to the party. Like Adams, Reiter could never become a Mob member because he lacked Italian heritage. But as the son of Gambino associate Mark Reiter, the younger Reiter had started making the connections he eventually needed to start his own stock-swindling business.

At some point at the beach house, Reiter introduced Adams to Charles Carneglia. The meeting wasn't anything unusual and was probably over lunch out on the porch. But Adams would eventually cross paths with Charles again and again. Eventually the contacts would develop to the point where Adams would have to rely on

Charles for help in his various illicit businesses. But that was a few years in the future. At the party, people were simply rubbing shoulders with the Carneglia family. With so many women around, it would have been foolish for the mobsters and their associates to talk about business. This was a time for everybody to show up, pay their respects, and do what they could to give a good send-off to a man who never turned into a snitch, and was destined to spend a lot of time in a prison cell.

Long in the shadow of his older brother, Charles was steadily making his presence known as a reliable worker for the Mob. True, he wasn't a made member of *La Cosa Nostra* at this point and wasn't capable of earning a lot of money for the bosses. But he had been delegated enough duties by his brother and Gotti that he was earning trust in key ways. Rumors abound that Charles liked to dispose of bodies; if the walls of his spooky, ramshackle shack in Brooklyn could talk, what stories of terror they might tell. Charles wasn't as gregarious as his brother and at parties kept a low-key presence. He knew enough to do his heavy drinking in private.

The high temperatures and hot sun sent some of the guests, mostly the women, to the chaise longues, where they were content to sun themselves at one end of the porch. Meanwhile, some of the men waded into the water. One particularly heavyset fellow, with tinted sunglasses, donned a child's inflatable life preserver and stuck it around his midsection. The effect on Angelo Ruggiero was comical, but in reality there wasn't much to laugh about with him.

Ruggiero had been one of the original members of John Gotti's crew when it was just a band of truck hijackers and burglars known as the Fulton-Rockaway Boys. Hijacking, particularly with all of the truck commerce in Brooklyn and Queens, was an easy moneymaker for Gotti and his gang. Ruggiero earned a reputation as being one of Gotti's musclemen, his imposing girth and scowling jowls gave him a fearsome look. He made his mark early when in 1974 he pleaded guilty, along with Gotti, for the attempted manslaughter of a man in a Staten Island bar. Police believed the killing of James McBratney was done as a favor to then-Gambino boss Carlo Gambino. After a plea bargain negotiated by lawyer Roy Cohn, both John Gotti and Angelo Ruggiero got lenient two-year state prison sentences.

Once Gotti and Ruggiero served their time, they went right back to the crime crew and had the good fortune—at least in the Mob—of being under the wing of Gambino crime family *consigliere* Aniello Dellacroce, who happened to be Ruggiero's uncle. Ruggiero had just gotten out of the manslaughter prison term when he had a hand in the killing of Vito Borelli, a hearse driver who had been dating the daughter of Paul Castellano. It turned out that Borelli had the poor judgment to make a joke about Castellano, who by then had taken over the reins of the crime family when Carlo Gambino had become sickly in 1975. Castellano heard about Borelli's transgression and ordered him killed. The job fell to Gotti and Ruggiero, as well as fellow Bonanno crime family members Joseph Massino and Salvatore Vitale, who helped dispose of the body.

Always Gotti's loyal acolyte, Ruggiero was believed to have orchestrated the abduction and murder of the Howard Beach man who accidentally ran over Gotti's twelve-year-old son, Frank, in 1980. Informants would later relate how it fell upon Charles Carneglia to dispose of the body in his particularly macabre way through the use of acid. Then there was always the murder of Castellano: Ruggiero was one of the plotters. Ruggiero also orchestrated a few other murders, including the slaying of Robert DiBernardo, to whom he owed $250,000. DiBernardo was brutally killed by a gunshot to the back of the head as he attended a Mob meeting. There was also the attempt on the life of Lucchese boss Anthony "Gaspipe" Casso. But that incident went woefully wrong on a Brooklyn street and Casso survived—something that didn't improve Ruggiero's stature within the Gambino family.

But murder wasn't the main problem for Angelo Ruggiero. He just plain talked too much. His banter and nonstop conversation seemed almost compulsive— some thought he suffered from Tourette's syndrome— earning him the derisive nickname "Quack-Quack." The FBI picked up on Ruggiero's imprudent talking and in 1981 and 1982 bugged his homes in Howard Beach and Cedarhurst, Long Island. The tapes proved to be a treasure trove for the government, which used them to convict John Carneglia and Gene Gotti.

However, while Ruggiero was also indicted for the same offenses as John Carneglia, he discovered that he was ill with lung cancer. Though he would die six months after the Dune Road party, Ruggiero didn't seem any worse for wear as he waded into the ocean and soaked up the sun. If John Carneglia held any malice toward Ruggiero for all of the trouble his big mouth had caused, he didn't show it as he stuck a fork into a piece of layer cake and ordered his wife, Helene, to keep the coffee coming.

But for Gotti, Ruggiero was another matter. The crime boss had become furious with Ruggiero's incredible lack of discretion, both in the way he talked on the

telephone and in the way he seemed to botch things
like the Casso hit. Sammy Gravano said that at one
point Gotti, angry over the way the Ruggiero tapes
had implicated his brother Gene Gotti and John Car-
negelia, planned to have his old friend killed. But because Ruggiero had terminal cancer, Gravano said, he
talked Gotti into calling off any hit and instead settling
for stripping Ruggiero of any power in the crime family.
The banishment so devastated Ruggiero that he would
meet Gotti's wife, Victoria, on Cross Bay Boulevard and
cry as he beseeched her to convince her husband to
take him back into the fold. Gotti, of course, would not
be moved.

Another man who graced the table at the Hampton
Bays party was Peter Zuccaro, the same man who had
been with Charles that night in 1975 at the Esquire
when the fight erupted with the court officer Albert
Gelb. Ever since he was a kid growing up in Brooklyn,
Zuccaro wanted to be a gangster, and in the ensuing
years made good on that aspiration in his association
with Charles. The men became close friends: Charles
was Zuccaro's best man, although he declined to sign
the marriage license so as not to have his signature in a
place where law enforcement could find it. Though he
got arrested numerous times in the 1970s for assaults,
robberies, drug dealing, and car thefts, Zuccaro didn't
serve any time in jail. But in the 1980s, after pulling
off two armored-car robberies, Zuccaro was convicted
and sentenced to a seven-year stretch behind bars, getting out in 1988.

Associates do a lot of crimes for the Mob, but they are
basically indentured servants who can be sold and traded
by the crime families like baseball players. Such is what
happened to Peter Zuccaro in 1986 while serving time

for the robberies. Ruggiero and Bonanno boss Joe Massino hashed out the trade while both were spending time, awaiting trial, in the federal jail in Manhattan in 1986. Both men then told Zuccaro, who was also being held in the same detention center, about the switch.

"After they had a discussion, they called me in to where they were discussing this situation, and they told me I was now switched from the Bonanno family to the Gambino family," Zuccaro remembered.

Zuccaro was told that his boss was to be John Carneglia and got the brush-off from Massino when he asked why he had been traded, so to speak. Already established with the Bonanno family, and with hopes of becoming one of its made members, Zuccaro wasn't thrilled with having to switch allegiances. He had grown up as a criminal with the Bonanno clan and had close family involved with the *borgata*. The move was out of his comfort zone. But there was nothing that Zuccaro could do, and so he showed his allegiance to Carneglia any way he could, including by showing up at Dune Road. When John Carneglia went away to prison in a short time, Zuccaro would be reassigned to work with Charles. It would be a relationship that would later hold important consequences for both men.

Kevin McMahon was captured on a homemade video of the Dune Road party slathering himself with sunscreen as John Carneglia's wife, Helene, panned the camera.

"Hi, Kev," she said affectionately as McMahon's image filled the frame for an instant.

Known as "the Weasel" and "the Midget" because of his short height, McMahon was considered by Helene and her husband to be part of the family ever since they discovered him living in their backyard cabana in

Howard Beach. They gave him money, took him on vacations, and attended his wedding. Of Irish descent, McMahon had no chance of becoming a full-fledged *La Cosa Nostra* member. But he had his usefulness to both John and Charles Carneglia in various crimes involving the crime family.

McMahon wasn't a killer. He didn't have the lust for blood or the need to show he could take a life. But when John Carneglia and John Gotti were on trial in 1986 in Brooklyn federal court, it was McMahon, along with other Gambino crime family associates, who went about trying to tamper with the jury. But for the most part, McMahon was a guy who knew cars, how to drive them and how to steal them. He had perfected his skill as an auto thief since he was thirteen years old and bragged that he had stolen five hundred vehicles. He also had a lot of help in Howard Beach, where other aspiring Mob associates were willing to pop an ignition switch. When he needed a car and driver for an illicit job, Charles Carneglia knew he could turn to McMahon for help.

As he got older, McMahon would get involved with Charles in a host of crimes. But the real usefulness of McMahon was in the role of Charles's babysitter. As a man who abused alcohol, Charles would go on drinking binges, which left him near comatose in his apartment. As a drunk, Charles was also loud and obnoxious. Emboldened by alcohol, Charles would talk about things that any prudent mobster would keep under wraps—like where the bodies were supposedly buried. McMahon would make sure Charles could wake up, and took care that the inebriated gangster didn't have guns around when the alcohol was flowing.

Though a prison term was staring him in the face,

John Carneglia nevertheless seemed to have a devil-may-care attitude. Those who shared the weekend with him—mother Jennie, wife Helene, brother Charles, McMahon, Zuccaro, even the dying Ruggiero—by their presence seemed to form a tribute to John Carneglia's run in the Mob. He had a long tenure in the life, and now it was time to pay the price. Though life in the Mob could bring big money, the end result seemed to be decidedly grim. The *Cosa Nostra* didn't have a retirement plan and its members were more and more finding themselves pensioned off to a government old-age home surrounded by barbed wire and tall fences. At one point, John Carneglia spoke to one of his guests in a way that seemed to foreshadow what the future had in store for those, particularly his brother, who continued to live the gangster life.

Unlike the days of the old *Cosa Nostra* bosses from Italy, theirs was a life in which loyalties were tentative, shifting, or nonexistent. The stand-up guys, those who could be counted on to never betray the Mob's oaths, were in short supply. Turncoats—"canaries," as Charles called them—would rule the day. In his own way, even John Carneglia acknowledged the new reality.

"I stick up for you whenever I can," said John. The qualification in that remark seemed to unsettle the guest.

"What do you mean *whenever you can?*" the man answered. He said it with a nervous, disconcerted laugh.

No sooner had the Hampton Bays party ended than the Carneglia family got a rude awakening back in Brooklyn. Judge John Bartels had decided to revoke the bail of John, as well as Gene Gotti, pending their July 7 sentencing in the heroin case. Bartels ruled that since both men placed their allegiance to the crime family above all else, they should await their sentencing in jail. But Bartels allowed both defendants to have one more night to say good-bye to their families. They were to return to court the next day at 10:00 A.M.

The next day proved to be a bit of a nail-biter for defense attorneys Gerald L. Shargel, who represented John Carneglia, and Ronald Fischetti, who was the lawyer for Gene Gotti. The deadline was approaching for the defendants to surrender, and neither defendant was in sight as the lawyers, reporters, and others gathered outside the Brooklyn federal court. But with eight minutes to go before Bartels's deadline, Gotti and Carneglia arrived outside the courthouse, clad in nylon jogging suits and new Reeboks.

"Afraid we weren't going to show up?" Gotti remarked to the lawyers.

A week later, Bartels sentenced Gotti and Carneglia to fifty-year terms, and some of the spectators gasped at the severity of the prison terms. Neither man spoke.

Even behind bars, John Carneglia and Gene Gotti never lost touch with the Gambino family, and law enforcement officials said that Gotti made sure his loan-sharking racket continued to generate money. With his brother effectively off the street, it was up to Charles Carneglia to keep John abreast of Mob business, which he did in regular telephone calls with the inmate. But now it was Charles's time to try and step up and show his mettle as mobster material. He still had a powerful ally in John Gotti. Not before long, he would be asked to prove he could handle a special job for the Gambino boss.

5

The Albanian

John Alite was a guy who grew up in Queens, and as they say in Howard Beach, he was very "street."

That meant in his stomping grounds around Forest Park and Ozone Park that Alite survived well by his wits, guile, bravado, and plain brute force. Growing up the son of a cabdriver and a secretary, Alite, whose name is of Albanian origin, knew about crime from a very early age. His uncle ran a card game with Charles Luciano, not the legendary gangster from the 1930s, but a Gambino soldier whose territory was part of Queens. With such role models, Alite began to think at the age of seven that being a gangster was an honorable way to live.

"I looked at [it like] somebody that goes to the army, the armed forces," said Alite later of the wiseguys. "You look at it as if something to look upon as a good thing, something with respect and honor. And I wanted to do the same. I wanted to join those forces."

While working in a delicatessen, Alite began doing a

little numbers running for a local bookmaker linked to
the Lucchese crime family. That was pretty tame stuff in
the world of crime. But then Alite got into trouble with a
local merchant, who began threatening him because he
thought the Albanian kid was laughing at him. The
threats escalated to the point where the merchant turned
up one day at Alite's home with an automatic weapon!

It was then that Alite turned to his old baseball coach
Anthony Ruggiano for help. As it turned out, Ruggiano
was the son of the well-known Gambino crime family
captain Anthony Ruggiano. At first, Ruggiano asked the
merchant to stop bothering Alite. That didn't work, so
a sterner warning was given. When that had no effect,
the merchant's son was abducted and thrown off a
building, sustaining severe injuries, such as a broken
neck and skull fracture, Alite told police. His problem
with the merchant stopped.

Since some of his friends were criminals, it was only
a matter of time before Alite would run into Junior
Gotti, the son of the man everybody knew to be the up-
and-coming power in the Gambino crime family. The
first real encounter between Alite and Junior took
place at the Finish Line, a bar in Queens not far from
Belmont Park, a racetrack. Aside from some small talk,
there wasn't much to it. Both men, then in their late
teens, became friends. Alite wasn't doing anything
much as a criminal except for moving small amounts of
cocaine to make some money before he went away to
attend the University of Tampa, Florida, where he
hoped to make a mark for himself as a baseball player.
But after one semester, an arm injury sidelined Alite's
career as a college athlete and he returned to New
York, where he enrolled in Queens College.

After his father discovered that Alite was moving

drugs, he gave his son a good beating and then sent him to live with an uncle in California, thinking that might keep his son on the straight and narrow. Combative and unable to avoid trouble, Alite got arrested for assault and came back after a year to Queens. Once back in the Woodhaven area, adjacent to Forest Park, Alite got reacquainted with drug dealing on a larger scale with an old friend, Kevin Bonner. It was after that, Alite would later tell the FBI, that he and Bonner started kicking up some of their drug money to Junior, who by then was an associate of his father's crime family.

In later debriefings with the FBI, Alite insisted that Gotti not only demanded a share of his drug sales but was also running a marijuana distribution racket with John Gebert, another of Alite's friends. (Gotti would deny the allegations of drug dealing when he went on trial years later.) Alite and Junior's friendship went to another level of trust when, according to Alite, the younger Gotti enlisted his help in a drive-by shooting targeting some Jamaican marijuana dealers who had robbed Gebert. Alite said he was the driver, and Gebert the shooter, as they cruised by a location in Jamaica at about 118th Street. When they found their targets, Alite slowed the car down to a crawl, and Gebert rolled down his passenger-side window and fired his handgun at the Jamaicans. Two men were hit, although it was unclear if they died. The shooting in mid-1984 apparently did wonders for Alite's esteem in Junior's eyes.

"He didn't look at me as some college kid now," Alite would say later. "Now he seen that I was capable. That I did a good job. I didn't panic. And I was able to commit a hit if he needed it, or he could start using me for strong-arming things."

When Alite got married on February 14, 1989, it was

Junior who stood up for him as his best man, and along with another Gambino crime family member, "Johnny Boy" Ruggiero, son of Angelo Ruggiero, he signed the marriage license as witnesses. The Valentine's Day date of the nuptials wasn't picked for sentimentality: it happened to be Junior's birthday, and he asked Alite to hold the wedding then out of respect for him.

It wasn't long before Alite's connection to the Gambino family brought him into contact with Charles Carneglia. At first, it was mostly on the basis of reputation and various rumors flying around the neighborhood. One: Charles had fled upstate to avoid prosecution (true, since that is what happened during the 1985 federal indictment). Two: Charles had been wanted in the stabbing to death of a court officer who was going to testify against him (not true, since Albert Gelb was shot to death). Three: Charles would boast about killing the officer and was overheard saying, "That's what should happen to all cops." (Such a statement is unverifiable.)

There were a number of other things Alite picked up among the whispers on the street and in Queens bars about Charles, all of which made him sound like a man who liked to kill and inflict physical pain. There was the murder of Sal Puma, an old friend of Charles, who the crime family leadership said was stabbed by Charles on the streets of Howard Beach. The Puma stabbing seemed like a personal vendetta to Alite. But when Senior Gotti needed something done about Carmine Agnello, the man who was dating his daughter Victoria and allegedly struck her, he turned to Charles's crew, which included Steven Zuccaro, to do the dirty work. Agnello, who ran an auto salvage business near the old Shea Stadium, was chased down as he drove one of his tow trucks. Attempting to flee on foot, Agnello stumbled to the ground and began to cry out for his mother as his assailants beat him and stabbed him in the buttocks. Under Senior Gotti's orders, Agnello wasn't supposed to be killed and he did survive, later marrying Victoria, who finally divorced him in 2003 after it was revealed that the FBI had tapes of her husband having sex with a woman who worked for him.

From about 1983, and for about ten years, Alite was one of the largest cocaine dealers in the city, he said. Neighborhoods like Howard Beach, Ozone Park, and Woodhaven in Queens, as well as East New York in Brooklyn and Valley Stream on Long Island, were Alite's drug turf. Just how big Alite was in the drug racket is open to debate, and there is some evidence he wasn't raking in nearly as much money as the $1 million-a-month profit he would later claim to the FBI. At this point, Charles was an associate of the Gambino *borgata,* just like Alite. But whatever he was doing with drugs, Alite could rely on the power of the crime family for help.

"When I needed guys, I had guys. When I needed somebody to go do something, I had people to do something. If I had a problem with another crew, another family, I had my umbrella," said Alite.

The Gambino family, led by John Gotti Sr., was Alite's umbrella. For that protection, Alite claimed he paid Junior Gotti money from the drug dealing, something that flew in the face of the Mafia ban. Senior Gotti suspected Alite was a major drug dealer and said that while he didn't know exactly what the Albanian was doing, if he got caught, the Mob would kill him. Alite took that to mean that Senior Gotti was willing to look the other way on the cocaine trafficking, but that Alite would take the fall if the police got wise to him.

Charles, also an associate of the Gambino family, had his own crew of criminals to work with, reporting in this period to his brother, John. But Charles's main value was as a source of muscle to carry out beatings or whatever strong-armed tactics Senior Gotti needed. Alite also was given the power by the Gambino family to run his own crew of associates, something that didn't happen often to somebody who wasn't of Italian lineage. Alite was valuable because he led a drug operation that provided an important source of revenue for the *borgata*. He was also a man who could be counted on to help out in a murder.

People usually don't get killed by the Mob for no reason. The motivation may seem trivial to law-abiding people, but to the killers, and to the Mafia, a breach of respect and protocol are just as likely to get a person murdered as more serious reasons, like a Mob war. John Alite made himself useful to the Mob by arranging hits and even doing them himself. It didn't matter if you had been a friend or if you were an enemy, Alite was an equal-opportunity killer, no matter who the victim might be.

In the Mob drug culture in Queens, George Grosso made a big mistake when he said he was dealing cocaine for the Gottis, which he apparently wasn't doing. Grosso only compounded his problems when he took a shot at Alite in an apparent assassination attempt. Grosso had to go, and Alite got permission in December 1988, so he said, from the Gambino crime family to carry out the hit and arranged it with some ingenuity to take place during a night of barhopping. Despite Grosso's attempt to shoot Alite, both men were among a group of Gambino associates who started drinking at a bar known as the Light Horse. Everybody was downing shots of vodka, but Alite kept a clear head by drinking just water. As Alite would later tell the FBI, he arranged to have the bar close early so that the group would have to get in a car and seek out libation elsewhere. Grosso sat near Alite while someone else drove. With his victim in the car, Alite turned and pumped three bullets into Grosso's skull.

Bruce Gotterup was a low-level Gambino associate who, in 1992, was misguided enough that he started shaking down one of the crime family's protected bars. He wasn't subtle about it, spraying the place with a machine pistol as he demanded a $500-a-week payoff. The *borgata* leadership told Alite to make Gotterup disappear, and he again lured the victim into a false sense of security to set him up for the hit. Alite did that by having the bar owner make a couple of weekly payments to Gotterup. Alite then said he arranged for another Gambino associate to get Gotterup drunk, take him to the beach, and then kill him.

Frank "Geeky" Boccia was dating the daughter of Fat Andy Ruggiero, a major captain in the Gambino crime family, when he made the stupid decision to strike not only the young woman but also her mother. To make matters worse, Geeky ran into Gambino *consigliere* Joseph Corozzo and threatened him with a machine gun, Alite told the FBI. Lured into a Mob social club on Springfield Boulevard, Geeky was shot dead in a back patio area, right next to the tomato plants, which were used to make the pasta sauce. Geeky's body was never found, and government witnesses said it was taken out on a boat into the Atlantic Ocean and dumped.

So Alite was capable of getting his hands dirty with

murder or arranging others to carry out the deed. He had a certain way of finessing things, and when Senior Gotti needed a way of teaching a lesson to a recalcitrant captain named Louis DiBono, he knew who it was that he could turn to for getting the job done. DiBono was a corpulent captain whose girth earned him the nickname "Jelly Belly." He was not an insignificant member of the Gambino hierarchy, and he had told the elder Gotti that there was a lot of money to be made at the World Trade Center because drywall had to be replaced. As Sammy Gravano remembered things, DiBono proposed that Gotti become his partner in the drywall business.

A big job at the World Trade Center and whatever scam DiBono could have pulled off while doing it could have meant a lot of money for Gotti. But in a move that proved an insult to the Gambino boss, DiBono constantly failed to keep meetings with Gotti.

"John was insulted," said Gravano.

Gotti then wanted DiBono killed for the transgression and farmed out the hit contract, according to Gravano, to Gambino capo Pat Conte. But Conte's contacts never carried out the murder, in large part because DiBono was constantly moving around New York and New Jersey and confusing his pursuers. Finally, according to what Alite would later allege to the FBI, Gotti asked his son to assemble a hit team to take care of DiBono. Charles was among those enlisted in the murder plot, which included Bobby Boriello, an old friend of Junior Gotti's, Alite told the FBI. In fact, Alite said, he was supposed to be on the hit team but was replaced by the diminutive Kevin McMahon, who had a certain skill as a getaway car driver.

The slaying of DiBono took place at the World Trade

Center parking lot on around October 3, 1990, some three years before the first terrorist attack set off a bomb that destroyed that underground garage. Police found DiBono lying on the front seat of his car. The autopsy found seven gunshot wounds, five penetrating the body and two more that went completely through DiBono. The shooter didn't want to leave anything to chance and approached very close to DiBono, possibly as near as a foot, based on gunshot residue found on his skin. DiBono had four shots to the head, three of which entered from his left side, consistent with his being in the driver's seat. One shot went through DiBono's brain, while three others slammed into his skull at various points. Another bullet entered the chest and damaged a major artery.

Alite wasn't there when DiBono was killed, but he remembered Junior Gotti saying everything went as planned, and being very pleased that he was able to carry out an assignment given him by his father. It was the younger Gotti's way of proving his worth to his father as a leader, said Alite. Several months later, Charles got his reward, Alite told his FBI handlers, when he was inducted into the Gambino family for carrying out the DiBono murder. The secret ceremony took place at a house in Howard Beach, where Kevin McMahon had the house swept for electronic surveillance devices, and Alite said he was told by Junior Gotti to clean the dwelling so that it looked spiffy for the induction. Howard Beach streets generally have enough parking, but Gotti wanted McMahon and two others to make sure that not only was there enough spaces for vehicles but that they should keep a lookout for law enforcement surveillance cars and vans. Charles Carneglia, Thomas Cacciapoli, and Jackie Cavallo were all in-

ducted that day, said Alite. So, although he might not
be a big money earner, Charles proved, based on what
had happened to DiBono, that he would carry out a
deadly assignment. That was enough, for the Gotti
regime, to make him a full-fledged wiseguy.

Though Alite wasn't part of the DiBono hit team, his
relationship with Junior Gotti continued unabated. But
the bond between the two men was doomed to fail, as
many do in that life. Some of the problems, based on
what Alite later told investigators, was the way he took
abuse from Senior Gotti for things that the crime boss's
son had been involved with. Junior Gotti, said Alite,
didn't step up and take responsibility when he should
have. For instance, during a fight at a nightclub in the
Maspeth section of Queens, sometime around 1984, it
was Junior Gotti who allegedly pulled out a derringer
and fired a shot at someone, Alite told the FBI. Since
Alite had also been in the melee, the elder Gotti summoned him to a meeting at the Our Friends Social
Club, a place run by the crime boss's brother Richard,
and a few doors away from Bergin Hunt and Fish.

Arriving at the Our Friends Social Club, Alite noticed that Senior Gotti was there, and sitting next to
him was his son. It was an angry Senior Gotti who
started out by yelling at a couple of other mobsters in
the club about the shooting. Turning his attention to
Alite, the crime boss accused him of doing the shooting, which Alite denied. Still furious, Senior Gotti told
three of his key associates—Angelo Ruggiero, Tony
Rampino, and Wilfred "Willie Boy" Johnson—to take
Alite out and give him a beating so he would have to go
to the hospital. The trio gave Alite some abuse but
didn't hurt him too much. Instead, Alite felt more
wounded by the way Junior Gotti just sat quietly while

Alite was being berated. Later, when Alite asked Junior Gotti why he didn't defend him in front of his father, the younger Gotti replied that to do so would have brought the wrath of his father on him as well, Alite said to investigators some years later.

There was a second beating incident that Alite said he suffered at the hands of Senior Gotti over the Mob boss's anger with Alite because of a shakedown of a bar owner. Alite told the FBI later that he was confused over the Gotti tirade because Junior Gotti, who, he alleged, told him to go to the bar in the first place, didn't do anything to stop his father. But what really marked the point at which Alite's relationship with Junior Gotti soured was around 1996. It was then that Alite's free-ranging ways got him into a festering dispute with Junior Gotti, who Alite suspected was trying to have him killed. As Alite would later tell the FBI, a federal agent played a tape that purportedly contained a conversation between Junior Gotti, his uncle Peter, and Carmine Agnello, which appeared to contain threatening words about the Albanian. Streetwise and perceptive about threats to his well-being, Alite began to absent himself from Queens, avoiding Gotti and his men. But the need to generate money for his own family—he had a wife and child in New Jersey—made Alite agree to meet Junior Gotti at Aqueduct Racetrack in Jamaica, Queens. It wasn't that Alite liked to play the horses, but the Man O' War Room, where he arranged for the meeting to take place, had magnetometers, which would detect anyone attempting to enter with a metal object, like a gun or a knife.

Junior Gotti arrived at the track with three friends, including his brother-in-law Carmine Agnello, while Alite had two buddies with him. The conversation between

Gotti and Alite took place away from the table where the other men congregated, and according to an FBI report, it didn't start off very well. Gotti thought Alite was being paranoid and told him so, assuring him that no one wanted to kill him. Alite thought otherwise and brought up the tip he received from the FBI agent. Because Junior Gotti never expressly denied threatening him, Alite became more confrontational, telling Gotti that while he wasn't looking for trouble, he would take the initiative strike first—presumably at Gotti—to protect himself.

Both men continued to exchange sharp words, and Alite threatened, at one point, to kill Gotti's brother, Peter. Eventually, after much chest thumping, tempers cooled. Alite said he would stay away from Queens. Perhaps as a peace offering, Gotti invited Alite to go hunting with him. Given their strained relationship, Alite asked Junior Gotti in jest if he preferred that he wear rabbit ears to make himself a better target.

Things didn't improve between Alite and Gotti after the racetrack meeting. Alite heard from his Howard Beach contacts that rumors were spreading that Gotti had run him out of Queens because he was a "rat." Infuriated by the gossip, Alite tried to track down the low-level Mob associate who had been spreading the stories, something that others in the Gambino crime family perceived as a threatening and disrespectful action. As a result, Alite was summoned to a meeting at a Cross Bay Boulevard pizzeria with Thomas "Tommy Sneakers" Cacciopoli, who told him that he was nuts to come back into Queens and start threatening people.

No sooner had Tommy Sneakers made reference to Gotti by saying "Junior said" than Alite went ballistic.

"Fuck Junior, he's your boss, not mine," Alite responded sharply.

Finally, around 1996, Alite again broke his agreement and returned to Queens to visit his family and afterward got called to another meeting with Gotti. Wary of being set up, Alite contacted a friend who arranged through Charles Carneglia to have the meeting on the boardwalk in Atlantic City, where Gotti was planning to attend a prizefight. Charles was often used by Gotti to convey messages, Alite recalled in conversations with investigators.

The meeting started off well, with Gotti trying to be diplomatic, thanking Alite for some help he gave the crime family about two or three years earlier. The particular assistance involved a dispute between a friend of Gotti's and a reputed drug dealer known as "George the Albanian" over a $60,000 debt. Unimpressed by the clout of the Gambino crime family or with Junior Gotti, George demanded the money and allegedly threatened to kill Gotti's friend if he didn't make repayment. To defuse the situation, Alite had cautioned Junior Gotti that Albanians were violent and would think nothing of shooting him and disappearing into the Bronx, a place where many Albanians lived. Junior eventually repaid his friend's debt, funneling the payments through Charles Carneglia, Alite told investigators.

But if Junior and Alite were grateful that the problem with the Albanian had been solved peacefully, that didn't solve a more substantial problem both men had with each other. During the talk on the boardwalk, Gotti made the point again that Alite was to stay out of New York. With a family to feed, Alite wouldn't accept Junior Gotti's command and told him so.

Gotti now knew that his old friend Alite was somebody who could prove to be a big problem. He and the rest of the Gambino family would find out the hard way just how much trouble Alite would become.

6

The Weasel

They called Kevin McMahon "the Weasel" because he was one of the shortest guys who ever hung around Bergin Hunt and Fish on 101st Avenue in Ozone Park. About the only person he was taller than was the elderly Jennie Carneglia. He also earned that nickname because he always seemed to be conniving about something.

The child of a drug-abusing mother, and a father who was a criminal, McMahon didn't have much going for him until the Carneglia family took him in as a street urchin who had been living by his wits. In many ways, his informal adoption by John and Helene Carneglia was one of the best things that ever happened to him. He had a roof over his head and was treated like family. When he got married, it was the Carneglia clan, including Charles and his mother, who beamed with delight over McMahon's happy day. John Carneglia wasn't in the wedding picture for the simple reason that he was just starting a prison sentence that would last a good twenty-five years at least.

Yet, in other ways, McMahon's absorption by the Carneglia family would turn out to be one of the worst things that ever happened. Certainly, that was how he felt for a time in the days soon after Gambino captain Louis DiBono was shot dead in the underground parking lot of the World Trade Center in October 1990. McMahon knew exactly what happened then because of the simple fact that he was there when the killing took place. The murder wasn't something he expected, and he knew when it happened that he was then an accomplice. As he later told the FBI and testified to in federal court, McMahon sat in one of two getaway cars for the two men most directly involved in the actual hit: Charles Carneglia and Bartolomeo Borriello.

The slaying of DiBono, according to the FBI, was done at the command of John Gotti Sr., and farmed out to his son Junior Gotti. McMahon was picked as somebody whose expertise in finding and equipping stolen cars was well known to the Gambino family. He also had a knack for evasive driving and avoiding surveillance. Since Charles had a lot of wrecked cars at his auto salvage yard on Fountain Avenue, McMahon went there to get a couple of license plates off a couple of wrecks and transferred them to two stolen vehicles that matched them in make and model. McMahon wasn't a killer, but he sure knew how to get those "work cars" for the Mob. In the summer of 1990, he had a good handful of cars that could be used for surveillance, robberies, kidnappings, beatings, and whatever else was required. Within the Gambino crime family, DiBono was a hunted man for weeks. As far as McMahon knew, DiBono was supposed to be kidnapped and brought back to Senior Gotti. Reputed Gambino soldier Iggy Alonga, using one of the work cars stolen by McMahon, tried to grab DiBono but never found him. So, after Alonga made a mess of things, the job was passed on to Borriello, who happened to be Senior Gotti's driver.

McMahon was Charles's constant shadow, his minder who watched him to make sure he didn't do crazy things when he was drunk or high. There were other times that McMahon was somebody Charles wanted around, sort of like a security blanket. So, on October 14, McMahon was sitting inside the home Charles shared with his mother when a call came in that DiBono had been spotted. It was then that McMahon, Charles, Borriello, and a man known as "Harpo," because of a bushy head of hair that made him look like one of the Marx Brothers, got into two cars and drove to Manhattan.

McMahon was not somebody the Mob utilized to do a piece of work, a murder. During the slaying of DiBono, he sat in a gray Cadillac as the man who had slighted Senior Gotti drove into the World Trade Center parking lot in a smaller blue Cadillac. It was then, McMahon would later recall, that Charles got out of the car after being alerted by Borriello through a two-way radio, walked toward DiBono's vehicle, and appeared to wrestle with the obese capo who sat in the driver's seat. McMahon said he heard popping sounds, as if someone was being struck on the head. Actually, it was the sounds of gunfire.

Louis DiBono was dead, and Kevin McMahon had never expected that to happen. He thought Charles and the others were going to bring DiBono back to Senior Gotti for a beating for having not obeyed the crime boss's request to come in for a meeting. Instead, McMahon found himself an accessory to murder.

"Don't tell nobody," Borriello warned McMahon. "You will end up like Louis DiBono."

Being a car thief is one thing; being part of a murder is something McMahon wasn't prepared to handle. The fact that his old friend Charles had put him in that position—had placed him in jeopardy—angered McMahon, since he really didn't have to be present at the parking lot at all. McMahon held his tongue and kept his feelings to himself. But for Charles the world changed dramatically. How much so became apparent a few days after the newspapers reported about DiBono's slaying, and he and McMahon walked over to Bergin Hunt and Fish. Rather than his usual perfunctory greeting, Senior Gotti gave Charles a big, warm hello and a kiss.

It doesn't seem like he's mad at him, thought McMahon after seeing how the crime boss treated Charles.

Perhaps to soothe his anger, or maybe just to keep him quiet, a few weeks later McMahon got a handsome $10,000 diamond bracelet as a gift from Charles and Boriello. Charles had never given McMahon any gift before, so this was a big deal. But not as big as what would happen a few months later when Charles became a made member of the crime family. Now the Carneglia family had two certified gangsters in the household. McMahon's status remained the same, although he had slightly more clout because he was now part of the crew of a made man who was virtually his own family. On top of that, the Mob looked to McMahon as being stable enough to play a role in keeping Charles under control. Both Peter Gotti, the brother of the Gambino boss, and John Carneglia had told McMahon to keep an eye on

Charles at functions like weddings, and to a lesser extent funerals. Given his propensity to drink and get out of control, Charles needed a babysitter now more than ever, and it was up to McMahon to make sure his friend remained calm and lucid.

McMahon also saw how Charles easily developed a paranoia that, if unchecked, had the potential to make him do strange things. Worried that police dogs might sniff around his cars, Charles put pepper on the ground outside the vehicles to deter the animals from getting too close. If he was feeling threatened or feared that he might be attacked at his house, Charles also put up plywood on the windows. McMahon also noticed that Charles always carried a switchblade, which he called a "poker," in his waistband.

Although Charles Carneglia had a reputation for being a killer, that alone wasn't enough to pay the bills. Charles never had a steady racket providing him with a reliable cash flow, at least not like the big money the other gangsters were making. He still had to hustle to make a buck and took some bold and dangerous steps with Kevin McMahon to do that. Twice in the days before he became a made member of the Mob, McMahon said, Charles turned to him for help in setting up robberies of armored cars. Those kind of heists are among the most risky any criminal can take part in. The vehicles are difficult to penetrate, the guards are armed, and the action usually takes place on a public street, where there is a greater chance of being seen by a lot of witnesses. Trouble can also develop if other vehicles or police arrive unexpectedly.

One heist, according to McMahon, took place near the sprawling Western Beef outlet store in Brooklyn, not far from the border with Queens. As McMahon later remembered for the FBI, the theft was pretty easy as those things go as four of them, including Charles, pulled up next to the armored car as it pulled into the parking lot. McMahon said he held a shotgun on the armored-car crew as they came out of their vehicle with cash in bags. Charles, McMahon remembered, floated around the area in a different car with a portable radio, serving as a lookout. The guards gave up the cash haul, which amounted to about $180,000, of which McMahon got about $33,000.

While the money from those kinds of robberies could be substantial, they took a lot of planning, and despite all of McMahon's babysitting, Charles still managed to get drunk and take drugs in such quantities that he was unable to plan or think straight. This became evident during a yearlong attempt by McMahon and others under Charles to pull off a robbery of an armored car at JFK. For months, various loose groups of constantly changing participants scouted out an armored car as it made regular drops at the airport. They were trying to figure out the best place to do the robbery. At times, the gang would follow the vehicle as it went from JFK to LaGuardia Airport and then upstate, where often they lost track of it. Charles didn't help things when he crashed one of the cars used in surveillance while he was in one of his drunken states, said McMahon. With constant infighting and apparent lackluster leadership from Charles, the groups fell apart in late 1990.

But Charles wouldn't give up. One December morning in 1990, McMahon said, he awoke to the sound of Charles at his apartment door. It was early, around 4:30 A.M., and well before sunrise. It was a pity to let that armored car servicing JFK to become a lost opportunity, said Charles (according to McMahon). Dressing for the weather, which was seasonally cold, McMahon and Charles doffed baseball caps with American Airlines logos and got into a brown Cutlass Ciera, where Bobby Borriello, the Gambino soldier who had taken part in the DiBono slaying a few months earlier, already sat in the backseat. Borriello had a shotgun and Charles, who sat in the front passenger seat, carried a pistol, McMahon remembered.

The drive from McMahon's apartment to the parking lot of American Airlines couldn't have taken very long. On arriving, McMahon drove the Cutlass behind the armored car, which had arrived earlier. McMahon parked close, but not too close, to the armored vehicle, because he wanted to be able to speed away without having to back up. Having to back up in an escape situation wasted precious seconds and that could prove to be the margin between getting away or getting caught—an experienced escape driver like McMahon knew that.

Jose Delgado Rivera, a forty-seven-year-old father of seven, had driven the armored truck that morning to the parking lot. He wasn't supposed to be working that particular early-morning shift but had filled in for another driver. He stepped out of the cab of the truck and had in his hands two canvas bags containing cash. Intent on going into the American Airlines office, Rivera didn't notice two men who exited the vehicle that was parked a short distance behind his truck.

McMahon had been watching Rivera leave his vehicle when he noticed that Charles and Borriello got out of the Cutlass and crept around the truck from the left side just as Rivera passed to the front of his vehicle. In the instant after both men disappeared from his sight,

McMahon heard a lot of shots—he wouldn't recall how many or if they sounded like they came from the same firearm. Some of them sounded like firecrackers. When the noise stopped, Borriello came running back to the Ciera with the two canvas bags, which McMahon knew from his past sneaky surveillance of the location contained cash.

Borriello jumped into the backseat. However, with Charles nowhere in sight, McMahon left his car and ran around to the front of the truck. It was there, he later told the FBI, that he saw Charles standing over Rivera, pistol-whipping the kneeling driver in the head from behind. McMahon knew he had to get Charles out of there fast and ran up to him and grabbed him.

"Let's go!" yelled McMahon.

As they fled, Rivera fell facedown on a grassy verge near the truck. He wasn't moving at all.

Charles and McMahon made it back to the Ciera and it was then McMahon pulled away at great speed, past a guard booth by the lot entrance. Adrenaline rushing through his veins, McMahon pressed the accelerator as much as he could under the confines of the road and sped back to his apartment. The only words McMahon heard anybody utter in that drive were "slow down," since it would have made for a very bad day to get stopped for speeding with two guns and cash stolen from a robbery.

Back at McMahon's apartment, Charles came in for a little while and seemed troubled by the turn of events.

"I don't know what happened. Don't say nothing," Charles finally said, according to McMahon.

Fishing around in one of the closets, Charles gathered up some American Airlines baseball caps, which the crew had planned to use when there were more people to be involved in the preparation for the heist, and left.

McMahon didn't see Charles for at least a week after that, because he had gone to his own apartment and made it like a cave by boarding up the windows. Then, in what served as his own peculiar hideaway, Charles coped by sinking the ship, emptying a bottle of Chivas Regal and waiting until things died down.

But things really never die down in Howard Beach. The death of Rivera, who sustained not only a shotgun blast to the abdomen but also a single gunshot wound to his back, was all over the news. Peter Zuccaro had never much liked the idea of a robbery of an armored car. Ever since he saw how drunk Charles was while trying to do a surveillance of the American Airlines facility, he had a bad feeling. When Charles stumbled out of the car, Zuccaro had said to himself that he was through being part of his motley crew. Zuccaro didn't dwell on a lost opportunity but just went to his regular construction job in Queens and put the idea of a robbery out of his mind.

But when the news had the report of Rivera's death in the armored-car robbery, Zuccaro had a pretty good idea of whom to approach for information. Seeing McMahon driving in Howard Beach, Zuccaro flagged him down and both men started talking. McMahon seemed a bit nervous. Zuccaro was upset, not because of the fact that he lost out on an opportunity to make a score but because a working guy like Rivera had died. The killing seemed an unnecessary act to Zuccaro. Guards are trained to give up the cash and not risk their lives in a gun battle. The FBI would take care of the investigation. Nobody had to kill a working stiff.

Standing on the sidewalk at around Ninety-fifth

Street, Zuccaro and McMahon had a hurried conversation about the robbery. McMahon, according to Zuccaro, said Charles and Borriello killed the guard. In fact, it seemed that it was Borriello who did the shooting, said McMahon. Zuccaro had an interesting morsel of information: somebody had dropped a baseball cap at the crime scene. (This unnerved McMahon, who denied losing his hat.)

A week after the armored-car robbery, McMahon got a pile of cash, $20,000, from Charles, who seemed preoccupied with fiddling with the baseball caps to see if fingerprints could be lifted from them. He also mentioned that DNA technology might be able to extract evidence from something as small as a hair root. But what really made Charles mad wasn't the fact that Rivera had died but rather that McMahon was keeping his share of the money in a pile, with all of the bills in sequence. That would be a tip-off if the cops ever came and found the money.

Neither the police nor the FBI ever got wind of McMahon's role in the robbery at that time. But in the street gossip of Howard Beach, it seemed clear to some in the Mob that McMahon and Carneglia were involved in what had happened. It was a secret both men would bear uneasily, and it created a wariness of each other that would persist for years.

McMahon also had other reasons to be leery of Charles Carneglia. Since 1984, the word on the street among the Gambino crime family was that Charles was the one responsible for yet another stabbing death. Salvatore Puma was one of the young knockabout Mob associates who was part of Charles's crew. Another one

of the handsome, dark-haired young men who aspired
to a life of crime, Puma had been stealing cars with
Kevin McMahon since the age of about thirteen. His
cousin was Joey Cavalcante, who was involved as far
back as the late 1970s and early 1980s in some armored-
car robberies with Peter Zuccaro. Both Zuccaro and
Cavalcante spent some time in prison for the robberies.
Despite Cavalcante being in prison, his cousin Puma
stayed in contact with him, providing him with prison
commissary money, the kind of cash placed into the accounts of federal inmates so they could buy sundry
items, snacks, and toilet articles while in custody. The
commissary money Cavalcante received, McMahon remembered, actually came from Charles, who gave it to
Puma for deposit in his cousin's prison account.

In July 1984, Howard Beach was rocked by the news
that Puma was stabbed to death right in broad daylight
on the street. His wake drew scores of young people
from the community. Among the mourners was a young
neighborhood woman named Kim Albanese. Like many
of the girls growing up in the neighborhood, Albanese
had been drawn to some of the more feral young
bucks in the area and had dated Puma. She proved to
be devastated, as many were, by the young man's slaying. (Albanese would later go on to date and marry
John A. Gotti, the son of the crime boss, and have six
children with him.)

McMahon was also upset with Puma's killing. As soon
as he heard about it, he called Charles. The reaction he
got was puzzling. *What has that got to do with me?* was
Charles's reply before hanging up. Then, speaking to
John Carneglia, McMahon was told to lose Charles's
number—in other words, not call him again. Shortly

after the slaying, Charles went on the lam, disappearing to Florida.

Gossip about the Puma killing permeated the neighborhood for weeks. But whenever McMahon went up to a group of people talking about what had happened, they clammed up and changed the subject when he was around. It didn't take much for McMahon to get the feeling that Charles might know more than he was letting on. Though Charles never said anything directly implicating himself at the time, McMahon remembered he talked derisively about Puma, claiming that he had stolen some of the commissary money meant to go to Cavalcante. On top of that, there was talk that Puma had been fooling around with Cavalcante girlfriend, said Charles. It seemed clear to McMahon that there was little sense of loss in his old friend about Puma. So much for loyalty.

In the Gotti homestead in Howard Beach, an oil painting of young Frank Gotti is the biggest picture in the house, even larger than a photograph right next to it of his father. It is the closest thing to a shrine for the child, who was like any active schoolboy with an interest in sports.

In Mob lore, the facts surrounding the death of twelve-year-old Frankie Gotti are well known. The youngster was biking with some friends in Howard Beach when he borrowed a motorized minibike from a slightly older Kevin McMahon. Gotti's mother had often warned him about scooting around in those devices because she viewed them as inherently unsafe within the confines of the narrow, sometimes busy neighborhood ~~eets~~. Ignoring his mother's long-standing warning,

Frankie Gotti took McMahon's bike, and on a March day in 1980 started tooling around the blocks near where he lived.

John Favara, a neighbor, had turned into the residential area after exiting from the Belt Parkway when he accidentally ran over the young Gotti on Eighty-seventh Street. Victoria Gotti and her younger daughter, Vicky, ran to the scene in time to see firefighters working on the injured boy. Frankie's mother cradled his head, beseeching him with screams of "Frankie, it's Mommy—can you hear me?"

Frankie Gotti died a short time later in the hospital trauma unit, and his death sent his father and his mother into deep depression. John Gotti, a man who many feared, was consigned to sitting alone in his den on the first floor of the family house and, nursing a drink, crying with the door closed. Victoria, the grieving mother, came close to a nervous breakdown. She would wander late at night through the neighborhood and walk to a nearby ball field in the vain hope of finding her son alive. Her daughter Vicky, in her own account of the hours after the child's death, said Victoria Gotti attempted to slash her wrists with the jagged pieces of her mirror she had smashed. When that failed, she attempted to overdose on sedatives, said her daughter.

After the funeral and burial of Frankie at St. John's Cemetery in Middle Village, in the tranquil confines of the indoor crypt area known as the Cloisters, the anger started to erupt in the Gotti household. When the Favara house had a party, with loud music and beer, a few days after the funeral, it proved too much for Victoria Gotti to handle. She stood in her front yard and glared at her seemingly remorseless neighbor. Nothing happened at that moment, but later that evening Victoria left her house with a baseball bat and started smashing Favara's car, which she believed still had some of her son's blood on it. She also lunged at Favara with the bat when he came out of the house—but missed—and then was hustled away by her daughter.

Favara eventually was told by some acquaintances that he should consider moving from the neighborhood. He was thinking about doing that when in July 1980 a group of men abducted him from the parking lot of the Castro Convertibles store in New Hyde Park, where he worked, and put him into a van. That was the last time anyone ever saw Favara alive. His body was never found.

Like the New York mystery of long-missing Judge Crater, there are plenty of theories about what happened to Favara. Some believe John Gotti himself, angered and watching the devastating effect the death of the child had on his wife and family, ordered the killing of Favara in retaliation. Others think that Gotti's associates, notably Angelo Ruggiero Sr., seeing the grief and anger in the Gotti household, easily took matters into their own hands, with the crime boss's suggestion, much as did the knights in *Macbeth* who slay a rival on their king's subtle suggestion. There is also the possibility that Ruggiero and the others in the Bergin crew took it upon themselves to act.

Although Gotti was traveling in Florida and wasn't around when Favara disappeared, it is highly unlikely that he didn't know at least something about the abduction and murder plot. Mob associates don't carry out killings, especially one that would naturally bring law enforcement attention to a boss, unless they get clearance. Gotti would later tell the FBI and the cops that he didn't know anything about what had happened to Favara, and pointed out that the Gotti family was in Florida when the abduction occurred. But even Gotti's son John, years later, would say that he thought it probable that his father had arranged the Favara abduction.

"You don't harm one of his own without consequences," Junior Gotti said in a television interview.

But what happened to Favara's corpse? A number of stories surfaced, mostly citing law enforcement sources. One had Favara killed with a chain saw, his body hacked to pieces and put in an auto that was then pressed in a giant cube of scrap metal. Another had Favara kept alive until Gotti returned from Florida so he could personally cut him to death with the chain saw. Still, another alleged Favara was put in a fifty-gallon drum filled with concrete and dumped out at sea.

It was in connection with the continuing investigation of Charles Carneglia that federal investigators believe they hit upon the true story of the disposal of Favara. It came from Kevin McMahon himself, who was forever wedded to the tragic death of Frankie Gotti because he had been riding the bike just before the young Gotti rode to his death.

Charles was the kind of drunk who would become loud and obnoxious, his friends remembered. Some drunks get very loose lips and talk about things they shouldn't. Charles was that way: boisterous, pugnacious, and much too talkative for a man with some skeletons in his closet. McMahon remembered Charles in one inebriated state finally telling him what had happened to John Favara. It wasn't pretty. Charles stated that Ruggiero had turned over Favara's body to him for disposal, McMahon told the FBI after he was arrested in an unrelated federal case in Florida. The substance of the gruesome body disposal method was also spelled out in a letter filed in Brooklyn federal court in 2009 by federal prosecutors. The technique used, according to McMahon, was placement of the body in a barrel of acid, which had the effect over a period of days in dissolving much of Favara's corpse. Charles was getting some criticism from the Gambino family as a drunken incompetent for the length of time it took for the body to disintegrate, McMahon told the agents. Charles said that he didn't use the right kind of acid at first but changed the formulation to speed up the process, according to McMahon. Eventually, Charles said, the body dissolved enough that he finally took a piece of finger bone and dropped it in a bowl of soup Ruggiero was eating at the Lindenwood Diner, said McMahon.

This wasn't the only time acid baths for body disposal had been linked to Charles on the recollection of McMahon. According to the 2009 prosecutorial memo, it was in the late 1970s that Charles admitted to McMahon that he had a corpse wrapped in a blue tarp under the floorboard of a barn at his property on Pine Street in East Brooklyn, a location about two blocks from the large Fountain Avenue junkyard owned by the Carneglia family. The body was that of a heroin junkie killed by someone Charles said he knew and that he was doing a favor by disposing of the body, according to the memo. Folding the corpse in half, Charles explained, he placed it in a large plastic barrel, which was used to store pickles, poured in the acid and waited several days, said the investigators' memorandum. Moving the barrel with a backhoe, Charles said, he poured the liquid contents down a sewer and as a result stunk up the neighborhood, according to investigators.

The macabre body disposal tied to Charles came

almost entirely from the mouth of McMahon. Quite apart from whether McMahon's recollection of what Charles said to him about the acid is accurate, given that they may have been said under the influence of drugs or alcohol, there is the question about whether it is plausible that a corpse can be disposed of in such a way.

Can a corpse really be dissolved to nothingness as seen in horror movies? Back in 1897, Adolph L. Luetgert, the so-called sausage king of Chicago because he owned a sausage-packing plant, murdered his wife, Louisa, and then dissolved her body in one of the vats at his facility. During the investigation of Luetgert, Chicago police found that he had purchased large quantities of arsenic and potash before the killing. Detectives also discovered in the factory furnace burned sausage and human bones, as well as two of Louisa's rings. Among the bones were a female skull, ribs, and metatarsals.

Trial evidence showed that Luetgert put his wife's dead body in a vat filled with a solution of potash and continuously stirred the mixture. The result, according to an account of the celebrated murder case written by Elizabeth Royte for *Smithsonian* magazine in 1996, was a mass of gelatinized bones, some of which had leaked onto the factory floor. The trial was noteworthy because it involved the testimony of a forensic anthropologist who said the bones found were human. Though he protested his innocence, Luetgert was convicted and died in an Illinois prison in 1899.

Aside from Luetgert, British killer John George Haigh used sulfuric acid to dissolve the bodies of six victims in the 1940s. There were also reports that Mexican drug cartel killers in 2009 have used sodium hydroxide or potassium hydroxide, which when heated to about three hundred degrees can turn a body into an oily, tan liquid. In a more acceptable practice, American funeral directors were considering using a process known as "alkaline hydrolysis" in a heated and pressured container to dissolve bodies in lye as an environmentally safer alternative to traditional cremation. The process, which has been used to dispose of cadavers, leaves a liquid, which can be poured away, as well as some dry bony residue.

So, could Charles have disposed of bodies with acid? He would need the right kind of acid, of course, something he might easily be able to get from a metal-plating company or a chemical supplier. He would have needed sufficient quantities to cover the body, which in today's post-September 11 world might trigger a suspicious report to law enforcement. But in the 1970s and 1980s, that wouldn't have been a concern, particularly since he dealt in scrap metal. Based on the Luetgert and Haigh cases, as well as acceptable disposal practices in the medical profession, bodies can be disposed of with acid. But any of the methods leave some kind of residue or bone matter—in the Luetgert case, his wife's skull was found. If Charles did act as the Mob's ghoul, he would have been left with skull and bones to deal with. Maybe East New York is still hiding some secrets.

But Charles was also said to have used acid for more than just body disposal. According to Kevin McMahon again, Charles Carneglia had a sadistic streak and he wouldn't shy away from any method for inflicting pain on a victim.

* * *

Justine Carneglia, the pretty niece of Charles and the daughter of his brother, John, graduated high school around 1992. As in most households, the Carneglia family held a party to celebrate the graduation. But trouble developed when someone fired a shot outside the house in Howard Beach. Rumors began to fly, McMahon told investigators, that the one pulling the trigger was Christopher Carneglia, the son of John and the nephew of Charles.

A shooting at the home of a powerful Mafia member like John Carneglia isn't something that passes without repercussions, and the hunt began for the foolhardy person who fired the handgun. One of the names rumored to have been the culprit was that of Joey Scopo, the son of the late Colombo crime family boss Ralph Scopo. Christopher Carneglia denied he did anything, and his father, according to Kevin McMahon, wanted Charles to get to the bottom of things. The Albanian renegade gangster John Alite also recalled for the FBI that Charles told him his brother had placed an angry call from prison, fuming over the disrespect showed to his family at their home.

Charles enlisted McMahon to get a camcorder and show up at the Fountain Avenue junkyard. Once he got to the yard, McMahon found a belligerent and yelling Charles, who appeared to have been drinking, which didn't help his disposition at all. If two or three of the kids who had attended the party didn't volunteer to come and talk to him, Charles swore that he would bring them in forcefully, McMahon told the FBI.

The young men didn't come in on their volition. McMahon was standing by the junkyard when a car drove up containing two or three passengers (McMahon wasn't sure of the exact number) who had white bags over their heads and their hands tied. The prisoners—which is what they appeared to be to Mc-Mahon—were brought into the junkyard office. Mc-Mahon recognized two of the boys, one was Danny Cassara from the neighborhood and the other was Alite's friend David D'Arpino. Both had their shoes and socks removed.

As McMahon recalled, Charles had a special interrogation technique that would have made the Gestapo proud. When Charles didn't get an answer to the question about who did the shooting at Justine's party, he took a turkey baster, filled it with acid, and dropped some on the feet of the two bound men, said McMahon to investigators. That caused a great deal of pain and left scars, which years later were apparent on D'Arpino's foot when the FBI photographed it. McMahon said he had a good view of what was going on because he was filming the scene with the camcorder, as Charles had wanted. (Alite also told the FBI that D'Arpino related to him that Charles had poured acid on his feet.)

"It was getting all red and bubbly," McMahon recalled in court testimony about the effect of the acid on the skin of the feet. "As they were rubbing it, the skin was coming off."

Still, D'Arpino and Cassara didn't drop the name of the person who did the shooting, preferring to endure the pain of the acid, remembered McMahon.

Charles had enough. He pulled down the trousers of both men and had them bend over.

"I am going to stick the turkey baster up your ass," he threatened, according to McMahon.

That was enough for D'Arpino and Cassara, who couldn't bear the idea of going through such a rectum-wrecking experience.

"Chris did it!" the prisoners screamed in unison, remembered McMahon.

After the name, apparently referring to Chris Carneglia, was mentioned, Charles had the two men try and wash off the acid from their feet, said McMahon. Whether it was true or not that the younger Carneglia had fired the shot that started the whole torture incident almost didn't matter after what D'Arpino and Cassara had gone through. It was never revealed what Christopher's father may have done once he learned of that information.

McMahon recalled that he and Charles watched the video, and that others may have done so as well, to laughter. But McMahon also knew that the video was an indictment waiting to happen, should the police or FBI get their hands on the tape. He said he destroyed it because of that. Sometime later, McMahon would recall, he and Charles ran into D'Arpino and Alite at Philly's Bait and Tackle Shop, a fishing-supply store on Cross Bay Boulevard. Charles was solicitous of D'Arpino's well-being and asked to see his injured foot, which by then had a healing wound, said McMahon.

7

"A Sad State"

The evening of December 11, 1990, was a very cold night, even for so late a time in the fall. On Mulberry Street, at the Gambino crime family club the Ravenite, people started to arrive by around 4:00 P.M. But it wasn't because of the weather that the men were gathering in suits and expensive overcoats. Their boss John J. Gotti had long ago decreed that his captains and other underlings had to appear at least once a week at the brick-faced building to pay their respects and report to him.

Most of the Gambino *borgata* would arrive that night before Gotti, who liked to make big entrances. Keeping tabs on who was showing up were FBI agents of the C-16 squad, who were watching the club from some carefully hidden observation posts along Mulberry Street. By 6:30 P.M., Gotti's ruling group of *consigliere* Frank LoCascio and underboss Sammy Gravano had arrived at the Mulberry Street club. At 6:52 P.M., Gotti himself arrived, an event that set off a terse, coded radio message from the FBI observation post by Special Agent Bruce Mouw informing the FBI car coming down the street that Gotti—known as "number one" in squad lingo—had entered the Ravenite.

Gotti barely had time to get his own cup of coffee when the FBI, led by Special Agent George Gabriel, burst in and commenced the long night that would become the start of the Gambino boss's life behind bars.

Charles Carneglia wasn't at the Ravenite the night his boss was arrested. Charles wasn't really a Manhattan guy, preferring to stay away when he could from the club show-ups in Little Italy and instead do his business with Gotti at Bergin Hunt and Fish in Ozone Park. Like the rest of the city, Charles learned from a combination of news flashes and calls from the Ravenite to Queens that Senior Gotti had been arrested. The FBI bust shouldn't have come as a surprise because grand jury subpoenas had been served weeks earlier on Lo-Cascio and Gravano, as well as others in the crime family. Newspapers also carried stories about the fact that a federal investigation had targeted Gotti for racketeering.

But now it was real. Gotti had been arrested, and Charles, who had worked so hard over the years to get in the good graces of the Gambino boss, felt a deep sense of loss. Gotti thought he was smart when he told Gravano and LoCascio they would be running things if he ever got arrested. However, he hadn't counted on all three key men in the Gambino administration being grabbed together. The decapitation of Gotti's ruling committee meant that the *borgata* had to scramble to come up with a working structure. Eventually Jackie "the Nose" D'Amico, Peter Gotti, and Gotti's son John became an acting hierarchy. Nevertheless, the entire family entered a period of increased instability made worse by the fact that some captains disagreed with the way Gotti's family members had been forced upon them as the acting leadership. Clearly, the glory days of Gotti, who had beaten two attempts to convict him (each time with jury tampering, as it turned out), were over.

Further knocking Gotti off balance were some big setbacks in the federal case. Brooklyn federal judge I. Leo Glasser agreed with a government request that Gotti's two main attorneys, Bruce Cutler and Gerald Shargel, should be disqualified because they might be called as witnesses. Prosecutors said that both lawyers had given the kind of advice to Gotti that made them virtual "house counsel" to the Gambino crime family, a claim both men denied—but to no avail. They were bounced from the case, to be replaced by Albert Krieger, of Miami. But the real blow came in November 1991 when, in one of the biggest coups in law enforcement history, Gravano agreed to enter the witness security program and became a cooperating witness against Senior Gotti.

Nevertheless, Gotti still held sway over the crime family, communicating orders and messages through his brother Peter and Junior Gotti. Among the business Junior Gotti took care of was to induct new members, which he did by holding the spring 1991 ceremony for Charles at the home of Claudia DiPippa, an old girl-friend of John Alite's. Charles didn't get that much notice of the event. Bobby Borriello told him one day to clean the axle grease from his hands and put a suit on. Then he drove him in a van to the Howard Beach house for the initiation.

Being made as a full-fledged member of the Gambino family meant that Charles had at last earned some respect. Forget about the derisive comments about his supposed incompetence and drunken bouts, from the likes of Angelo Ruggiero, who was dead more than a year now. Like all the soldiers, Charles worked for a captain, which in this case was Junior Gotti, who had earlier been elevated in rank quickly on Gravano's insistence. Now Charles was no longer an associate but directed a bunch of them in *borgata* endeavors. If he was smart, Charles could make money.

But things were hardly going on an even keel for the Gambino crew, particularly for those who were the mainstays of Gotti's Bergin Hunt and Fish club. Change and instability often signal problems for the Mob, and that means people die. It proved no different for those who were part of Gotti's world.

Like many of the Ozone Park faction of the Gambino family, Bartolomeo "Bobby" Borriello would show up for the usual Saturday-night dinners at Bergin Hunt and Fish. A big, beefy man, Boriello had started out with Joey "Crazy Joe" Gallo's crew in the late 1960s and early 1970s in Brooklyn. When Gallo was shot dead at Umberto's Clam House in 1972, Boriello gravitated to the Gambino family and became a member of the Mob in a wave of 1980s initiations. Later, Boriello served as one of the gatekeepers watching the doors on Christmas Eve, 1988, inside the Little Italy apartment of Joseph "Joe Butch" Corrao when Junior Gotti, Michael "Mikey Scars" DiLeonardo, and a wiry, bespectacled man named Dominick "Skinny Dom" Pizzonia were inducted into the Gambino family. Pizzonia had taken part a few years earlier in a murder at his social club in Queens, a place where he earned fame as being one of the best cooks in the city's Mob clubhouses. Administering the oath that night was Sammy Gravano.

Saturday nights at Bergin Hunt and Fish were known for pasta and sausage dinners, which drew a lot of the made men from the neighborhood. What seemed to really make the meals more than the average pasta night was the sauce. After eating, everybody would take some home in a jar. So, on the night of April 13, 1991, Borriello was given a jar of the Bergin's finest sauce by one of the club regulars to take back to his wife in the Bath Beach section of Brooklyn. Arriving sometime around 7:30 P.M. in his driveway at Bay Twenty-ninth Street, Borriello got into an argument with someone after he exited his car. The next thing Boriello's nephew saw when he came outside to see what the commotion was all about was his uncle lying beside his car. Though the nephew didn't hear any shots, cops found that Borriello had been shot ten times. The pasta sauce jar was found broken, its contents spilled, next to his body.

Charles was in Terre Haute, Indiana, along with Kevin McMahon, visiting his brother John at the federal prison there, when word reached him that Borriello had been killed. Charles and McMahon cut their visit short and raced back to the airport in order to get back to Queens to find out what was happening with the Bergin Hunt and Fish crew out at Ozone Park. A Mob rubout always started the hushed conversations about possible perpetrators, and Charles needed to be there to pick up intelligence and relay it back to his brother. The crew also needed people around in case of further trouble.

Borriello had been very close to Charles. Both had been at the World Trade Center parking lot when Louis DiBono was killed. But no matter how close Charles might have been to Borriello, McMahon remembered that he had a very cold, matter-of-fact reaction to the news of the hit.

"One less guy to worry about," said Charles, an apparent reference to the DiBono homicide, remembered McMahon.

Such an esteemed member of the Bergin crew drew a big funeral crowd in downtown Brooklyn at St. Stephen's Church. The funeral was directed by one of Carroll Gardens' funeral directors, Vincent Raccuglia, whom a number of families of local mobsters, such as Joey Gallo, had for their wakes. Just about the entire Gambino family attended, except for those, like John Carneglia, John and Gene Gotti, who were incarcerated. The centerpiece of the multitude was Junior Gotti himself who exited the church, surrounded by the likes of Jackie "the Nose" D'Amico, the Albanian John Alite, Dominick Borghese, and, of course, Charles Carneglia, with Kevin McMahon in tow. The funeral was Junior Gotti's first major public appearance for the media as one of the de facto leaders of the Gambino ruling administration. Junior wasn't warm and fuzzy, glowering at the photographers who had packed Carroll Street.

Back at the club on 101st Avenue in Ozone Park, the word on the street was that Borriello had been killed by Preston Geritano, a hanger-on and associate with the Genovese crime family. A hot-tempered man, Geritano had been among those considered part of the late Joey Gallo's unofficial "Sixth Family" working out of Brooklyn. After Gallo was murdered in 1972, a number of his people were taken under the wing of the Genovese crime family and among them was Geritano, who functioned as an associate. Geritano's reputation as a hothead only intensified when he started abusing drugs, said one former Gallo associate. "He was crazy to begin with, but that (drugs) made him crazier," the old Gallo associate told the author.

Despite all of the grand theories that Borriello's murder might have been ordered by Senior Gotti himself or because he had stolen money, it turned out that he and Geritano had some bad personal history. According to an old member of the Gallo crew, Borriello had given Geritano a beating a few months earlier on Smith Street in downtown Brooklyn; Geritano vowed to get revenge. Junior Gotti, infuriated at the murder of his close friend, demanded and got a sit-down meeting with Liborio "Barney" Bellomo, one of the reputed leaders of the Genovese crime family. The Genovese faction agreed that something had to be done about Geritano, but he proved elusive. Nothing ever happened to him until a relative killed him in another private dispute in 2004 and then got a twenty-five-year prison term.

If the loss of Bobby Borriello didn't bother Charles very much, what government attorneys had in store for him, his brother, and mother certainly did. The Fountain Avenue junkyard had been a staple of the Carneglia clan for decades. The facility had been pieced together over the years with property purchases until the yard covered a city block in East New York. Although Jennie wasn't involved in the day-to-day running of the junkyard, her name appeared on all of the land transactions and deeds surrounding the property.

Police and federal investigators had believed for years that the Carneglia junkyard was a place where stolen cars were taken so that they could either be chopped up for parts or sanitized with new vehicle identification numbers for later sale to unsuspecting—or perhaps complicit—purchasers. Of course, McMahon would spell out for the FBI how the facility was supposed to be a Mob mortuary, where bodies were dissolved in acid for unceremonious disposal elsewhere. The focus of the macabre activity was said to be a ramshackle house near the property known as "the Barn," which outsiders were loath to enter, even when Charles did some barbecuing there. The basement was the spookiest because, as McMahon recalled, there were trophies of body disposal. On the walls of the building, hanging on nails, were pieces of jewelry that allegedly came from the various victims whose bodies had been given the Mob's brutal last rites.

In late 1991, it became clear that law enforcement was looking at the Fountain Avenue location as the suspected location of a car theft operation. In December, federal and local investigators from Long Island filed a lawsuit against a number of people and companies, accusing them of running a sophisticated scheme. Because their property on Fountain Avenue was allegedly used by one of the companies accused of taking part in the scheme, Charles, John, and Jennie Carneglia were named as defendants as well.

In an affidavit filed in Brooklyn federal court, Thomas Keteltas, a detective with the Nassau County police, said that four companies in particular were believed to be involved in the illicit operation. The companies, said Keteltas, would buy badly damaged late-model luxury cars from insurance companies. This was not an uncommon practice, and if done correctly, it would allow the buyer to scrap, sell, or rebuild the vehicle lawfully. Any sold or rebuilt vehicle then needs to have proper Department of Motor Vehicle forms filled out for it. Those cars need to be inspected and have their VINs checked.

But, according to the government, the four companies sued didn't operate legitimately but instead were
involved in "laundering" stolen cars by claiming they
were rebuilt insurance wrecks, according to investigators. This was done in a number of steps. First the vehicle identification number was removed from the wreck
and placed upon the undamaged stolen vehicle. Then
the stolen car, complete with the new VIN, was presented to a local state motor vehicle office for inspection as a rebuilt wreck, said Keteltas. An official at the
local DMV office who was corrupt would then certify
that the car passed inspection, when it had not. After
passing the bogus inspection process, the car's title was
effectively laundered and the vehicle could be sold.

Of the four companies cited in the lawsuit, one,
known as Citiwide Auto Parts, Inc., was working out of
the Fountain Avenue location. In a court hearing at
which time federal prosecutors sought to seize the
Fountain Avenue property and other assets of the defendants, Assistant U.S. Attorney James Catterson said
the practice was making it very difficult for legitimate
businessmen to compete.

"By the way, no taxes are paid on this type of income,"
said Catterson in court. "They are stolen cars. There's
no question that these are stolen cars. And every car
that we have inspected . . . has been a retagged vehicle."

While neither Charles nor anyone else in his family
was accused of actually taking part in the stealing of the
cars, the Carneglia family had leased the Fountain
Avenue address to Citiwide, which was accused of being
part of the scheme. Court records showed that this
property had been leased as far back as October 1984
to Citiwide for the annual rent of $60,000, or about
$5,000 a month. John Carneglia had signed the lease

on behalf of his brother and mother. In the government's eyes, since the property was being used for an illegal purpose, it could be seized. This was true for other locations as well that had been linked by investigators to the scheme.

In danger of losing Fountain Avenue, Charles and his family hired high-powered attorney Benjamin Brafman to fight the seizure attempt. Brafman filed legal papers that pointed out to the court that the elderly Jennie Carneglia and her son Charles didn't appear to have been directly involved in the purchase of the property. Brafman also noted that the government's complaint didn't allege that any of the Carneglias were aware of the illegal business that might have been going on at Fountain Avenue. How could they, when anyone driving by the address wouldn't have noticed anything but an automobile junkyard business, the very kind of permissible business specified in the lease, argued Brafman.

Brafman and other defense attorneys fought the effort to seize locations like Fountain Avenue and to get a dismissal of the complaint. But Judge Eugene Nickerson thought otherwise and sided with the government because of the pervasive problem posed by rampant car theft.

"The United States had an interest in stopping the trafficking in stolen motor vehicles and motor vehicle parts with vehicle identification numbers removed or altered," said Nickerson. "The United States had a reasonable concern that the property would continue to be used as an instrumentality of crime."

The government didn't have to prove that the Fountain Avenue property owners—the Carneglias—knew that their land was involved in the trafficking of stolen cars, Nickerson indicated. Since the government was attempting to seize the land in a special so-called in rem proceeding, all it had to do was show that the property was tainted by illegal conduct upon it, ruled Nickerson. It was a pretty drastic and draconian legal principle, but it had been employed for decades in many kinds of seizure cases.

After the U.S. Court of Appeals upheld Nickerson, Charles and his family were in danger of losing the entire parcel that made up Fountain Avenue. But as often happened in civil forfeiture cases, the government decided to settle. In an order signed by Brafman on behalf of Charles and his family, and attorney Gino Josh Singer for Citiwide Auto Parts, the government agreed to close out the case. All of the assets of Citiwide were forfeited to the government, with some exceptions for equipment like a crane, backhoe, and racks used to store automobile parts. More importantly for Charles, the government agreed to drop its attempt to seize the Fountain Avenue location, which would stay in his family's hands. Given the kind of ghoulish evidence Kevin McMahon said was kept on the land, that was a significant win.

With the Fountain Avenue property having lost a tenant, Charles needed to assure the place was used for something, and it seemed that he lost no time taking over the facility to use for his own junkyard. But junk and scrap was a very competitive business. Charles needed other sources of income, and it seemed he turned to his friends on the street for that.

In 1992, the Gambino family, already in a state of flux because of Senior Gotti's indictment, was dealt another blow when the "Teflon Don," who had dodged convictions with a little help from some jury tampering, was convicted by a federal jury in Brooklyn. With the testimony of Gravano and Gotti's own tape-recorded words to go on, the anonymous jury convicted him of thirteen racketeering counts after a mere fourteen hours of deliberation over what amounted to a two-day period. The conviction assured that Gotti would be spending the rest of his life in jail.

While jury tampering had been the norm in Gotti's previous cases and had worked, the jury in the 1992 trial wasn't touched. But apparently the Gambino family made an attempt. In April 2010, federal prosecutors indicted a number of reputed Gambino gangsters and their associates on a variety of charges, including sex trafficking. Also included in the indictment was a charge of jury tampering that alleged that the *borgata* tried to influence the panel with much the same tactics employed in the case of John Carneglia. One Gambino soldier was charged in the 2010 case with having followed sequestered jurors in Gotti's 1992 trial as they stayed at a Manhattan hotel to deliberate. But the crime family ultimately didn't do anything beyond tailing the jurors because it was believed that there would be a mistrial because of a hung jury, said investigators. Why any rational person who followed the evidence presented against Gotti would think he had a shot of getting a hung jury was mystifying. The case against the "Dapper Don" was rock solid, and anyone who thought otherwise must have been delusional.

The conviction of Gotti devastated Charles and the rest of the Bergin crew. Gotti's son lost his crime mentor and protector on the street, a situation that seemed to make him headstrong and suspicious of many of his father's old associates. With the Gambino family in danger of disintegrating into a fractured leadership, Charles found himself drawn more and more into the devious maneuverings that developed over proceeds from the family rackets.

Daniel Marino and John "Johnny G" Gammarano were two seasoned veterans of the crime family and had been relied upon by the elder Gotti. Marino, in particular, had his hand in the setting up of trade show exhibits in New York, of which there were many every year. But it was also Marino who, law enforcement officials said, as far back as 1986 had been in talks with the Genovese crime family to assassinate Senior Gotti. With Gotti dead, Gambino capo James "Jimmy Brown" Failla would be installed as the new boss, with the blessing of the Genovese family, which was led by Vincent "the Chin" Gigante.

Around the time Senior Gotti was convicted in 1992, his son began seeing cheats and enemies around him. His old friend and confidant Mikey Scars DiLeonardo later turned government witness and testified in federal court that Junior Gotti suspected that Marino and Gammarano were skimming substantial amounts of construction industry extortion proceeds and not kicking the cash up to the Gambino family leadership—of which the younger Gotti was a part. An incensed Gotti asked DiLeonardo to set up a meeting with the two men and indicated that if things went bad, both would be killed, said DiLeonardo.

At Gotti's request, DiLeonardo said he found an apartment of a friend on Bay Eleventh Street in Brooklyn. Gotti drove up to the building and in the car were two others whom DiLeonardo recognized: Charles Carneglia and Tommy Sneakers Cacciapoli. They were both armed and in the car were some body bags, said DiLeonardo. Both DiLeonardo and Gotti walked over to the apartment, which was close to where Mikey Scars lived.

"He wasn't happy when he seen it. It wasn't a place conducive to killing two guys," DiLeonardo testified later about Gotti's reaction to the apartment, which was in a row house, with another apartment downstairs. If anyone was planning a hit, doing it in a row house with neighbors close by was a sure way of getting attention when the time came for killing.

Still, Gotti, Charles, and Cacciapoli entered the premises, recalled DiLeonardo. Both Charles and Tommy Sneakers went into a bedroom area off from the dining room and closed the door, with instructions to stay there in case things went wrong, according to DiLeonardo. A little later, Jackie the Nose D'Amico, who was part of the committee running the crime family, along with Junior Gotti, showed up.

Arriving in a limousine driven by a livery driver were Joseph "the German" Watts, Marino, and Gammarano. Also in the vehicle was an unexpected fourth person, George Lombardozzi, a cousin of Gammarano's. Seeing the presence of Gammarano and the limo driver, Di-Leonardo figured that the situation was now too complicated for anything murderous to happen.

Nobody is getting killed, DiLeonardo thought to himself.

With a family name that wasn't rooted in Italy's *mezzogiorno*, there was no way that Watts would ever become a made member of *La Cosa Nostra*. But he was nonetheless one of the most respected, if not most powerful, non-Italians associated with the Mob. His counsel and advice were often sought by the wiseguys. He even had his own crew of associates, much the same way as Alite. Because of that, Watts, who was very close to Senior Gotti, had his own power base. It was for that reason that he came to the meeting with Junior Gotti to argue the case for Marino and Gammarano in the dispute, which in Mob lingo was known as the "beef."

Watts wasn't intimidated by Junior Gotti or by D'Amico and spelled out his position. It turned out he had a very big trump card. Watts said that it had been Senior Gotti who had given him carte blanche over the years to handle some of the construction payoffs. It was his to do with it as he wanted. Some money was clearly going to the Gambino family, but Watts said he decided how much, according to DiLeonardo.

"Once Joe Watts tells that to Junior, it is over, because of the relationship Joe Watts had with Senior," DiLeonardo later testified. "His father wanted it that way, and John respected it, so there was no need to kill anybody."

Lombardozzi, Marino, and Gammarano then left the apartment, leaving behind Watts, Junior Gotti, and his little entourage. At that point, Charles Carneglia and Tommy Sneakers came out of the back bedroom. Watts, who was wise to the way the Mob killed people, was startled and upset to see them break their cover. Watts let Junior Gotti know the rashness of what he apparently planned to do to both men, according to DiLeonardo.

Watts wasn't the only person upset by the incident. By being called out of the bedroom by Junior Gotti and exposed to Watts, Charles felt that he had been compromised by his role as a potential assassin, McMahon would later testify. It turned out Charles feared that Marino, who was very powerful in the crime family, might retaliate against him for the way he laid in wait for a possible hit, said McMahon. For a man who was already paranoid enough about everything, from hound dogs to eavesdropping devices, Charles now apparently had to be wary about Marino as a possible threat. This wasn't just an idle fear. Marino and Junior Gotti were shaping up to be rivals for control of the family at a very treacherous time. With Charles aligned with the Gotti faction, things could get precarious for him if the struggle became violent. Marino also had various allies outside the Gambino family, notably the Genovese group, which had a reputation for viciousness and had already once schemed to bump off Senior Gotti.

The abortive hit plot against Daniel Marino was just another in a series of episodes that was making Charles Carneglia uncomfortable with Junior Gotti's attempt to control the family. He felt Gotti's son had risen prematurely to the position and hadn't seasoned enough along the way. A number of older captains and soldiers in the family also believed that Senior Gotti had improperly advanced his son to a position of power, and resentment was growing. The younger Gotti, whose public image in news photographs was one of a beefy, muscle-bound thug who paraded around Ozone Park, was also known to become a little volatile and hot tempered. It was a trait that followed the younger Gotti from his youth, as McMahon found out the hard way.

Because he had given the twelve-year-old Frankie Gotti the motorized bike he was riding when he was run over and killed by a car, McMahon wasn't liked among the Gotti household. The one exception seemed to be Senior Gotti, who, according to McMahon, thought the young man brought him luck so he insisted that the young man sit next to him during card games as a lucky charm. Gotti still lost more than he won. Gotti also was superstitious about boats and insisted that McMahon go with him on Sunday pleasure rides on the powerboat *Not Guilty* as a form of insurance against the craft sinking.

But Junior Gotti apparently didn't share his father's view of McMahon, and, according to one Gambino associate, was envious of the way McMahon seemed in such good graces with Senior Gotti. He also seemed to hold McMahon responsible for the death of his brother Frankie. With such tension between them, something finally happened during a visit Junior Gotti and Alite made to McMahon's apartment. Gotti became irritated when McMahon, who had a habit of bothering people with silly remarks, badgered Gotti.

"John took it personal," Alite later recalled in court. "Kevin didn't mean it personal, but then it got heated a little bit and Kevin wouldn't shut his mouth. This is one of the reasons I said I didn't like him. He can irritate the shit out of someone. He irritated John."

In a private conversation with investigators, Alite said that Junior Gotti warned McMahon during the escalating argument with words to the effect that "you're lucky I haven't killed you already, after what you did to my brother," a reference to the deceased Frankie.

McMahon still didn't shut up and answered the young Gotti back. By that time, Junior Gotti was reaching the boiling point and, according to Alite, pulled a small weapon, like a derringer, pointed it at McMahon, and said, "There is nothing John (Carneglia) is going to do about [it]." The size of the handgun drew a laugh from McMahon, which Alite told the FBI further goaded Junior Gotti, who then picked up a rifle leaning against the wall. Gotti was fuming by now. He told McMahon that if he didn't shut up, he would shoot him with the rifle, recalled Alite. Gotti again took the opportunity to trash John Carneglia, saying the imprisoned mobster was nothing but a drug dealer, according to Alite. McMahon didn't stop hectoring Gotti, and then the rifle Gotti was holding fired.

Perhaps it was a problem with the weapon or its safety mechanism. Nevertheless, Gotti, according to Alite, was stunned that the weapon had discharged and immediately said it was an accident. McMahon would later tell investigators that he also thought it was an accidental discharge. On Gotti's advice, he went to the hospital, where he told doctors that some black youths had mugged and shot him.

John Carneglia quickly found out about the shooting of McMahon and confronted Alite. But still loyal to Junior Gotti, Alite wouldn't give up his friend, instead telling Carneglia to ask McMahon about what had happened. However, Carneglia apparently had a sense of who fired the shot and grew very angry, calling Junior Gotti a "spoiled-brat motherfucker" whom he would have killed if it were not for his father, recalled Alite.

John Carneglia's intense dislike for Junior Gotti continued beyond the McMahon incident, and the relationship between the two men further deteriorated, spilling over to envelop Charles. Another flash point in the Carneglia-Gotti feud came when Helene Forgione, John Carneglia's mother-in-law, died in January 1996. According to Alite, both John Carneglia and Gotti were in the middle of a dispute over money. As a result, Gotti ordered that members and associates of the Gambino family not attend the wake. In Mob life, wakes and funerals are among the most important events at which crime family members show their respects, particularly if the bereaved is a key player in the crime family. If Gotti had told people to stay away, it was a big sign of disrespect.

By the time of the wake and funeral, Alite was already on the outs with Junior Gotti, having defied him by returning to New York to do business. So in another act of defiance, Alite said he and a number of his associates in the crime family showed up at the funeral home to pay their respects to the Carneglia family. While Alite was at the wake, John Carneglia telephoned the funeral home to thank him for the gesture.

Alite was a free agent and essentially ignored Gotti at will. But it wasn't easy for Charles Carneglia to do that. On the one hand, Junior Gotti was his boss and demanded respect—no matter how unfit Charles thought the younger man was for the job. But there was also pressure coming from John Carneglia, who not only disliked Gotti but wanted his brother to stand up to him. Had John Carneglia been able to do so, he would have probably killed Junior. Instead, he had to try and use his brother, Charles, as a proxy in disputes with the crime boss's aggressive son. It was an uncomfortable position for Charles. With his brother in prison, he had to try and make things work with Gotti, who he knew was ultimately carrying out the wishes of his imprisoned father.

It wasn't just Charles Carneglia who had problems with Junior Gotti. The Albanian renegade John Alite was in a constant state of psychological warfare with the acting boss of the crime family. Alite was trying constantly to outfox him in meetings so that there was never a situation where an ambush could be set up. With Alite not spending much time in Queens after his falling-out with Junior Gotti, Charles, Tommy Sneakers, and another friend, Jackie Cavallo, visited him at his home in New Jersey, where he was living with his pretty wife, Carol. From the visits, a closer friendship and rapport developed between Charles and Alite. Since the Albanian was such a useful associate of the crime family, and so efficient as a killer, Junior Gotti agreed to have Alite come back into the crime family fold, this time under the wing of Carneglia as part of his crew.

But although Alite was seemingly back in the good graces of the Gambino family, he learned that he couldn't let his guard down. As Alite would later recall for the FBI, he had just been allowed back into the fold, when he learned that there was apparently another hit attempt on his life. One day in 1995, Charles gave Alite a machine gun and two handguns. Why? According to Alite, Charles said that Junior Gotti allegedly wanted him killed. (Ironically, the weapons were supposedly given to Charles by Gotti, with the implication they were for the purported assassination attempt.) Alite didn't need to be running around New York City with unlicensed firearms, particularly an Uzi. So he went to a tattoo parlor on 101st Avenue and stored them, never having to use them.

Throughout the 1990s, Junior Gotti's hold on the Gambino leadership spot of acting boss was becoming shaky. His father's communication with the outside world was severely restricted, with visits only from his lawyers and relatives, like his eldest son and his brother Peter, allowed under the tight restrictions at the maximum-security facility at Marion, Illinois. He was also only permitted to make two monitored telephone calls a month to relatives, and had his incoming and outgoing mail screened. This limited communication with the street didn't permit Senior Gotti to get decisions passed along quickly to his associates outside the prison walls. According to law enforcement officials, the disarray in the Gambino family caused by the conviction of Senior Gotti and others was weakening the Mob's hold on various rackets. The FBI began to pick up intelligence that the leaders of the other *Cosa Nostra* families wanted to remove Senior Gotti as the Gambino boss and replace him with a younger man, like Nicholas Corozzo.

As law enforcement saw it, Gotti's attempt to rule the crime family from prison was doomed. Bruce Mouw, the retired supervisory FBI agent who had arrested Gotti back in 1990, said that the Gambino leadership was hobbled as Senior Gotti tried with futility to keep some semblance of control.

"They are in a sad state," said Mouw. "They have no real boss, no underboss, and no *consigliere.*"

Adding to the Gambino leadership problems was the fact that federal prosecutors were zeroing in on the men who were running the day-to-day operations, along with Junior Gotti. One of them was Nicholas Corozzo, the Brooklyn gangster who had been acquitted with Senior Gotti in the infamous 1986 federal prosecution case in Brooklyn, where the jury had been fixed. Corozzo had been sunning and surfing at the Sonesta Beach Hotel in Key Biscayne on December 18, 1996, when he was arrested by the FBI as he emerged from the warm Atlantic Ocean. A federal grand jury in Florida had indicted Corozzo on charges he was running the South Florida operation of the Gambino family, primarily through a large loan-sharking operation. The indictment also charged Corozzo with ordering the abduction and murder of Gambino associate Louis Maione for stealing loan-sharking proceeds.

Troubles for Corozzo didn't stop in Florida. Up in

New York, the FBI focused on an obscure soccer club in Canarsie, which from outward appearances seemed to be nothing more than a social club for old Italian men who wanted cups of espresso and cappuccino. But the FBI had turned its attention to the club for a very good reason: The operation, complete with some used white couches, was in reality an FBI sting. The Portofino Soccer Club, named after a swank resort area on the Italian Riviera, had been set up by an undercover FBI agent who had posed for well over a year as a Mob associate. Gangsters felt comfortable enough in the club setting to arrange for the disposal of hijacked designer dresses, computers, cigarettes, and exercise machines. It turned out Corozzo had permitted the social club to open. As a result of secret videotapes made by the FBI, he and one of his top associates, Leonard DiMaria, were indicted on charges of racketeering, loan-sharking, and extortion.

A few months later, Junior Gotti also drew some unnecessary attention to himself with a strange encounter with police in April 1997. It was then that Gotti and an associate, Steven Kaplan, twenty-nine, were stopped by police officers in the Gravesend section of Brooklyn one night. Police said that Gotti and Kaplan were in a Ford Expedition sport utility vehicle when they appeared to be following undercover officers looking to set up a buy-and-bust operation. Earlier, undercover cops were allegedly harangued by a Gotti associate outside an auto glass repair shop in the same area.

The police had arrested the Gotti associate, John Ruggiero, thirty-two, and were leaving the Sixtieth Precinct station house to continue the undercover drug operation when they spotted the car containing Gotti following them. Both Gotti and Kaplan were charged with obstructing governmental administration, and the case made headlines, including in the *New York Times*. About a month later, the charges were dropped. "The evidence is not sufficient to sustain the criminal charges," Charles J. Hynes, the district attorney (DA) of Brooklyn, said in a statement.

However, Junior Gotti's Brooklyn case was a mere sideshow to what was in the works. His activities in Manhattan had come under another FBI investigation. In January 1998, he was arrested and charged with thirty-nine others, including former Major League pitcher Denny McLain, in an indictment alleging fraud and extortion. The most serious charge was that Junior Gotti and his associates took over the popular strip club Scores on the Upper East Side and shook down everyone, from the owners to the coat check girls. Included in the case were charges that Gotti extorted construction companies and labor unions, as well as taking part in a fraud scheme using prepaid telephone cards.

Junior Gotti was held without bail. He tried a number of times to post bail but failed after prosecutors made some bare-bones allegations that he had threatened to kill a witness. Prosecutors wanted him kept behind bars as he awaited trial because they believed that would deprive the Gambino family of key leadership. However, a tenacious effort by his lawyers, Bruce Cutler and Gerald Shargel, finally negotiated a deal in which Gotti was freed on $10 million bail, secured by the property of friends and the home of his sister Victoria and her husband (and mobster) Carmine Agnello. Nine months after he was locked up, Gotti walked out of a White Plains federal courtroom a free man—sort of. The bail conditions were tough in that Gotti was under home confinement at his palatial Oyster Bay Cove home on

Long Island, and he had to wear an electronic ankle bracelet to track his movements. Phone calls and visitors were monitored as well.

For seven months after he got bail, Junior Gotti and the federal government engaged in a game of chicken. A trial date was set for April 1999 and the stakes for Gotti couldn't have been higher. Not only did he face twenty years in prison but also risked losing $20 million in assets. But as the months wore on, the government's case became weakened with witness problems. While prosecutors did knock off a number of the defendants with guilty pleas, they still faced the reality that they might not convict Gotti of everything. He also had some tenacious counsel with Cutler and Shargel, who knew how to handle themselves in the courtroom and in the sometimes more important court of public opinion.

The case was literally on the eve of trial when on April 1, 1999, Gotti, his lawyers, and the prosecutors walked into the White Plains court of federal judge Barrington Daniels Parker and announced that Gotti would plead guilty that night to wrap up the case. A major impetus for Gotti to take the deal was news that prosecutors intended to indict him on federal tax charges. When he took the plea, Gotti admitted that he had paid bribes to an official of a labor organization, later identified as Local 445 of the Teamsters Union. The payoff was made, Gotti said, in an effort to get up to $10 million in labor contracts for construction at Stewart Airport in New Windsor, New York. Also cobbled into the plea deal was a loan-sharking count and one count related to federal income taxes. Not mentioned in the guilty plea was anything about the strip club Scores, which prosecutors had trumpeted as the centerpiece of the case when they originally announced the indictment back in 1998. (The case against McLain was dismissed.)

But while the government didn't get everything it wanted from Junior Gotti in the plea, he now faced up to seven years and three months in prison and had to pay a $1 million fine. Judge Parker cut Gotti a little slack when it came time for sentencing in September 1999, giving Gotti six years and five months and telling him, "You are going to repay to society over the next seventy-seven months the debt you owed to your community." Parker also told Gotti—who moments before sentencing said, "I am here to take my medicine"—that once he got out of prison, he would have to spend the rest of his life repairing a family life where his children would be without a father for a long time.

U.S. Attorney Mary Jo White, of Manhattan, said that Junior Gotti's conviction should "serve as the death knell to the control the Gottis have exercised over the Gambino family for fifteen years." History would show that White's statement turned out to be a bit of hyperbole. The Gottis would remain a power in the crime family for some years. But on the streets of Ozone Park, the conviction of Gotti left Charles Carneglia in a state of new uncertainty about how the shift in day-to-day leadership would affect him. One thing was clear: the crime family had lost a troublesome leader.

8

"He's a Rat."

For all of the talk about rich gangsters, like the late Meyer Lansky, John Gotti, and Joseph Massino, *La Cosa Nostra* doesn't make money for everybody who is part of the life. There are earners in the Mob, those who can come up with lucrative schemes to generate millions of dollars for themselves and their bosses sitting at the top of the food chain. Then, there are those who have to hustle constantly, to come up with schemes, any schemes, to make a buck. Their financial futures were always in terrible shape: there was no retirement plan or 401(k) for the Mafia.

Charles Carneglia earned his reputation as a killer, not an earner. He was one of those who had to work hard to grab a few dollars. The old marijuana business allegedly done with Peter Zuccaro dried up and was a point of friction between the two men. True, he had the junkyard business, which provided for his mother and the rest of his relatives. When things got slow, he also took on jobs with a concrete company. Despite the fact that he was a soldier in one of the biggest *La Cosa Nostra* families in America, Charles wasn't making the big scores.

Hunter Adams, who was under Charles as an associate, was a stockbroker who made millions of dollars in drug deals and securities fraud. But Charles's business sense was so limited that he allegedly only demanded and took $400 a week in protection money from his underling. Yet, it is the small stuff that gets people in the most trouble.

Kevin McMahon was minding his own business—such as it was—in late 1996 when he got an inquisitive telephone call from his friend Ronald DeConza, an old reputed associate of the Gambino family under Charles. As McMahon remembered the conversation, DeConza asked about an older, elusive Gambino associate who had a connection to a strip club out on Long Island known as Forbidden Fruit. The associate had been pulling extortion money out of the club for years, apparently, when a Lucchese crime family soldier muscled in.

Since McMahon had visiting rights to see John Carneglia in prison, he went and told his old mentor about the problem with Forbidden Fruit and the fact that a crime family associate was getting squeezed out of the picture. In Mob protocol, this conflict between two crime families over a shakedown was a beef, which had to be settled.

"Do you still play racquetball?" John Carneglia asked McMahon.

"Yeah," answered McMahon.

Carneglia then told McMahon to see if during a racquetball session at a Brooklyn court he could talk to Louis "Louie Bagels" Daidone, then the acting boss of the Lucchese family, and explain the situation. So, during a visit to the Paerdegat Racquet Club, McMahon ran into Daidone, whom he played a racquetball session with, and then casually broached the problem with the Forbidden Fruit, explaining what John Carneglia had said during the prison visit. That was enough for Daidone to hear, and the Lucchese family pulled out of the club, leaving it to the Gambino family. As compensation for his effort, McMahon took $250-a-week payment from what the Genovese associate was getting from Forbidden Fruit. Neither John nor Charles Carneglia got any money.

One other shakedown artist getting a cut from the strip club was Carl Kline, another hanger-on and associate of the Gambino family. Since the sex business was always a ripe field for the Mob to get into, usually by shakedowns but sometimes through direct ownership, Kline kept an eye out for new opportunities. He didn't have to look very far. Down the block from the Forbidden Fruit was a porn video store known as Cherry Video.

Like most sex shops, Cherry Video had a section for porn videos, sex toys, lotions, and other paraphernalia. It also had a segment of products for gays, including some booths that had "glory holes" cut in the partitions, round openings that allowed gay men to engage in anonymous oral sex, according to one law enforcement official. Danny Melendez was the owner of Cherry Video and tried to run it as a legitimate business. He had an uncomfortable run-in with Mob guys in an earlier porn store known as Tender Traps. So when Kline appeared one day in early 2000 and essentially told him that he was getting paid off from Forbidden Fruit and that it made sense that the video store also pay protection, Melendez knew he had some trouble. He especially knew there was trouble brewing because Kline had with him a beefy man with biceps the size of tree trunks known as "Louie the Lumper," who on his birth certificate was otherwise known as Louis Riccardi.

It was after an earlier visit by Kline that Melendez went to the FBI for help in an effort to head off the Mob at the pass. The FBI immediately made a series of recordings, including many of Kline's telephone calls, and discovered that Charles Carneglia was involved in what was going on. It wasn't easy to identify exactly what was happening, because Kline and the person with whom he was talking conversed in coded conversations in which everyone talked elliptically, referring to people only in pronouns. This was a kind of code that Special Agent Greg Hagarty referred to as "pronoun abuse."

As part of the investigation, the FBI determined that a weekly extortion payoff of $300 was to be made by Danny Melendez, a payment that was overseen by Charles Carneglia. Surveillance found Kline meeting with and calling Charles at the Fountain Avenue junkyard about the payments. The tapes also indicated that 15 percent of the business, about $7,500, was to be overseen by Gambino captain Salvatore Scala. Over the years, Scala proved himself to be a Gotti loyalist and was identified as one of the gunmen in place around Sparks Steak House the night Paul Castellano was assassinated.

But whenever the Mob smells the blood of an easy shakedown target, a lot of sharks want to take a bite. In the case of Cherry Video, a Bonanno crime family figure named Thomas DiFiore claimed his group had the right to extort Melendez. To iron out the dispute, Charles,

Mug shot of Charles Carneglia taken around 1986. *(Photo courtesy U.S. Attorney's Office, Eastern District)*

Charles Carneglia
"Charlie Canig"

"Charlie Canig"

Charles Carneglia
"Charlie Canig"

Mug shot of Charles Carneglia taken at the Manhattan office of the FBI when he was arrested on February 7, 2008 at his home in Howard Beach, Queens. *(Photo courtesy U.S. Attorney's Office, Eastern District)*

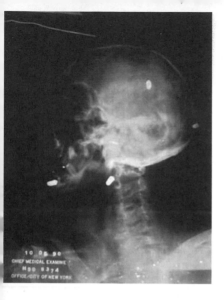

Autopsy X-ray of Louis DiBono's skull. The white rectangular objects are four bullets. *(Photo courtesy U.S. Attorney's Office, Eastern District)*

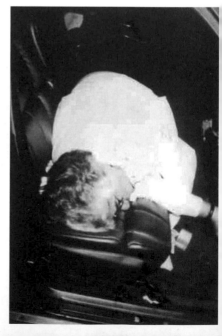

NYPD crime scene photo of the killing of Gambino soldier Louis DiBono in the World Trade Center garage on October 2, 1990. *(Photo courtesy U.S. Attorney's Office, Eastern District)*

Louis DiBono, whose murder in 1990 was ordered by John Gotti. Charles Carneglia was convicted in 2009 of being involved in the slaying. *(Photo courtesy U.S. Attorney's Office, Eastern District)*

Louis DiBono

Michael Cotillo, a Gambino associate who was killed in a stabbing incident outside a Howard Beach diner in 1977. A federal jury in 2009 found that Charles Carneglia was responsible for the murder. *(Photo courtesy U.S. Attorney's Office, Eastern District)*

Michael Cotillo

Salvatore Puma, a Gambino family associate who was stabbed to death on a Howard Beach street in 1983. In 2009 a federal court jury found that Charles Carneglia stabbed Puma in a dispute over the delivery of prison commissary money.
(Photo courtesy U.S. Attorney's Office, Eastern District)

Salvatore Puma

NYPD crime scene photo of the killing of Albert Gelb on March 11, 1976.
(Photo courtesy U.S. Attorney's Office, Eastern District)

Albert Gelb

Albert Gelb, a New York State court officer, was shot dead on a Brooklyn Street in 1976. In February 1975, Gelb got into an altercation with Charles Carneglia in a Howard Beach diner, an incident that led to Carneglia getting hit with a weapons charge. Federal prosecutors believed Carneglia was responsible for Gelb's death, but in 2009, a federal jury didn't find that Carneglia was involved. *(Photo courtesy U.S. Attorney's Office, Eastern District)*

MIchael Finnerty, a Gambino crime family associate who testified against Charles Carneglia. *(Photo courtesy U.S. Attorney's Office, Eastern District)*

Michael Finnerty

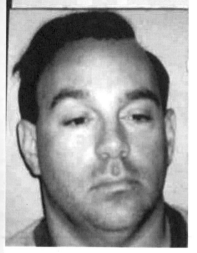

Kevin McMahon

Kevin McMahon, who as a Howard Beach youth was effectively adopted by the Carneglia family. McMahon became a trusted driver and associate of both John and Charles Carneglia in their criminal activities. He also took taking care of Charles when he was drunk. After being arrested by the FBI, McMahon turned into a cooperating witness and testified against Charles as well as John "Junior" Gotti. (Photo courtesy U.S. Attorney's Office, Eastern District)

Peter Zuccaro "Bud"

Peter "Bud" Zuccaro, a Gambino crime family associate who testified against Charles Carneglia. Zuccaro aspired all his life to be a gangster but passed up the opportunity when the Mob wanted to initiate him into La Cosa Nostra. (Photo courtesy U.S. Attorney's Office, Eastern District)

Michael DiLeonardo, known as "Mikey Scars" because of a facial disfigurement. A former Gambino captain, DiLeonardo became a witness against Charles Carneglia and Junior Gotti. *(Photo courtesy U.S. Attorney's Office, Eastern District)*

Michael DiLeonardo "Mikey Scars"

Eugene Gotti "Genie"

An aged Eugene Gotti, brother of late crime boss John Gotti. Like John Carneglia, Eugene was sentenced in 1989 to fifty years in prison for heroin trafficking. *(Photo courtesy U.S. Attorney's Office, Eastern District)*

John Gotti, Jr.
"Jr."

John Gotti, Jr., son of the late Gambino crime boss. Junior Gotti rose to the rank of captain and, according to federal court testimony, set up the murder of Louis DiBono in 1990, but was never convicted. From 2005 to 2009, Junior underwent four federal racketeering trials, which all resulted in mistrials. The government then decided enough was enough and gave up trying to nail Junior, whose main defense was that he'd left the Mob life. *(Photo courtesy U.S. Attorney's Office, Eastern District)*

John Alite, an Albanian associate of the Gambinos, who testified against Charles Carneglia in his 2009 federal racketeering trial. Alite also testified against Junior Gotti that same year. Alite proved a poor witness for the prosecution; a mistrial was declared. *(Photo courtesy U.S. Attorney's Office, Eastern District)*

John Alite

Angelo Ruggiero, Sr. "Quack Quack"

Angelo "Quack-Quack" Ruggiero, Sr., a powerful Gambino family member who was a trusted aide and childhood pal of John Gotti. Gotti soured on Quack-Quack (so-named because he could never stop talking). *(Photo courtesy U.S. Attorney's Office, Eastern District)*

John Gotti, Sr.
"Senior"

John Gotti, Sr., the late Gambino crime boss who died in June 2002 in a federal prison hospital. Gotti rose to power after he set up the assassination of then-Gambino boss Paul Castellano in 1985. Gotti's Queens-based crew included both Charles and John Carneglia.

(Photo courtesy U.S. Attorney's Office, Eastern District)

Domenico Cefalu, reputed acting underboss of the Gambino family, who was arrested by the FBI in February 2008. *(Photo courtesy U.S. Attorney's Office, Eastern District)*

Domenico Cefalu "Italian Dom"

John Carneglia "Johnny Canig"

John Carneglia, the Gambino captain and older brother of Charles Carneglia. He was sentenced in 1989 to a fifty-year prison stretch for heroin trafficking. *(Photo courtesy U.S. Attorney's Office, Eastern District)*

Joseph Corozzo
"JoJo"

The Corozzo brothers, Joseph (above) and Nicholas (right). Both men were rounded up in a February 2008 sweep by the FBI, two of sixty-two reputed members and associates of the Gambino family. Joseph was believed to be the consigliere of the Gambinos, while Nicky was a powerful captain. Both pleaded guilty in the case and received prison sentences. *(Photo courtesy U.S. Attorney's Office, Eastern District)*

Nicholas Corozzo
"Little Nicky" "Nicky"

From left to right: Kevin McMahon, John Carneglia, his mother Jennie Carneglia, and brother Charles. All were together during a visit to John in prison. *(Photo courtesy U.S. Attorney's Office, Eastern District)*

In happier times. The wedding photo of Kevin McMahon, who was essentially raised as a young teenager by John Carneglia and his wife, Helene. Charles Carneglia is on the far left and mother Jennie is seated in the front row. Chris Carneglia, Justine Carneglia, and John Jr. are all children of John Carneglia, Sr. Helen Forgione is the mother of Helene Carneglia. *(Photo courtesy U.S. Attorney's Office, Eastern District)*

Charles Carneglia, center, with Anthony "Blaise" Corozzo, brother of Nicholas, and Joseph, at left. The man on the right is unidentified.
(Photo courtesy U.S. Attorney's Office, Eastern District)

In this surveillance photo, circa 1990, are John "Junior" Gotti, left, and Charles Carneglia. Both are on their way to a funeral. Note the way they both seem to be adjusting their shirt cuffs. *(Photo courtesy U.S. Attorney's Office, Eastern District)*

using Kevin McMahon as an intermediary, got Scala to agree to meet with the Bonanno group. Why didn't Charles just pick up the telephone and call Scala? The FBI investigation revealed that both Charles and Scala had a dislike of each other. Scala believed that Charles, because of his instability, couldn't be trusted, according to a law enforcement official involved in the investigation.

The Mob sit-down over the Cherry Video dispute took place between Charles, Scala, DiFiore, and Ronald DeConza on May 3, 2000, in a parking lot on Long Island, court records show. By then, the FBI had enough to file a criminal complaint on May 8 charging everybody who had been at the sit-down, as well as Kevin McMahon and John Dwyer, with involvement in the extortion plot.

The amount of the extortion payment charged in the original criminal complaint and indictment didn't amount to very much. But the Mob generally made its money by pulling similar amounts from a number of businesses so that the accumulation did come to some serious money. "They do this every day, day in and day out, with five places and it comes to twelve hundred dollars [a week]," said Hagarty later.

The Cherry Video case didn't get much news coverage at the time, but it would prove to be the beginning of a key shift in the alliances of the Gambino faction, which Charles directed. For as the case developed, suspicions began to grow with Charles about those around him, particularly McMahon. As was his tendency, Charles started to become paranoid and abusive. As it turned out, the way Charles reacted would become part of a vicious circle, a self-fulfilling prophecy of things Charles feared the most about the treacherous way *La Cosa Nostra* had changed.

The troubles began as soon as McMahon ran into a problem getting bail after the government said he might prove to be a flight risk. Although Charles and the other defendants were able to post bond, McMahon was ordered held at the Nassau County Jail, a local lockup that wasn't the normal federal detention center. As it turned out, McMahon was held at the Nassau County facility because the case was assigned to a federal judge at the Central Islip courthouse, some distance away from the usual Metropolitan Detention Center in Brooklyn. A lot of Central Islip federal defendants found themselves taken to the local jail instead of the Brooklyn center. There really wasn't anything sinister about that move.

But the placement of McMahon in the local jail appeared to get Charles and others in the Gambino family suspicious. Even John Carneglia was overheard questioning why McMahon wasn't kept in the usual federal lockup: "What is going on with him?" With even his brother raising questions, Charles easily became suspicious about the way McMahon was being housed in a local jail.

Paranoid about McMahon, Charles visited him at the county lockup and gave him a warning, which wasn't very subtle. As McMahon later remembered, Charles said that if Kevin implicated him in the DiBono hit, Charles would turn around and say that McMahon played a role in the armored-car heist, presumably the one where the guard died. "I'm a good fellow and you're nothing," Charles said, according to McMahon.

McMahon festered in the Nassau County facility until November, when prosecutors consented to a $1 million bail package. By then, McMahon had some damage control to do, not only Charles but with his own wife, who had listened to some of the surveillance tapes turned over by the government as part of the normal pretrial discovery process. On one snippet of the tape, McMahon was talking to a friend about the oral sex he supposedly got at one of the strip clubs, and his wife went ballistic upon hearing that and screamed at him during one of his jailhouse calls home. Confronted with the recording, McMahon admitted he was in the strip club, but he explained that his talk about sex was done simply to entice the guy to come and meet him. The wife believed McMahon's denial, which he later insisted in court was truthful.

But McMahon had less success with Charles over a more serious issue. Following a pretrial hearing in the extortion case, where all of the defendants were present, McMahon ran into Charles in the parking lot of the Central Islip courthouse. By that time, Charles had been telling anyone who would listen that he thought McMahon was an informant. Outside the courthouse, McMahon and Charles got into a furious argument over the surveillance tapes turned over by prosecutors. Charles basically couldn't afford to pay up to $2,000 for his copies and demanded McMahon give them to him, along with the guns used in the DiBono homicide a decade earlier.

Rather than continue to argue in the parking lot, McMahon and Charles agreed to meet at the Carneglia house in Howard Beach on Eighty-fifth Street. McMahon drove as fast as he could in the hope that Charles wouldn't start drinking and get volatile. He was too late. Arriving at the house, McMahon found that Charles already had been drinking.

"He was all wound up, and he did something, some

kind of drug, and he was screaming I killed his mother," McMahon later testified.

Charles feared that the arrest and his possible conviction would pull him away from Jennie and that the elderly woman wouldn't be able to cope with the stress of another son in prison. When Charles stuck his hand under a pillow and pulled out a gun, McMahon figured it was time to go. He ran out the door to his car, where his wife was waiting.

"Don't come back," Charles yelled out the window. McMahon never did.

Charles, nevertheless, kept the pressure on McMahon, enlisting the help of Peter Gotti, the brother of the Gambino boss, to help get the guns back. Even that didn't stop Charles's harassment. McMahon later recalled how the man whom he once considered his "uncle" would drive to his house in Howard Beach and yell out how he had become a rat, which in that neighborhood was like being branded with the "Scarlet Letter."

The trial of the Cherry Video extortion case took place in the spring of 2001. But McMahon wasn't part of it. He had decided to plead guilty and did so on April 11, 2001, to one count of interfering with commerce with threats or violence. He received a thirty-three-month prison sentence, which Judge Arnold Spatt recommended be done in a shock incarceration unit, a prison boot camp, near New York City. McMahon was then sent to Fort Dix, the former military base that had been converted to a low-security correctional center.

Charles, Scala, and the other defendants went to trial over the porn shop extortion. To prove its case, the government called Ricciardi, the hulky big guy whom Kline used to threaten Melendez. Since Charles's name wasn't mentioned by Kline in his talks with Melendez—he used the term "friend" to signify his Mob connection—prosecutors had to build their case with circumstantial evidence about what those vague words meant. Ricciardi's testimony established that Kline had said to him that Charles was his Mob connection. Both men even went to see Charles, who was known as "Charles from 101" because of his ties to the Bergin Hunt and Fish social club, at his junkyard in East New York.

Prosecutor Andrew Genser called Hagarty as an expert witness about the Mob to give his opinion to the jury about what he believed Kline and the others were talking about on the tapes when they referred to other participants in the scheme with pronouns or coded words. The added problem for Charles in the case was that he was also picked up on wiretaps and bugs talking with Kline and McMahon about the shakedown. From January until about March 2000, Melendez paid over to Kline the weekly shakedown fee, which, in reality, was FBI money. At one point, at the direction of the FBI, Melendez stopped paying, forcing Kline and McMahon to pay him a visit to get the money.

The defense conceded that Kline was extorting Melendez—there was no way around that fact because of the tapes. But the lawyers tried to argue that neither Charles nor Scala were involved in the shakedown and that the tapes were too vague. However, it became clear to the jury that Charles and Scala were part of the Mob after prosecutors played a compilation of police surveillance videos made of the Ravenite from 1988 to 1990 that showed Scala and Charles talking with Gambino crime family members. Charles may not have liked going to the Ravenite, but he had the bad timing to be there when the cops were running their video cameras.

However, Charles didn't concede things, particularly

about his Mob membership. His defense attorney, Joseph Corozzo, the attorney son of the Gambino captain with the same name, said the Ravenite videos and other evidence proved nothing about membership in the Mafia. The only evidence that Charles was in the Mob, argued Corozzo, was that of an FBI agent who wrote out the original application to get the wiretaps and said informants claimed Charles was in the Gambino family.

"Not one of the made members mentioned or whoever cooperated never came in and said Charles Carneglia is a member of the Mafia and committed a crime," Corozzo argued to the jurors.

Corozzo also stressed that just because Hagarty said Kline was tied to Charles, that didn't mean that Charles was involved in everything Kline was doing. Kline was doing things early in the case in which he never mentioned Charles doing anything with Cherry Video, said Corozzo.

"They all go back to Agent Hagarty's expert opinion that if Carl (Kline) was doing it, Charles was doing it. There is no evidence of that," said Corozzo.

As convincing as the tape recordings of the Cherry Video shakedown by Kline were to prosecutors, the jurors weren't fully persuaded of the government's argument. The panel acquitted Charles and Scala of all but one of the extortion counts involving Cherry Video. The jury also acquitted defendant John Dwyer of the two counts he faced. (Kline had pleaded guilty to seven counts before the trial.)

But a conviction on a single count of interference with commerce by threats—the same charge McMahon pleaded guilty to—was still serious for Charles. While he had some relatively small prior convictions, Charles was still considered a key figure in the Gambino family, and the courts generally were weighing in with significant prison sentences on Mob cases. Charles was no exception. On November 2, 2001, Charles was sentenced to sixty-three months in prison—five years and three months—by Judge Jacob Mishler. As it turned out, the Federal Bureau of Prisons (BOP) sent Charles to Fort Dix, the same facility as his old "nephew" Kevin McMahon.

Charles Carneglia and Kevin McMahon never came into contact while both were serving their time at Fort Dix. But it didn't take long for McMahon to pick up on the anger Charles held toward him. When other prisoners would come over from the section of the institution where Charles was held, McMahon recalled that he heard them say how Charles was branding him as a "rat" and wanted to kill him.

With his world in shambles and having lost the camaraderie he once had with the Carneglia clan, McMahon saw how empty the Mob life had become. Around 2002, he thought about becoming a cooperating witness for the government. But even when some FBI agents came to visit him at Fort Dix with news he could be arrested in a Florida case, McMahon kept his own counsel and didn't cooperate. The fact that the FBI came to interview him also stoked the Fort Dix rumor mill because several inmates saw McMahon go to the special facility where government officials met with prisoners.

The FBI officials who visited McMahon were in the process of building a criminal case against a Florida offshoot of the Gambino family led by a transplanted New York gangster by the name of Ronald "One Arm"

Trucchio, so named because of a withered right arm he had as a result of a childhood accident. Trucchio, a Gambino captain, had already pleaded guilty to gambling charges in a New York State prosecution by Queens DA Richard Brown and was serving a sentence of up to three years when federal prosecutors in Tampa brought some bigger guns to bear. In August 2004, the Tampa grand jury charged Trucchio, Michael Malone, Steven Catalano, Pasquale Andriano, and Terry L. Scaglione with racketeering conspiracy.

There was also a sixth person charged in the Tampa case, the Albanian hothead from Queens, John Alite. It seems that when Alite split with Junior Gotti, he bounced around; prosecutors said that he carried out his own brand of extortion, home invasion robberies, and drug dealing in the Sunshine State. It was also in the Tampa area that Alite infiltrated a number of valet-parking businesses, which he sometimes used, along with a glass business and nightclub, to launder drug proceeds.

But when the FBI went to pick up Alite, he was nowhere to be found. Sensing trouble brewing, Alite packed up in March 2003 with his pretty Brazilian girlfriend he had been living with in Florida and took off to Brazil. Living overseas wouldn't be a problem, since Alite had millions of dollars, so he said, to tide him over. Settling in the Copacabana section of Rio de Janeiro, Alite started teaching boxing lessons to keep busy. Some fugitives—like Ronnie Biggs, of the "Great London Train Robbery" fame—were able to live on the lam in Brazil for years. But in Alite's case, homesick for the United States, and eager to stay in touch with his Mob cronies, he started taking foolish risks with his telephone calls and Internet links back home. For ten months, Alite used Internet cafés to make his connections with friends in New York. The result was that the FBI, with the help of Brazilian federal police, were able to get a line on where Alite was staying and arrested him in Copacabana in November 2004.

For the next two years, Alite would fight extradition, although it is hard to fathom why he wanted to stay in a Brazilian jail. The conditions there were odious—with crime rampant in the jails, where the daily diet was rice and beans, and toilets overflowed from above your cell. Alite was a bit of a rake and had actually fathered a child while he was in Brazil (he already had two with his first wife, Carol, and another with girlfriend Claudia DiPippa) and thought it might help him stay in South America. While he was spending millions of dollars on lawyers to fight extradition back to the United States, Alite began to think about the possibility that his only way out of the predicament was to become a cooperating witness. But before he even approached the FBI, Alite tried to squeeze hundreds of thousands of dollars in hush money from old Mob cronies back in the United States. Yet for all of the lawyers he hired, Alite lost out in the extradition fight and found himself back in Florida in December 2006.

Perhaps Kevin McMahon should have decided to cooperate when the FBI came to see him in 2002 at Fort Dix. For in April 2005, McMahon was arrested in Brooklyn in the Tampa case involving Trucchio, Alite, and the others. A free man for about two years after serving his sentence in the Cherry Video case, McMahon found himself again facing the serious prospect that his future held nothing for him other than a prison cell. The main case against McMahon involved two robberies that took place over ten years earlier in New

York and New Jersey. One involved a September 5, 1995, rip-off of a Sears department store in Vineland, New Jersey; the other was two months later of the Papavero Funeral Home in Maspeth, Queens, a family-run business that would later get publicity as the place that handled the funeral of John Gotti when he died in June 2002. Both robberies involved McMahon as a lookout.

McMahon tried to get the Tampa indictment against him dismissed on the grounds that a delay of about ten years in voting the indictment hurt his chances of defending himself. Some witnesses had died or relocated, while the memories of others had faded with time, McMahon's attorneys argued. But the court rejected McMahon's argument, and in November 2006, he rolled the dice and decided to go to trial. After prosecutors presented their case, McMahon's attorneys asked that he be acquitted by the court. Their argument was a simple one: McMahon was part of a crew of Gambino associates who worked under Charles Carneglia and Salvatore Scala—not John Alite, as the Florida indictment charged. "The Carneglia crew worked separately and independently from the Alite crew allegedly managed by Ronald Trucchio and John Alite," argued McMahon's lawyers. They also noted that the two robberies happened more than five years before the indictment, and thus were outside the statute of limitations.

The result of the trial was a disaster for McMahon. The court not only rejected his attempt to get a judgment of acquittal, but the jury rejected his defense, convicting him on November 27, 2006, of the sole count of conspiracy. McMahon now faced a possible prison term of twenty years. His lifelong status as a fellow traveler with John and Charles Carneglia had earned him nothing more than the hope of a prison cell and the company of other criminals.

McMahon got a taste of what his life would be when he was ordered jailed immediately after his conviction and was sent to the Hernando County Jail, outside of Tampa, where federal prisoners were held. He arrived around the same time as Alite, who had been brought back to the United States from Brazil in early December after losing his extradition battle. One Sunday morning, while standing in a line inside the jail waiting to go to church, both Alite and McMahon bumped into each other. The reunion wasn't pleasant. McMahon berated Alite for labeling him a "rat" in Howard Beach. Taken aback, Alite got defensive and denied branding McMahon as an informant, saying someone else had done that.

The conversation then took a turn that, when it was over, likely got both McMahon and Alite thinking about the futility of their current situations. It was probably the moment when, despite all of their bluster, both men realized they were vulnerable to being saddled with responsibility for numerous murders and other crimes, which could mean a lifetime in jail.

"I don't know why you didn't cooperate," said Alite. "Nobody helped you or anything."

"Why would I cooperate? You are facing life, not me," shot back McMahon.

Both men at this point, waiting to go to church, were playing a mind game with each other. Alite was subtly seeing if McMahon had considered cooperating with the government, while McMahon was saying it was Alite who should be the one to think about becoming a witness. Perhaps unwittingly, both men were suggesting reasons why the other should abandon the Mob life and cooperate with the FBI.

The rhetoric intensified. Alite reminded McMahon that rumors had been rampant that Peter Zuccaro, the old partner in crime with Charles Carneglia, had decided to cooperate. This meant that Zuccaro would provide evidence about the DiBono homicide, as well as the armored-car robbery that took the life of guard Delgado Rivera. Alite said he knew McMahon had been involved in both incidents.

"I don't know what you are talking about," responded McMahon, trying to evade the issue. Finally McMahon took his own shot at Alite, telling him that the evidence in the Tampa case against him was overwhelming. "You are dead at trial," said McMahon. "You should cooperate."

Even before his trial, the FBI had tried in earnest to turn McMahon into a cooperating witness. At one point, the Tampa FBI office pulled him in for a talk and the only thing McMahon would say was that he wanted to talk with Special Agent Hagarty, who was back in New York. Though nothing happened immediately, the telephone conversation with Hagarty proved pivotal to McMahon's future. Hagarty was a down-to-earth agent who not only had an encyclopedic knowledge of the Gambino crime family but had the professional sense— honed from years of experience—on how to rope in a cooperating witness. Some witnesses aren't ready to take such a step until they become self-aware about what is part of their past and where their future lies. If the potential witnesses have wives and families on the outside of prison, they may be reluctant to take such a big step. From the hesitation in McMahon's voice, it seemed to Hagarty that the defendant wasn't ready to become a cooperator, a step that would rip out his whole prior life and change the way he lived forever.

After his conviction, McMahon knew he was facing some heavy prison sentence. Why, then, should he hold out on cooperating? Hagarty had also told him back in the Cherry Video case that he was already perceived as being an informant because of the way he was captured on so many surveillance tapes. True, it wasn't the same thing as signing on the dotted line and agreeing to be a cooperator, but the effect on people like Charles and others in the Gambino family was the same. There was no way he would have respect in the gangster life. Putting that together with his sense of abandonment by the Carneglias, and the realization that he could be saddled with responsibility for the DiBono and Delgado Rivera murders, Kevin McMahon made the decision to become a cooperator.

Because he had fled to Brazil and went through two years of extradition proceedings, John Alite was going to be tried separately for the Tampa conspiracy case. By the time his trial was scheduled in 2007, Alite had a pretty good idea of the strength of the government's case. He knew things weren't looking good. Alite kept switching defense attorneys, which further delayed the trial. But the extra time also gave Alite the opportunity to work out his own deal with the government; after numerous postponements in his case, he decided to throw his lot in with the FBI. On January 16, 2008, at the age of forty-five, Alite pleaded in a sealed court proceeding in Tampa to a racketeering conspiracy count. The result was no different than if he had gone to trial and lost, since he was still facing the potential of a life term in prison. But if he testified truthfully and helped the government, Alite just might get the Holy Grail of all federal cooperating witnesses—a break on his prison sentence and might even be able to walk out with time served.

With John Alite and Kevin McMahon now cooperating, federal prosecutors back in Brooklyn and Manhattan were ecstatic. They had good reason to be. The government had something very big brewing back in New York on a number of fronts, and the two new witnesses would have crucial roles to play.

9

Code Name "Zipper"

Charles Carneglia came back to Howard Beach in May 2006 at age sixty after spending just about five years in federal custody for the Cherry Video extortion. He found a lot of changes. The old Bergin Hunt and Fish social club was long gone, and the premises had turned into a dog-grooming salon. Senior Gotti was dead four years already, and Gotti's brother Peter in prison for life. Junior Gotti was struggling under a new federal racketeering indictment. Despite two mistrials, Junior had to face a trial for a third time that fall.

Charles's mother Jennie was pushing ninety-one. While she was still living in the house on Eighty-fifth Street, she really couldn't care for herself. It was a good thing that her youngest son was now home. Charles loved cooking for her and making sure her diapers were changed. He did the shopping and made certain Mom had what she needed. He tried like hell to be a good son.

There were other familiar faces no longer around. Kevin McMahon, who had not talked to Charles since 2000, was awaiting trial in Florida. John Alite was working out with boxers in Brazil and picking the best spots to sunbathe on the wonderfully curved beach of Copacabana with his lithe and curvy Brazilian girlfriend.

Back in Howard Beach, Charles fell into a routine of going to the Carosello Restaurant on Cross Bay Boulevard just before lunchtime. He preferred going in the back door by the parking lot. On some days, he didn't even go in; on other days, he had two-hour or more lunches, with the tab picked up by people who knew him. He might then sit on a bench in the parking lot and smoke—not the smartest thing for a man with emphysema. He would talk with people he knew, and sometimes the conversations would take a morose turn.

"He was tired," Charles's old friend Mark Gioia recalled. "He used to sit there for hours. We were in the back of Carosello's, sitting on the benches next to the parking valet hut, and just sitting there for two and a half hours. He would drink. You would see tears in Charles's eyes. There was nothing left to him."

What disturbed Charles the most was the way the new generation of mobsters would at the drop of a hat become cooperating witnesses to save their skins, making up stories if necessary, remembered Gioia some years later. Charles had a name for them, Gioia said, "inmates of the new millennium."

But other days, Charles was feeling more sociable and would get a ride in a car registered to the wife of a local realtor and go to another well-known local eatery, Don Pepe, where he met some more men his age. Charles didn't work, and he supported himself, so he said, with the proceeds of a life insurance policy he had cashed in.

The world knows so much about Charles's lifestyle and eating habits after he got out of prison because— unbeknownst to him—there was constant surveillance of his activities by the FBI. A surveillance team known as SO-3, a unit assigned to follow organized crime figures in the Gambino family, started tailing him in earnest, shooting videos and taking still pictures. Charles's probation officer also followed him to see if he met with any people on a special list of prohibited persons he wasn't supposed to consort with on probation. But it was the FBI that began watching Charles with added interest, particularly in 2007 and in 2008, because of the unfinished business of five homicides that had been nagging investigators for decades. Then there was also the dirty dealings of the Mob across the bridge on Staten Island, things that Charles may not have played a role in but were all coming together in a way that would drastically affect his newfound liberty. There was no way in a hundred years Charles could have seen what was coming.

Federal prosecutors love sexy Mob cases, with lots of homicides, high-profile defendants, and lots of media coverage. But the routine bread-and-butter things that come across the desk of most federal investigators are more mundane tax, drug, and fraud cases. For Burton Ryan, an assistant U.S. attorney in the Eastern District of New York, the particular tax case that landed on his desk in 2000 involved two brothers from Long Island, Fortunato "Fred" and Guisseppe "Joseph" Scalamandre. Both men owned several major construction companies and were involved in large public projects in New York City, including renovation of subway and railroad lines, as well as roadway improvement on the Long Island Expressway and Seaford–Oyster Bay Expressway.

To make sure they had peace with their unions, the Scalamandres devised a way of generating kickbacks and, at the same time, avoided paying federal taxes on the money generated. Federal investigators also discovered that they used a couple of minority businesses as fronts on public projects. During the investigation, Ryan uncovered evidence that the kickbacks—which were generated by paying false invoices to subcontractors—were being passed on for a while to acting Lucchese crime boss Alphonse D'Arco and underboss Anthony "Gaspipe" Casso to influence construction trade unions. The aim of the payoff, which amounted to about $40,000 a year from 1991 through 1998, was to avoid having the Scalamandre companies pay into the union benefit funds and the payment of dues for the workers.

The payoff scheme was a common ploy used by the Mob to generate cash in return for influencing labor unions. What made the Scalamandre case out of the ordinary was that it involved such big mobsters as D'Arco and Casso. Faced with evidence developed by Ryan and government investigators, the Scalamandre brothers quickly pleaded guilty in early 2001 to tax evasion conspiracy and admitted to conspiring to pay the two Lucchese bosses. They were both sentenced to four years' probation and agreed to turn over to the federal government $5 million, representing the proceeds of their cash generation scheme.

Burton Ryan's case emboldened a newly formed federal construction industry task force on Long Island, which involved a bunch of agencies, including the FBI, Department of Labor, along with state agencies, like the Metropolitan Transportation Authority of New York. Agents started digging into leads, executing search warrants, and coming up with a series of suspected labor payoff schemes. One case in particular involved a trucker from Staten Island named Joseph Vollaro, son of a Gambino crime family bookmaker who once used his boy as a runner for the numbers operation. Vollaro was suspected of "double breasting," a particular labor crime in which a union company devised a way not to pay the correct scale on wages dictated by the labor agreement. There are a number of ways a double-breasting scheme works; sometimes they involved two different groups of workers, some of whom are paid lower wages through a shell company. At other times, the union officials are paid off, which is what investigators thought Vollaro was doing.

But no sooner had Vollaro come into focus as a target of the investigation of Ryan's task force than Ryan's boss, the U.S. attorney in Brooklyn, abruptly decided to pare down the construction task force. Under the new regime, Department of Labor investigators didn't want to work with the Brooklyn federal organized crime prosecutors, so the Vollaro case was in danger of withering on the vine. To avoid killing the investigation, as well as other cases that had been under way, Ryan began to visit friends in other investigative offices to find a home for his orphaned investigations.

The Vollaro probe was very close to dying when the New York State Organized Crime Task Force (OCTF), part of the attorney general's office run at that time by Eliot Spitzer, decided it would take over the investigation and try to find a state crime. Meanwhile, federal agents with the Department of Labor agreed to continue their own look at the double-breasting union fraud.

As the Vollaro investigation got under way in its new home at OCTF in 2005, there were some other big events in the Mafia that same year, notably the decision by Joseph Massino to become a cooperating witness. That led to nothing but trouble for the Bonanno crime family. But the old crowd that had been around the late John Gotti on 101st Avenue in Ozone Park had been relatively immune from the effects of turncoats since Sammy Gravano surfaced back in the 1990s. The result was that individual prosecutors started looking at the Gambino family in piecemeal fashion. Here and there smaller cases were prosecuted. Then, in 2002, the Havana-born FBI undercover agent Joaquin "Jack" Garcia, posing as "Jack Falcone," penetrated one wing of the Gambino family and made a case against crime captain Gregory DePalma. Still, the Gambino family went along as usual with up-and-coming boss Nicholas Corozzo and those close to him making moves, and making money. Included in that group was Vollaro.

Like many connected to the Gambino *borgata*, Vollaro was born in Brooklyn and later moved to Staten Island as a young boy. His bookmaking father introduced him to the Mob on the ground level with bookmaking being a stepping-stone. By his early twenties, Vollaro started dealing drugs; in 1987, he was arrested in New Jersey for selling cocaine. Court records show that in 1989 Vollaro was convicted and sentenced to a three-year term in New Jersey.

Back home on Staten Island, Vollaro's father became one of the largest bookmakers in that part of the city and came under the control of Jerome Brancato, a diminutive Gambino soldier who helped the elderly Vollaro with collecting gambling debts, court records stated. According to federal prosecutors, Brancato demanded $1,000 a month from the Vollaro gambling ring as payment for mediating disputes that might arise with other mobsters, collecting monies, and insulating the operation from shakedowns.

It was Brancato who also suggested to Vollaro's father that his jailed son seek out another Gambino associate who was also housed in the same facility. The younger Joe Vollaro managed to hook up with the associate Sam Corsaro, and the two became fast friends. At that point, Vollaro had some important connections to the Gambino crime family, which would prove to be pivotal to his life, although not the way he first imagined.

By the time Vollaro hooked up with Corsaro, the older Gambino associate had become a reputed soldier in the crime family. Now a full-fledged associate of the Gambino family under Corsaro's crew, Vollaro took part in loan-sharking, gambling, and fraud. As might be expected, such a lifestyle got Vollaro in trouble again, and he was convicted in 1996 of a federal extortion charge and given thirty-seven months in prison. It was while he was in federal custody at Fort Dix that Vollaro had another auspicious linkage when he struck up a friendship with Gambino capo Nicholas Corozzo, part of the Brooklyn wing of the crime family. Though nominally loyal to Senior Gotti when he was alive, the Corozzo group didn't have much love for the Bergin Hunt and Fish crowd after the Dapper Don was gone. In fact, it was the Corozzo crew that considered—but ultimately rejected—the idea of killing Charles Carneglia because he was suspected of stabbing to death the young Michael Cotillo, one of the faction's associates. If there was anyone who held the potential of becoming a leader in the Gambino family after the time of Gotti, it was Nicholas Corozzo.

Ties people make in prison can bind, particularly if they involve the Mob. In Fort Dix, Corozzo advised Vollaro to keep a low profile and not commit any crimes once he left prison. That sounded like fatherly advice, but investigators believed that Corozzo had a more sinister purpose, particularly since Vollaro had so many persistent old ties to the Gambino family that he seemed like a moneymaking machine. One of his partners in a trucking company, which he had started just before being jailed on the federal case, was a Gambino associate. On top of that, once Corsaro died, reputed Gambino soldier Louis Filippelli assumed control over Vollaro, court records stated.

After he was freed from prison in 2005, Corozzo summoned Vollaro to a meeting and, according to federal prosecutors, said that he, Corozzo, would be taking over control of the trucker. Since he was on parole and couldn't openly associate with convicted felons, Corozzo said that Vollaro was to deal with Leonard DiMaria, an old Gambino captain out of Brooklyn, according to investigators. At this point, all Vollaro had to do was run his businesses, which he had expanded into the cement industry, pay his Gambino overseers, and keep his pretty wife, Trisha, happy.

Back in New York, DiMaria had been in and out of trouble so many times that during one federal court hearing about one of his violations of probation, a judge remarked that the Gambino gangster essentially couldn't be supervised. He had been acquitted with Senior Gotti in the infamous 1986 federal trial, but he was prosecuted a number of times, spending over ten years in prison. Finally freed from prison in 2005, DiMaria was in turn able to introduce Vollaro to other reputed Gambino members, who had their own ties to the construction industry.

Corozzo was being touted as the next true boss of the Gambino crime family, the person who had outlasted the Gotti regime and in the end would prevail over the Bergin crew. But his decision to reach out and contact Vollaro turned out to be a case of very bad timing. Vollaro just couldn't keep his nose clean; and although there was no way he would have known, his telephones were being tapped by the OCTF and the federal labor agents.

The wiretap on Vollaro's phone got some unexpected results. The tap picked up that Vollaro not only was in touch with a number of mobsters but was also still involved in cocaine trafficking. Some guys just don't learn. Even though Vollaro talked in code in his telephone calls, agents were able to decipher what he was saying and learned when and where he was planning a drug delivery. In January 2005, Vollaro was cruising in his car near Amboy Road in Staten Island when investigators pulled him over. Vollaro had a little over a pound of cocaine in the car, and his stunned customers watched from nearby as he was hauled away in handcuffs. Faced with being a three-time loser because of two prior felony convictions, Vollaro quickly agreed to become an informant, a fact that escaped the notice of his customers when he was promptly freed on bail in the drug investigation.

Investigators who listened in on Vollaro's telephone calls noticed that he had a particular way of telling his drug customers that he was ready to make a delivery. "I am zipped up, ready to go," Vollaro was overheard telling his cocaine contacts. The constant use of the words "zipped up" inspired OCTF agent George Pagnotta to dub Vollaro with the special code name "Zipper." So, throughout the law enforcement hierarchy, Vollaro became known as Zipper, the valuable source who was getting the goods on the Gambino family.

Agents told Vollaro that he was to go about his normal trucking business, but he had to check in every day. With a recording device provided by the agents, Vollaro agreed to tape his conversations with mobsters. Whenever he had meetings with crime figures, Vollaro not only taped the talks but was shadowed by agents, who verified with whom he met. The telephone tap remained in place and gathered additional evidence. For a three-year period, Vollaro secretly taped nine hundred hours of his conversations with Gambino crime family members.

Vollaro already had a long-standing relationship with the Gambino family, making it money through protection payments he made over the years. Anyone listening to his banter with the Mafiosi on the wiretaps and body wires could hear the ease and familiarity that they had in talking to him. Sometimes gangsters like Leonard DiMaria talked in a fatherly way to him, as if to try and steer Vollaro from doing anything illegal. Other times, the Mob associates sounded angry that Vollaro was expanding his businesses into areas that competed with other gangsters. Over the three-year period, Vollaro was so convincing in gaining the confidence of the Gambino family members that one tape recording showed that he was going to be proposed for membership in the *borgata*.

That particular tape was made by Vollaro as he talked to one of his government overseers and he only recorded his end of the conversation. Vollaro never mentioned the words "made" or "initiation," but it seemed from the context that he was talking about being proposed for membership in the Gambino family.

"George told me a little while ago there might be a gift for somebody," Vollaro was heard saying on the recording, using an apparent code word for Mob initiation. Repeating what he had heard, Vollaro then got an indication from the government agent that investigators would want him to go through with any initiation. The tip that he would be initiated would come from a request for him to get dressed up, said Vollaro.

"We are having a party, come dressed" would be the code word for the initiation ceremony, said Vollaro, who saw his potential initiation to the Mob as a major development for the investigation.

"That's batting a thousand (percent) and hitting four home runs," he said. "They think I have big, big pull with everything on Staten Island."

Having Vollaro in the bag as an informant was an important development for the OCTF, which over the years had played roles in a number of major organized crime cases but never got much of the glory or fanfare. Most of the accolades went, instead, to the FBI or federal prosecutors. The capture of Vollaro raised the game of the OCTF and forced other agencies to take notice of the fact that they had an intelligence asset that could pay dividends in the investigation of the Mob. Thanks to Ryan's diplomacy, the OCTF didn't feel like it was going to be shut out of any big cases and kept his office apprised of what was going on with Vollaro. As Ryan would find out later, it sometimes paid to be nice.

While his bosses had turned down the heat on Ryan's construction task force, the unit really didn't disappear. Instead, it stayed in business and worked hand in hand with yet another task force that for years had been monitoring the Gambino family rackets on the New York waterfront. If it seemed like there were too many investigators poking around, Ryan and his colleagues knew from their experience that the Mob wove some very tangled webs where it was sometimes difficult to find out exactly where they would lead, unless you had enough resources.

Following the money in one investigation, Ryan uncovered checks that led to a suspected drug operation. What made this interesting to the Drug Enforcement Agency (DEA) was that the business seemed to be a very large hydroponic marijuana operation in Brooklyn. Hydroponic marijuana, unlike the conventional weed, is grown indoors on moist beds that are constantly beamed with artificial sunlight.

The Brooklyn marijuana-growing business was in a warehouse about a thousand feet away from Public School 109 (P.S. 109), an elementary school. Since 1997, informants said, the business had been growing one thousand plants, which in turn produced over two thousand pounds of pot. The DEA estimated the operation grossed $12 million. The growers had used a fenced-in toolshed as a grow room, which was sixty feet deep and had all the tools needed to get a good marijuana crop. The electricity needed to power the lamps was stolen from a nearby street pole and amounted to $800,000 in purloined power. An illegal gas hookup was also in use.

Who was behind such a large-scale marijuana business? Witnesses and informants said it was none other than Peter Zuccaro, the old East New York Gambino associate and onetime business partner of Charles Carneglia. The Mob's ban on drug dealing be damned,

Zuccaro was a perennial pot entrepreneur for years, including a period in the 1970s when he partnered with Charles and Carneglia's brother, John. Back in 1997, Zuccaro had been arrested and pleaded guilty on Long Island for dealing in hydroponic marijuana and got a 120-day sentence.

The investigation of the Brooklyn operation didn't lead into Charles Carneglia: Zuccaro claimed he kept his drug business a secret from the Gambino family because he didn't want anyone meddling with his business. But it did lead to the arrest of Zuccaro's brother-in-law Michael Lezamiz and Angelo Ruggiero Jr., the son of the late Gambino captain who had been a close friend of the late John Gotti and part of the Bergin crew. His son, it seemed, was a bad apple that had not fallen very far from the tree.

In court records, federal prosecutors said that the younger Angelo Ruggiero was a soldier in the Gambino family under the command of captain Michael "Mickey" Paradiso. Ruggiero started out providing protection for a door-to-door drug delivery service known as Smiles, which used motor bike couriers to make deliveries throughout New York City, court records stated. Sometime between 2002 and 2003, Zuccaro and Ruggiero agreed to a deal in which the Smiles courier operation distributed Zuccaro's marijuana, the documents stated.

Zuccaro wasn't arrested in the Brooklyn investigation—he was already under indictment in the Florida case involving Ronald Trucchio, John Alite, and others. But Zuccaro didn't need anyone to draw him a picture about what the drug case meant. Facing a federal racketeering case in Florida, as well as the likelihood of a drug conspiracy charge in New York, Zuccaro made the decision to become a cooperating witness. That was the only way he could save himself from spending the rest of his life behind bars.

So, in a convoluted series of events, investigators developed two crucial witnesses with substantial links to the Gambino crime family. Vollaro had been making hundreds of hours of recordings, some involving the key street bosses of the crime family's Brooklyn faction. Then there was Zuccaro, a man who was feared on the street in his own right, who knew a lot about some unsolved homicides and other family business that traced back to Gotti's old Bergin crew—the most tempting target being Charles Carneglia.

When it rains, it pours. With Vollaro and Zuccaro on the government's side, another witness came out of the woodwork. For years, the late John Gotti's confidant Lewis Kasman was an informant, agreeing to provide information but not serve as a witness in court. One of the first contacts with Kasman was developed in April 1997 when then-supervisory special agent Bruce Mouw learned from him that Joseph Corozzo Jr., the attorney, was going to fly out to see Gotti in federal prison, according to federal court documents. According to Mouw, Kasman alleged that Gotti used such visits to pass messages. In fact, Kasman was claiming all sorts of lawyers were passing messages to the outside world from Gotti.

Kasman was passing along information to the FBI as an informant for years before Gotti died. Then, in 2005, Kasman agreed that he would testify for the agency in its investigation of Junior Gotti and the rest of the crime family. Junior was at that point in a battle with Manhattan federal prosecutors who had him on trial for racketeering in a new indictment, which came down in 2004. One of the key reasons the FBI was talking to

Kasman in this period was to try and build evidence to discredit Gotti's defense attorneys. Kasman went as far as to try during a conversation at the urinals in a courthouse men's room to get lead Gotti defense attorney Jeffrey Lichtman to take a $10,000 cash payment for legal fees—presumably to see if Lichtman wouldn't report the money for tax purposes. But Lichtman later told the author that he told Kasman he would take the money and *report* it to the IRS—at which point Kasman didn't make the payment.

The fact that Kasman was willing to cooperate and build cases was seen as crucial because there had never been an informant who had the ability to penetrate the affairs of so many of the late John Gotti's old Ozone Park clique. Federal prosecutors in Brooklyn were ecstatic that Kasman was their prime source and they started to prepare possible cases for prosecution. Though Kasman's cooperation would remain a secret for many months, a hint that he had become a witness surfaced when his name was mentioned as an investor in a Long Island fish restaurant. The restaurant, Hudson & McCoy, was at the center of a Colombo crime family extortion case. That particular case alleged facts that suggested that Kasman himself was being extorted.

Meanwhile, over in the U.S. Department of Labor, Joseph Vollaro, known by his code name Zipper, began also providing evidence of possible labor union bribery and commercial bribery. Vollaro's tapes revealed that he was paying over $6,000 a month to get work at a Secaucus, New Jersey, construction firm, according to an affidavit used to get wiretaps. Among the suspects targeted in this phase of the investigation were a number of Gambino crime family associates.

Back in the Brooklyn U.S. Attorney's Office, the

prosecutor also had a number of Gambino crime family investigations under way that were suddenly helped enormously by the decisions of Kevin McMahon and John Alite to cooperate. They both had been insiders at the Bergin Hunt and Fish social club and for the first time provided investigators with some important information about those who were involved in the old inner circle of Gotti. Charles Carneglia was one such person, all the more tempting a target because of evidence that he was Gotti's hit man of choice.

There was yet another witness who had the potential to cause trouble for Charles: Anthony Ruggiano, son of the late Gambino soldier Anthony "Fat Andy" Ruggiano. The father's sobriquet of Fat Andy was an amalgam of a childhood nickname and his later obesity after he became a made member of the Mob in 1953. The younger Ruggiano had twice been proposed for membership in the Gambino family, but he didn't get inducted because he got arrested both times his name was under consideration. Ruggiano worked under his father as a bookmaker and dealer in stolen merchandise, and eventually committed murders, including that of his brother-in-law Frank "Geeky" Boccia in June 1988. After his father's death in 1999, Ruggiano came under the command of Nicholas Corozzo.

Born and bred to the Mob, Ruggiano knew the old Ozone Park and Howard Beach network of mobsters, associates, and hangers-on that were all part of Charles's world. Ruggiano never committed any crimes with Charles, but he knew his fearsome reputation. Ruggiano also knew a lot of Charles's friends, his haunts like the Lindenwood and Blue Fountain, and everything from gossip to rumors about what he had done to cause trouble in the area. After becoming implicated in the death of Boccia, Ruggiano decided to become a government witness, giving prosecutors a lot of institutional memory about the cast of characters that populated Charles's world.

The mind-numbing flood of investigations continued with another Gambino probe under way in the Tampa U.S. Attorney's Office, which couldn't take its sights off Junior Gotti. By late 2006, Gotti had garnered three mistrials in his second major racketeering case involving the 2004 Manhattan federal indictment. But after failing three times to convince jurors unanimously of Gotti's guilt, Manhattan federal prosecutors decided to drop the indictment, which had accused him of extortion, loan-sharking, and arranging the beating of radio talk show host and Guardian Angel founder Curtis Sliwa. Gotti had argued that he had left the Mob life in 1999, when he went to prison for his earlier federal conviction, and thus was outside the five-year statute of limitations on the racketeering charge. Enough jurors gave credence to this so-called withdrawal defense that prosecutors couldn't get a unanimous decision for conviction.

After the third mistrial, Junior Gotti walked out of court a free man. He had a celebratory dinner with his attorneys Charles Carnesi and Seth Ginsberg at the Altadonna Restaurant in the Douglaston section of Queens and started planning a new life, with musings about leaving New York and writing a children's book. However, federal prosecutors had other ideas. With Kevin McMahon and John Alite as cooperating witnesses, federal investigators began to brag quietly in the fall of 2007 that they had a stronger, bigger case against Junior Gotti in the works. It was actually Alite who was doing the most damage, alleging in his FBI interviews that Gotti had engineered the George Grosso and

Bruce Gotterup murders nearly two decades earlier in connection with drug dealing.

Clearly, state and federal investigators had a lot of balls in the air when it came to the Gambino crime family. Sometimes law enforcement agencies come to blows over who has priority in an investigation, particularly if the targets are similar. But this time egos took a backseat. In the Brooklyn U.S. Attorney's Office, Ryan, who was actually assigned to the Central Islip office on Long Island, met with the OCTF and agreed that with a big Gambino indictment in the wings that it made perfect sense for both offices to cooperate. The OCTF threw its cases and its witness Vollaro into the pot, along with his tapes that provided strong evidence of extortion and payoffs among Nicholas Corozzo's arm of the Gambino family. Peter Zuccaro, John Alite, and Kevin McMahon, all of whom had been more closely involved with Charles Carneglia and the Bergin crew, were providing evidence of murders, drug dealing, and other crimes. All the agencies decided to pool their efforts and try and come up with a large, sweeping case that would bring in scores of defendants and get a big bang in the news media. "There was no big fighting on anything," said one former prosecutor who was involved in the government strategy meetings. The idea was to get as much evidence as possible against the Gambino family, he said.

Prosecutors had tried these kinds of sprawling cases before with mixed results. In 2007, the Brooklyn U.S. Attorney's Office charged eighteen members and associates of the Bonanno crime family in a large extortion and bookmaking case. The case came about after a Howard Beach housewife named Yvonne Rossetti became indebted to a reputed Bonanno loan shark, in part because her own real estate investment scheme turned out to be a fraud and she needed a quick infusion of money to turn things around. The arrests were highly publicized, but the case didn't live up to its hype. Eventually all of the defendants agreed to take pleas for various counts, some with little or no prison time. Only one low-level defendant admitted to being involved in attempting to extort Rossetti.

But prosecutors believed the Gambino case would be different. Joseph Vollaro had provided his handlers with so many hours of recordings of mobsters that the FBI believed it had a treasure trove of material showing extortion across the construction, trucking, and cement industries. On top of that was evidence from another side of the investigation that a group of the Gambino family, notably *consigliere* Joseph Corozzo, Vincent Gotti (brother of the crime boss), and his nephew Richard G. Gotti, as well as Charles Carneglia, were involved in drug dealing. But the real cream rising out of the investigation—thanks to the other cooperating witnesses—was evidence that Charles was involved in five murders and that Nicholas Corozzo played a role in the 1996 slaying of Lucchese crime family associate Robert Arena.

The morning Charles was arrested at his mother's house turned out to be a bad day for scores of others in the crime family as FBI teams hauled in a wide range of Gambino crime family members and their associates. Among those arrested were the crime family's acting boss Jackie "the Nose" D'Amico, underboss Domenico Cefalu, *consigliere* Joseph Corozzo, captains Leonard Di-Maria and Frank Cali. Also grabbed were soldiers Vincent and Richard G. Gotti and Vincent Dragonetti. The news media had a field day with the story. THE END OF THE GAMBINOS, crowed the *Daily News* front-page headline, with an amusing and unflattering photograph of the fat rear end of one of the minor defendants stepping into the FBI van taking prisoners to court.

Another key defendant named in the indictment was Nicholas Corozzo, who was identified in the case as a major crime family captain. But while Charles and all of the other defendants were paraded before the news media outside Federal Plaza in Lower Manhattan, Nicholas Corozzo was conspicuous by his absence. Earlier in the morning, FBI agents had gone to the home of Corozzo's daughter, Bernadette, who happened to be married to Dragonetti. When the agents locked up her husband, it was natural for Bernadette to call her father and tell him what had happened. That was all the sixty-seven-year-old crime captain needed to hear as he then promptly disappeared.

Most of the charges in the case involved extortion counts tied into attempts by the Mob to squeeze Vollaro and his companies. But, ironically, the most severe charges involving the five murders blamed on Charles Carneglia had nothing to do with the Vollaro investigation but instead came from corroborating evidence of McMahon and Alite. Nicholas Corozzo also had two murders attributed to him, the 1996 double slaying of Robert Arena and Thomas Maranga, who just happened to be an innocent bystander. Prosecutors claimed that Corozzo ordered the slaying of Arena in retaliation for the earlier murder of his close associate Anthony "Tough Tony" Placido, a hit the Gambino faction blamed on Arena. Rather than stick around and face the music, Corozzo went on the lam, becoming a feature on the television program *America's Most Wanted*. There were a hell of a lot better places for Corozzo to be than in solitary confinement in a federal lockup.

Nicholas Corozzo wasn't the only person who dropped out of sight with the unveiling of the Gambino indictment. As soon as his name was unveiled as the main informant, Joseph Vollaro disappeared. With the terse remark "I'm leaving," Vollaro walked out on his wife, Trisha, who was pregnant with twins, leaving her to run what was left of his businesses, as well as a popular restaurant, Docks. About a week before he left, Vollaro sold his cement business for about $1.8 million. Under the control of the FBI, Joseph Vollaro went into hiding in the federal witness protection program, turning his back not only on his wife but also a large Staten Island home and a forty-foot speedboat named *Cat in the Act.*

10

The Letter

Jodi Ryan had been to Jennie Carneglia's house on Eighty-fifth Street in Howard Beach so many times that she could find her way blindfolded. In all of the years when Charles was incarcerated, he relied on friends like Ryan to take care of his elderly mother. He might be a son in absentia, but Charles had his priorities right about Momma.

Ryan, a mother of five who lived with her common-law husband, Allen Mershanski, in a condominium complex about a mile away from Jennie's home, had taken care of her in those years of Charles's absence any way she could. Jennie, like some other elderly folks, liked to go to the bank in person to get the interest posted on her accounts, and Ryan took her there. To save a penny, Jennie would like to browse in the local 99 Cent Store, and Ryan took her there as well. Doctor appointments, food shopping: those were all things Ryan helped Jennie perform. Ryan's husband, Allen, also tried to help out if he could.

But he suffered from a chronic degenerative condition of the spine, so his mobility was limited, and it fell to his wife to do the heavy lifting to take care of Charles's mother.

On a particular day in April 2008, Ryan found herself going yet again with Allen to Jennie's house. But this time the trip had a special urgency. The couple was on a quest to find the letter, a typed document that Charles thought would help him deflate one of the prosecution's key witnesses against him, Kevin McMahon.

Held without bail since February 7, and with no prospect that he was going to be free to do things for himself, Charles relied on Ryan, her spouse, and his lawyers to do things to help his legal situation. Ryan had already taken care of his leased car and a parking ticket: Charles didn't want his credit rating to be hurt by appearing to renege on the lease or to lose his driver's license because of nonpayment of the ticket. Ryan also made sure Charles had enough money placed in his jail commissary account to buy sundry items. Now the question of the letter had come up and Charles had to rely on Ryan to try and retrieve it.

According to Charles, the document had come from Kevin McMahon after the young man had been arrested in the Florida federal racketeering case against Ronald Trucchio, John Alite, and the others. As Ryan would later recall, the letter mentioned how federal prosecutors wanted McMahon to provide evidence against Charles and his imprisoned brother, John. McMahon had written that all he needed was $10,000 to cover his hotel costs during the Florida trial (he had been free on bail) because he didn't have the money, said Ryan.

To Charles, the missive from McMahon seemed like

nothing more than a crass attempt at a shakedown. The remarks that investigators were looking for Charles's head on a platter, combined with a request for money, equated to extortion, said Charles.

"Can you believe the balls of this guy? He is threatening me," said Charles after he initially got the letter, according to Ryan. She recalled glancing at the document before giving it back to Charles.

While his room might have looked like a sloppy bachelor pad to the agents who arrested him in February, Charles was actually a neat freak about his personal affairs. It seemed almost like an obsessive-compulsive disorder (OCD) to his friends. He kept meticulous files, which he maintained in his own peculiar system of organization. The letter had been placed in one of them, Charles recalled, and he remembered placing it in the attic—the very place where Detective Steve Kaplan caught him looking anxiously the morning he arrested him. Charles asked Ryan to go to the house and retrieve the letter. If there was ever a trial, the letter could very well prove to be dynamite evidence that would be useful to undermine Kevin McMahon's credibility.

Rushing to Jennie's house, Ryan and her husband also remembered the specific instructions Charles had given her about how the letter should be handled. Rubber gloves had to be used when touching the document, and it had to be placed in a ziplock plastic bag to protect it. Since the letter wasn't signed, Charles believed the only way to prove it came from McMahon was to find his fingerprints on it. The fewer people who actually touched the paper, the better, he said.

Once inside Jennie's home, Ryan went straight to the attic. Her husband, Allen, because of his spinal condition, really couldn't climb around, so Ryan climbed up the ladder. She had seen the letter months earlier and believed that it could be found, since Charles was so compulsive about his possessions. But her attic search found nothing. She went to Charles's room, where his files were also kept, but found nothing there, either. Glancing around the bedroom, a frustrated Ryan had a sense that Charles wouldn't be happy. It seemed like an omen of what was to come.

11

Let's Make a Deal.

The indictment against Charles Carneglia and his sixty-one codefendants was assigned at first to Judge Nicholas Garaufis. Sworn in as one of Brooklyn's federal jurists in 2000, the affable Garaufis had lots of experience in Mob cases: he had handled the trial of the former Bonanno crime boss Joseph Massino in 2004, a case that had numerous defendants. The Massino case had garnered lots of media attention and had become noteworthy when Massino himself directly approached Garaufis after his conviction and asked to become a cooperating witness.

Following Massino's trial, Mob cases were constantly on the horizon for Garaufis, who seemed to relish the publicity such trials generated. Even when a trial was completed, Garaufis would find himself years later having to sentence some of the cooperating witnesses. One Bonanno crime family defendant in particular, crime captain Vincent "Vinny Gorgeous" Basciano, would stay on Garaufis's docket for years. Basciano would face a death penalty prosecution, which was expected to go to trial in early 2011. (Displeased with the expense of the Basciano case and noting that the mobster already had a life sentence, Garaufis wrote Attorney General Eric Holder in the spring of 2010 to ask him to reconsider taking the death penalty off the table.)

But as soon as it became known that the big Gambino crime family case had been assigned to him, Garaufis was thrust into legal controversy. Usually, federal cases are assigned to judges randomly so that there can be no suspicion that a matter had been improperly steered to a particular jurist. However, with the Gambino indictment, federal prosecutors performed a move that defense attorneys later privately charged smacked of judge shopping. The government stated that Garaufis should get the assignment of the Gambino case because the indictment involved witnesses and events similar to some of what had cropped up in the Massino case. Federal court rules do allow for a "related " case to be assigned to a judge who already has a similar matter. The day before Charles and his codefendants were arrested, Assistant U.S. Attorneys Mitra Hormozi and Joey Lipton filed sealed court papers with Garaufis and Brian Cogan, another judge who had a related case, asking that they consider taking the Gambino indictment. Cogan declined. Garaufis accepted.

In a ruling, Garaufis noted that the case against Charles Carneglia and Leonard DiMaria involved allegations of securities fraud similar to another case already on the docket, which named Jonathan Winston and others as defendants. Two other Gambino defendants, Vincent Dragonetti and Steven Iaria, allegedly extorted a cooperating witness who had pleaded guilty in his courtroom earlier, said Garaufis. Finally, Garaufis said, the government reported that it was continuing its probe into the infamous May 1981 murder of three Bonanno crime family captains—Alphonse Indelicato, Philip Giaccone, and Dominick Trinchera—and the roles members of the Gambino crime family played in the killings. Garaufis noted that the three slayings came up in two other cases on his docket involving Massino and his trusted aide Anthony Urso. As a result of those various connections, the Gambino indictment was "related" to cases he already had, said Garaufis.

But to the legion of defense attorneys involved in the massive Gambino indictment, the prosecution's request to Garaufis, which was initially done before the indictment was unsealed, smacked of judge shopping. Led by attorney Joseph Corozzo, who was representing his father, Charles Carneglia, and thirty-five of the Gambino defendants filed papers objecting to Garaufis handling the case. While it was true that some witnesses had ties to a few Garaufis cases, the link was relatively minor, the defense attorneys argued. More to the point, the lawyers argued, it seemed like the Brooklyn U.S. Attorney's Office was trying to bypass the court clerk to get around the random assignment system and steer the big Gambino indictment to Garaufis. To avoid any appearance of impropriety, Garaufis should send the case back to the random system for reassignment to a new judge, the attorneys insisted.

In response, prosecutor Joey Lipton said that contrary to what Joseph Corozzo said the government followed court rules to the letter and filed its request at first with the clerk's office, which then assigned the case to Garaufis. While the government's argument was literally true, it seemed to ignore the fact that only a handful of the sixty-two defendants had any connection to cases on the Garaufis docket. It seemed like the minnow was swallowing the whale.

Though Garaufis insisted the Gambino case was related to his other cases, he nonetheless found a way to relinquish the matter barely a month after the indictment and put a rest to the claim of judge shopping, which would have persisted so long as he was involved. Using his discretion, Garaufis said in a ruling that he already had 356 pending civil cases and 142 criminal cases involving 289 defendants on his docket. Four of the criminal matters involved multidefendant organized cases, including two death penalty trials. In short, Garaufis now said he was really too busy to take on a sixty-two-defendant indictment. So, in the interest of helping to save judicial resources, Garaufis, on March 13, 2008, tossed the case back to the court clerk's office so it could be reassigned randomly.

Up until that time, the Gambino indictment was one of the largest organized crime prosecutions, in terms of the number of defendants, ever to hit the federal court system. With sixty-two defendants named, the sheer size of the case skewed the court statistics, putting the Brooklyn courthouse and Garaufis at the top of the list of assigned Mob prosecutions throughout the country. No other federal district came close.

But size isn't everything. The strength of a case is sometimes indicated by the plea bargains prosecutors are willing to offer. Good deals for the defendants (i.e., low prison terms) signal that the cases aren't considered very important or strong in terms of evidence. As a practical matter, it also made sense for Brooklyn prosecutors to close out as many cases as they could because their office in early 2008 was somewhat understaffed and laboring under a number of multidefendant Mob cases. Court statistics showed that for years the Brooklyn U.S. Attorney's Office was bringing fewer and fewer indictments; in part, it seemed because of fewer prosecutors and a large existing workload. By making plea deals early, the prosecution's docket was cleaned out, saving time and resources.

The first plea offers were made in letters to defense attorneys during the first court conference in the case. The offers ranged from four-month prison terms for some of the minor associates to as much as twenty years for the high-ranked mobsters, like Joseph Corozzo. "I am not unhappy," said one attorney. "I never got a plea agreement on my first appearance, that is the first," said another defense lawyer.

But lawyer Joseph Corozzo, who was representing his *consigiliere* father also named Joseph, said he disregarded the plea offer. As an attorney, Corozzo said, he was angered that his father was accused of drug dealing in the indictment.

"If they want to drop the drug charges, then I will talk to them," said Corozzo.

However, other attorneys saw the plea offers a sign that the government had bit off more than it could chew and wanted to get things down to a manageable level by weeding out defendants. The whole process of bargaining over the plea offers would take months.

Two defendants—Charles Carneglia and fugitive Nicholas Corozzo—didn't get any plea offers. Nicholas wasn't around in any case to think about an offer, and Charles had so many homicides in his indictment that there was no chance that any deal could be made. He would either have to go to trial or else plea to the indictment.

After Garaufis gave up the case, the random selection system assigned the Gambino indictment to Judge Jack B. Weinstein. Defense attorneys were happy, while prosecutors were somewhat chagrined. Appointed to the bench in 1967 by President Lyndon B. Johnson, Weinstein was one of the legal giants of the federal bar. A former U.S. Navy submarine officer in World War II and a graduate of Columbia University Law School, Weinstein had authored *Weinstein's Evidence*, one of the most influential treatises on the federal laws of evidence. As he grew older, Weinstein seemed to thrive on work and was one of the busiest judges in the Brooklyn courthouse, spewing out decisions that ran into the hundreds of pages in the most complex cases. He seemed to thrive on mass tort litigation, like the Agent Orange case, and coauthored another treatise, *Mass Torts: Cases and Materials,* as a result.

Weinstein also took time to smell the roses. On his lunch hour during the spring, he would walk around Brooklyn Heights, looking at the blooming trees and flowers. When there was a going-away party for one of his law clerks, Weinstein would take it upon himself to walk across Cadman Plaza Park to pick up a cake.

Weinstein was also known as an independent judge, who would ream out prosecutors and defense attorneys whenever he thought it necessary for being unprepared or positing silly legal arguments. He took on a project in 2004 to go through a backlog of over five hundred appeals of state court defendants and sometimes reversed the convictions where he found the evidence lacking or some error committed by the trial court. He also had, as everyone in the Gambino case would find out, a habit of pushing his cases along at a punishing, breakneck pace.

One of the first hot potatoes Weinstein fielded was a request by prosecutors to get attorney Joseph Corozzo disqualified from representing his father, the reputed *consigliere* of the Gambino family. As a lawyer, Joseph Corozzo had seen this move made by prosecutors many times before in other Mob cases. Sometimes it worked; other times he was allowed to represent the crime figures. But in this Gambino crime family case, things got particularly nasty. Perhaps it was a bit of payback for his filing the original motion questioning the giving of the case to Garaufis. In papers filed with Weinstein, prosecutors said that Corozzo was *not merely a lawyer who represents his father* but rather was *an associate of and "house counsel" to the Gambino family, involved in (the) Gambino family's illegal activities.*

In their papers filed with the court, prosecutors went on to describe various illegal acts that Joseph Corozzo allegedly participated in, including the collection of extortion payments, providing crime family monies to the imprisoned Gambino boss (Peter Gotti), and *used his status as an attorney to further the Gambino family's illegal interests.* Joseph Corozzo had heard some of these allegations before, particularly since they were raised in the 2007 trial of reputed Gambino soldier Dominick Pizzonia. Attorney Corozzo denied any wrongdoing, and Pizzonia remained steadfast in his desire to have Corozzo represent him. Weinstein happened to be the judge in the Pizzonia case and allowed the defendant his wish of having Corozzo stay on as his lawyer. But the various allegations must have made Weinstein, one of the country's preeminent jurists, wonder what kind of activity Corozzo had been doing as an attorney. Faced again with similar allegations in the big Gambino case, Weinstein was looking at some familiar territory.

But this time around, there proved to be a big difference. On March 25, 2008, prosecutors filed a letter with Judge Weinstein informing him what had been reported in the press just days earlier: the key informant for some of the allegations against Joseph Corozzo was none other than Lewis Kasman, the garment executive who had been the late John Gotti's "adopted" son. Initially identified as "CW#1" in court papers, Kasman was expected to testify about the senior Corozzo's association with the Gambino family, including his relationship with the late Senior Gotti and the current boss Peter Gotti, prosecutors stated. In particular, court papers said, Kasman would testify about the senior Corozzo's role in a conspiracy to shake down a Long Island fish restaurant known as Hudson & McCoy, one in which Kasman at one time had a hidden interest.

Three other witnesses, including former Gambino captain Michael "Mikey Scars" DiLeonardo and old associate Anthony Ruggiano, would testify about other allegations that tarred Corozzo, said prosecutors. With the expectation that Kasman would be making his first appearance as a cooperating witness, the news media jammed Weinstein's courtroom on March 27, 2008. Corozzo had attorney Henry Mazurek represent him. But the first witness didn't turn out to be Kasman but rather Salvatore Romano, an old Gambino associate. Under oath, Romano testified that he asked the lawyer Joseph Corozzo once to represent a man as a way of essentially ensuring that individual wouldn't become a cooperating witness.

Judge Weinstein had heard enough. To everyone's

surprise, he ruled that Joseph Corozzo couldn't represent his father because he had once allowed himself to serve as an attorney while being secretly employed by someone else with an interest in a case. The government didn't get to put on any of the other witnesses, like Kasman, whose evidence about Gambino crime family ties could have been much more embarrassing to Corozzo. In one sense, Weinstein did Corozzo a favor by truncating the hearing. He did call Corozzo a "brilliant" attorney, but he said he had to drop his father as a client.

There is no better way to get lawyers to come to an agreement than to confront them with a trial date. The prospect of actually having to get prepared for a court fight, in front of a jury, with all of one's evidence, is enough to get adversaries to see the light and settle. The same is true in criminal cases, like the monster Gambino indictment. Judge Weinstein seemed to relish trials and thought lawyers and prosecutors should be ready as soon as he was to take their fight to a jury. So, not even a month into the case, Weinstein started telling prosecution and defense attorneys that he was dividing up the sixty-two-defendant case for trial. By the way, said Weinstein, he expected the first of the trials to get under way by June 9.

Already working at breakneck speed, prosecutor Joey Lipton and the rest of his team begged Weinstein for some forbearance and slack. The Joseph Vollaro tapes alone encompassed nine hundred hours, and FBI agents were already working at breakneck speed to transcribe them and get copies to the defense attorneys. Weinstein listened but wouldn't relent. There were enough defendants in custody without bail and they deserved to have their cases heard quickly. Weinstein then divided the defendants into nine groups, with Group A including acting street boss Jack D'Amico, underboss Domenico Cefalu, and three others. That case would start in early June, and the next group of four defendants would be tried after a short break, ordered Weinstein. If the courthouse and government could handle it, Weinstein said, he would hold simultaneous trials with the help of other judges.

Charles Carneglia, Weinstein decided, would have a trial all by himself.

Weinstein also said that Nicholas Corozzo, if he should return from being a fugitive, would get his trial just before Charles. Maybe Nicholas Corozzo, who was on the lam for about four months, liked the idea of getting a fast trial before Weinstein. Perhaps he thought he might get a decent plea bargain from the government. In any case, a little before 9:30 A.M. on May 30, 2008, the sixty-eight-year-old Corozzo met his attorney Diarmuid White on Broadway in Lower Manhattan. They had talked for the first time by telephone a couple of weeks earlier. Together, both men walked two blocks north to the federal building where the FBI offices were, sharing some small talk about the nice weather. White, who didn't want to know where Nicholas Corozzo had been all of the preceding months, then escorted him to the government offices, where the reputed Gambino captain surrendered to four waiting FBI agents.

The torrid trial schedule Weinstein proposed had the effect of getting a lot of plea bargains. By July 8, Weinstein published a list of defendants who had pleaded guilty, and out of an original sixty-two defendants, an astonishing fifty-three had entered guilty pleas. This all had occurred within five months of the arrests in a case that could have trickled on for years. The government's generous plea offers had helped, but the way Judge Weinstein was cracking the whip also moved things along. D'Amico and Cefalu were among the first to take a plea, followed about a week later by reputed captain Frank Cali, a Staten Island man whom the Italian news media had touted as one of the big Mob connections between the United States and Italy, and stalwart captain Leonard DiMaria. Joseph Corozzo took his plea on June 6, admitting to shaking down Vollaro's concrete company. The drug charge was dropped against Corozzo, whose son Joseph, the lawyer, told reporters that his father "never allowed anyone who did drugs, or knew about drugs, to be around him."

The last man standing was Charles Carneglia. After watching all of his old friends and associates take pleas, Charles knew he was the last stand-up guy left from the old Bergin crew who was willing to fight the government. He might as well fight. The only guilty plea he could expect was to a charge that had life in prison, so it made sense for him to roll the dice and go to trial. If that was the case, then he might as well fight on every front he could muster.

Charles didn't have the money to hire his own lawyer. Forget about the fact that his brother's family seemed to have plenty of cash. Imprisoned John Carneglia and his wife controlled the property upon which the old junkyard once operated, according to property and business records. The land was soon to be used as a school bus depot, but that didn't mean Charles got any of the benefits. Friends said he was just scraping by before the arrest. Once he was jailed, Charles really had no family to rely on to pay for legal help.

People like Charles who can't hire a lawyer are assigned attorneys under the federal legal aid system. The day the Gambino case came down, it was Curtis Farber, a mild-mannered solo practitioner in Lower Manhattan who was assigned Charles's case. A former district attorney in the Bronx, Farber was also a member of the federal criminal justice panel, a group of private attorneys who were on call to provide legal help to indigent defendants. The work is paid at a set rate by the federal government, and some lawyers do quite well representing clients under the system.

But Farber, while experienced in a wide range of federal criminal matters, had never had an organized crime case the likes of which he faced with the Gambino indictment. Charles was accused not only of the racketeering charge but also at least nine distinct racketeering acts, including the five murders, a marijuana distribution conspiracy, robbery, extortion, and securities fraud. That list would grow slightly with the filing of a new indictment. Each of those crimes took a lot of work to investigate. It was as if Charles was facing nine or more trials. With the resources of the FBI and the Brooklyn U.S. Attorney's Office arrayed against him, Farber asked Judge Weinstein to appoint another active federal court defense attorney, named Kelley Sharkey, as co-counsel. One of the regulars around the Brooklyn courthouse, Sharkey not only was an experienced federal practitioner but had previously served with the state Capital Defender Office, a public unit set up to handle what had been expected to be a crush of death penalty cases in New York when capital punishment was reinstated in 1995. But after the New York Court of Appeals struck down capital punishment in 2004, Sharkey began to do more work in the federal courts, working out of an office in downtown Brooklyn. Known as a tenacious, patient litigator, Sharkey wasn't bothered by hard work. She would have plenty of it defending Charles.

One of the first big issues Kelley Sharkey and Curtis Farber faced in defending Charles Carneglia was to see if they could get the indictment dismissed. The indictment against him covered a period of time that stretched from 1975, when Albert Gelb was murdered, to February 2008, when federal agents raided Jennie Carneglia's house. That amounted to three decades, a long period of time, which Sharkey and Farber argued made the case more difficult to defend. With allegations stretching back so far, Charles faced an inability to defend himself.

It was Charles himself who weighed in and sent Weinstein an affidavit spelling out how the delay would hurt his ability to mount a defense. In particular, he had problems defending himself against the Gelb murder charge because a number of potential witnesses were dead. Among them was Charles Ball, an eyewitness to the shooting of Gelb who described to police an assailant whose physical description didn't resemble that of Charles at the time of the shooting, the affidavit stated. Also deceased was defense attorney Herbert Lyons, the New York attorney who represented Charles in the 1975 weapons case. Lyons had done the original investigation of the charges, but the results were now lost with the passage of time, said Charles.

The prejudice that has inured to me is real. As a result of the loss of key witnesses and investigation records, I will be severely restricted in my ability to defend myself, wrote Charles. *As such, I cannot receive a fair trial and request that instant indictment be dismissed.*

Farber filed his own papers with Judge Weinstein and

argued that by putting Charles in such a large group of
defendants as those in the Gambino case the government gained a major tactical advantage. The publicity
and spillover effect from having so many defendants together was something the government hoped would
lead to a successful prosecution, said Farber.

The defense attorney also raised the issue John
"Junior" Gotti had brought up with some success in his
previous three federal trials: withdrawal from the
Mob. Charles had effectively withdrawn from the big
Gambino crime family conspiracy in November 2001,
when he went to prison on the Cherry Video extor-
tion case, said Farber. Charles not only told his friends
and associates he wanted nothing more to do with the
Mob, he also led a quiet life, punctuated by dinner at
Carosello's.

Of course, the government didn't buy Charles's arguments. In a memorandum filed with Weinstein, Assistant U.S. Attorneys Roger Burlingame, Evan Norris,
and Marisa Megur Seifan (original prosecutor Joey
Lipton had left government service) said that Charles
was required under the law to show that he was actually
prejudiced by the long delay in his indictment. Specu-
lation wasn't enough, they said. In terms of the withdrawal defense, the law stated that was something that
had to be proven at trial and not before then, said the
prosecutors. There would also be evidence that Charles
consorted with Gambino crime family members after
he got out of prison in 2006, and didn't keep to himself
as he had argued, they said.

The law says you have a right to trial by a jury of your
peers. But you don't necessarily get to know who those

peers happen to be—particularly if the government says you are a dangerous mobster

In early December 2008, Burlingame and the rest of the prosecution team filed a request that Weinstein, who had already refused to dismiss the indictment, impanel an anonymous jury for Charles's trial, which was scheduled to begin in the upcoming February. The move wasn't unexpected. Anonymous jury requests have become the norm in Mafia cases in the United States, particularly in New York City. Weinstein had already granted an anonymous jury request in the 2006 trial of Dominick Pizzonia and was prepared to do so in the case of Nicholas Corozzo—although it was widely expected that he would accept a plea bargain and avoid a trial.

With anonymous juries, the names, addresses, and other identifying characteristics of the veniremen (as jurors are called) are kept confidential by the clerk of the court. Not even the judge knows the identities. Jurors are only identified by numbers when they are questioned and chosen for service. During the trial, the jurors are kept together by the U.S. Marshals and are taken to lunch or have lunch brought to them in a group. At the beginning and end of each day, it is the marshals who transport the jurors back and forth from a central location.

The main reason the prosecution asked for an anonymous jury for Charles was that the government thought he was just too dangerous. Added to that was the Gambino crime family's well-publicized history of jury tampering.

The murder of court officer Albert Gelb was one of the key arguments used by prosecutors for an anonymous jury. Charles Carneglia had murdered Gelb, a witness in a relatively minor firearms case against him, said prosecutors. That was *an act of obstruction far more depraved than jury tampering that the defendant committed to escape a far lighter potential sentence,* prosecutors wrote, referring to the short jail terms meted out on gun cases in the 1970s.

There was also the brazen history of the Gambino family when it came to jury tampering. First and foremost was the 1986 trial of the late John Gotti, John Carneglia, and six others, a case that actually involved an anonymous jury. But nevertheless, one of the impaneled jurors, George Pate, was identified and conspired with some crime family members to get an acquittal—a situation that led to Pate's conviction. Some of Charles's closest friends (including McMahon) were involved in tracing license plates to find a juror who could be corrupted, prosecutors told Weinstein.

Two of the 1980s trials of John Carneglia were also tainted by allegations of jury tampering. Then there was the 1992 trial of Senior Gotti. Informants and former members of the family said that the cousin of one of the jurors was paid $100,000 to get a vote of not guilty. But after the case led to a conviction, the cousin was killed. Other Gambino family members allegedly took part in obstructing justice, sometimes through witness tampering.

Prosecutors also pointed out that Charles seemed to look with disgust on the prospect of an anonymous jury and the trial process.

"They ain't got an ounce of evidence against me," said Charles in a taped jail telephone call to a friend. "They got these fuckin' paid fuckin'—they're not even rats—they're paid fuckin' witnesses."

Later in the same telephone call, Charles went on

about anonymous jurors and how he viewed them as sycophants for the government.

"They're gonna pick the jury," said Charles. "They're gonna have it anonymous. They're gonna have them sequestered. They're all gonna be government people on these juries. What do you think they're gonna be?"

But as cynical as those remarks might have been, Charles's attorneys said, there wasn't any possibility that he was going to interfere with the judicial process, since he was in jail. Just because he might be involved in the crime family didn't mean anybody in the Gambino family was going to try and tamper with justice on his behalf. Charles was also an alleged soldier in the Gambino family, not a high-ranked member who traditionally would have warranted anonymous juries, his lawyers argued.

Weinstein didn't have trouble coming to a decision. He wasn't going to take any chances. Some of the people Charles was accused of associating with in the Gambino family had tried to undermine judicial proceedings in the very Brooklyn court where the trial would be held, he said. Judge Weinstein granted the government's motion for the anonymous jury.

12

Soup Bones

In Mafia trials, the bad things the government tries to prove aren't limited to what is in the indictments. Prosecutors often try to bring in a wide range of bad acts that a mobster has done to prove that he was involved with the Mob and that a crime family functions as an organization. These are uncharged crimes that aren't in the indictment, and where there might not be enough proof ever to bring them as a formal charge.

While it seems unfair that allegations that couldn't make it into a formal charge can be brought in through the back door, the courts have a way of screening what kind of evidence is admissible by requiring prosecutors to file special requests *in limine*, Latin for "at the threshold" or "preliminary." Those requests, often filed shortly before a trial begins, have to spell out what evidence of uncharged crimes the prosecution wants to introduce and why. Most often, prosecutors argue that the evidence shows that a conspiracy—the Mob—exists.

On January 6, 2009, prosecutors Burlingame, Norris, and Seifan filed their *in limine* motion in Charles's case. They had some of the usual stuff in there, talking about the allegations of murder against him, as well as the extortion, kidnapping, robbery, drug, and securities fraud charges, which were already listed in the indictment. But on page nine prosecutors for the first time brought out into the open an amazing claim against Charles— one that would jolt Howard Beach, bring back some terrible memories, and overshadow everything else in the indictment.

In a paragraph titled "John Favara—Accessory to Murder," the prosecution said that a number of witnesses were prepared to testify about the gruesome fate that befell the man who disappeared in 1980 after accidentally killing the son of Mob boss John Gotti. Favara was ordered slain by Gotti, and it was Charles Carneglia, the witnesses would say, who disposed of the body by dissolving it in a barrel of acid. Charles had a constant fascination with body disposal and measured his worth to the Gambino family, a witness believed, by being its grisly mortician and making the corporeal remains of so many human beings disappear.

When Curtis Farber and Kelley Sharkey saw the government's motion, they went ballistic. By throwing into the case twenty additional crimes, some going back to the 1970s, prosecutors were going to make a trial that was already long get even more unmanageable.

This will effectively require over 20 mini-trials, which will seriously delay the proceeding and risk juror confusion: they will have to keep track of the proof relating to literally dozens of incidents, charged and uncharged, wrote Farber and Sharkey.

The extra danger was that the jury would look at the volume of uncharged crimes—which included a number of murders and attempted murders—and see them as evidence of Charles's propensity for violence and figure he must be guilty of the charged acts of violence in the indictment, argued the defense. The allegations of the immersion of John Favara's body in acid was one of those sensational things that had captivated the press and might drive the jury to convict, as was the claim that Charles was part of the group of men who chased down, beat, and shot at Carmine Agnello, the man who went on to marry Victoria Gotti, the Mob boss's daughter.

Farber and Sharkey, already rushing to get ready for trial, said that the revelations of the uncharged crimes were made so close to the opening statements that they couldn't be properly investigated with so little time remaining. "It is impossible to prepare to defend against such a disparate and far-ranging number of uncharged offenses—over twenty in all—as the trial goes forward," they argued to Weinstein.

Another problem facing the defense was that Charles wasn't the best client to help in his defense. The issue wasn't whether Charles wanted to help—he clearly did. But he wasn't a man with reading skills. Charles got through elementary school at St. Fortunata, but after attending Franklin K. Lane High School in Queens, he dropped out. To his credit, Charles went on to get a high-school equivalency diploma. However, he still wasn't the fastest reader and had trouble getting through the mounds of legal papers the lawyers needed him to examine. This also hampered the defense team as it moved closer to trial.

Judge Weinstein was a man with so many advanced degrees and scholarly credentials that he probably had a hard time comprehending how anyone could go through life without the love of the written word. But he wasn't an intellectual elitist and it showed in the way he treated the defendants, including Charles Carneglia, who appeared before him. Weinstein hardly ever wore a robe and he held pretrial conferences at a table in the well of the courtroom. The day after the government had filed its papers detailing the gruesome fate that John Favara suffered, the judge met with the attorneys and Charles in court. Listening to the problems that Charles had reading because of his interrupted education, Weinstein smiled and told him, "You should have stayed in school like your mother told you." As he smiled back, all Charles could do was nod his head in agreement.

Prosecutors kept the pressure on the defense. There are earners and killers in the Mob, and Charles's real problem, the prosecutors said in response to Farber and Sharkey's plea, was that he couldn't make money for the crime family. His real value—the reason Gotti kept him around and inducted him into the *borgata*—was his willingness to kill and commit other acts of mayhem, the government said. To take away all of that evidence would limit the prosecution's ability to prove Charles's role in the crime family.

The thing that troubled Judge Weinstein the most about the new allegations raised by prosecutors was the issue of the acid baths and additional charges that Charles had used acid or some kind of caustic solution to torture people. He saw the potential, as the defense had argued, that a jury would be prejudiced by such evidence. So on January 21, 2008, Weinstein decreed that the word "acid" or any reference to the use of acid for body disposal wouldn't be allowed at trial.

Where acid was allegedly used in the disposition of a body, the witness may indicate that the defendant helped dispose of that body. Where acid was allegedly used or threatened to be used for torture, the witness may indicate that the defendant used or threatened to use painful methods against alleged victims, ruled Weinstein.

The acid ruling was just about the only thing the defense won in its objection to the *in limine* motion. But the prosecutors still wouldn't stand for it. In response, they sent Weinstein an astonishing letter that gave graphic details, much more than anything ever revealed, about how Favara's body was dispatched. The source of the evidence was only identified in this new prosecution letter as "CW1," but clearly was referring to Kevin McMahon.

As described in the letter, McMahon said Charles would mention the disposal of Favara's body as an example of how he could competently do jobs for the Gambino family. The job of getting rid of Favara's corpse had been assigned Charles by the late Angelo Ruggiero, the letter stated.

At first the defendant said that he did not choose an appropriate type of acid, which meant that the disposal of Favara's body took much longer than he expected, the prosecution letter stated. *Ruggiero thus became angry and claimed that the defendant's heavy drug and alcohol use was interfering with his ability to capably perform his duties as a Gambino associate.*

To make amends and prove he could do the job, Charles changed the acid and succeeded in getting rid of the corpse, prosecutors said, relying on McMahon's recollection. When it came time for Charles to prove to Ruggiero that the deed was done, he told McMahon, he met the crime captain at the Lindenwood Diner and tossed some of Favara's finger bones into Ruggiero's chicken soup, said prosecutors.

The letter to Weinstein also related how Charles had allegedly told McMahon that the jewelry hanging from hooks in the basement of an old house known as the "body shop" were trophies taken from the bodies of murder victims before they were dissolved in acid. The problem with the jewelry, said McMahon, was that they were seen as bad luck. Andrew Curro, a friend of Charles's, had taken an item, wore it, and wound up getting convicted for murder and given a twenty-five-year prison term, said McMahon.

Prosecutors also described how John Alite, known as "CW2," would testify how Charles would say in drunken rants that he had disposed of bodies and favored acid as the best way of doing so. Peter Zuccaro, known as "CW3," was also prepared to testify, prosecutors said, that Charles told him how he had folded a dead heroin addict's body in a blue tarp, dissolved it in acid, and poured what was left down a sewer in East New York. Yet another surprise the government said it was prepared to prove at the trial was that Charles had kidnapped David D'Arpino and two others, dropping acid on their feet to get them to reveal who had fired a shot at John Carneglia's house in the mid-1990s.

All of the revelations about acid riveted the news media and promised to take the trial to another level of sensation. But Weinstein still wouldn't budge. Acid or any mention of it had to be kept out of the trial, which he scheduled to begin on January 29, 2009.

Try as he would to keep the mention of acid out of the trial, Judge Weinstein had no ability to control the spread in the public of the hideous details of the body disposal and torture allegations. Add in the fact that one of the bodies was that of the man who killed young Frankie Gotti, and the case was assured of being remembered for little else.

13

"His Executioner"

"We are going to give him the best trial he ever had."

When Judge Jack B. Weinstein told that to Charles Carneglia, there were no jurors present in the courtroom. In fact, the anonymous jury hadn't even been picked yet. But by February 28, 2009, everything was in place for what Weinstein promised would be a trial the likes of which Charles had never seen before.

With Weinstein's work habits, his trials didn't drag. He often asked attorneys to be in court early to argue any pretrial motions. If he didn't have enough information, the lawyers would have to see him in sidebars. Weinstein took a couple of ten-minute breaks and an hour for lunch, but generally he just plowed ahead. If nothing else, it would certainly turn out to be one of the fastest paced trials Charles had seen.

It was shortly after nine thirty, on what was a cold and wet morning that Weinstein's court deputy swore in the twelve jurors and six alternates who had gone through a careful selection process. Turning to Assistant U.S. Attorney Marisa Megur Seifan, Weinstein then raised the curtain.

"Proceed, please," Weinstein said.

Marisa Megur Seifan, a graduate of Georgetown University Law Center, and an attorney for six years, had been picked to give the prosecution's opening statement. These introductory remarks aren't evidence and generally try and set the table for the jury, sketching out what the government intended to prove and how it would do it. Great opening statements can be riveting and keep a jury's attention, or they can be boring orations. Seifan was well aware of that, as well as the fact that she would be talking to a full house.

Packed into Weinstein's courtroom on the fourteenth floor of the Brooklyn federal court were scores of New York State court officers. They were there to bear silent witness, as they had done during Charles's arraignment a year earlier, for their dead brother Albert Gelb. On Weinstein's instruction, the officers wore business suits—not their uniforms—in order not to appear to create any impression on the jurors. Their union president, Dennis Quirk, was expected to be a witness, so he had to watch the proceedings in the courthouse cafeteria, where the trial was being carried on closed-circuit television.

"The important thing is to convict this prick," the acerbic Quirk told a reporter. "The death penalty would be too good for him."

This was Seifan's first major organized crime case. To set the tone for the jury in the most compelling way with her opening statement, she drenched things in blood—Gelb's blood.

"Albert Gelb was a court officer. He worked in Brooklyn night court, just down the street from here. On March 11, 1976, he left work and drove home. He never made it," she said.

"The evidence will show that man, the defendant Charles Carneglia, gunned Gelb down in his car. Gelb was shot seven times in his face, in his chest, in his arm," she said.

Such slaughter, Seifan told the jurors, was carried out because Gelb was scheduled to testify against Charles. The killing was the only way that Charles could silence the man who had the temerity to stand up to him, she argued.

The murder of Gelb was just one of many crimes Charles had committed for the Gambino crime family, said Seifan. There were four other killings—Michael Cotillo, Salvatore Puma, Jose Delgado Rivera, and also that of Louis DiBono, who was killed on the orders of John Gotti. DiBono died because he had disrespected Gotti by refusing to meet with the crime boss.

"Disrespecting John Gotti got DiBono a death sentence," said Seifan, "the defendant was his executioner."

With each of the homicides, Seifan spelled out just enough of the gory details—the knife to the heart for Puma and Cotillo, the shotgun to the back for Rivera— to let the jurors know how the victims died. She also said that Charles stood accused of extortion, fraud, armed robbery, and drug dealing. Those crimes would also be proved, said Seifan.

The government's opening remarks by Seifan were direct and to the point. She kept things mercifully short, about twenty minutes, ending by saying the evidence would prove Charles Carneglia's membership in the Gambino family and his guilt beyond a reasonable doubt.

* * *

Charles sat back in his chair during Seifan's opening, his beard and hair neatly trimmed, wearing a suit. His attorney Kelley Sharkey would now have a chance to give the defense version and she started by attacking the turncoat witnesses, all criminals, who were going to march to the witness stand.

"There is a line outside of that door," said Sharkey, gesturing to the hallway, "of men who don't want to die in jail.

"They will do anything to get out from under and shift the blame to an easy target, Charles Carneglia," said Sharkey. The witnesses the government was going to bring into court were criminals, murderers, liars. There was nothing, Sharkey stressed, to assure that what those miscreants said in court was truthful.

Sharkey already knew that one of the first turncoats to take the stand was Michael "Mikey Scars" DiLeonardo and she had some special words about him, calling him "the dean of the college of cooperating witnesses."

Responsible himself for three murders, numerous beatings, and decades of making fast money through extortion and loan-sharking, DiLeonardo spent little time in jail because he thrived by testifying, said Sharkey. She didn't bring up the names of John Alite, Kevin McMahon, or Peter Zuccaro, but Sharkey told the jury that they were "cold, calculating liars" who wanted to please the government with their testimony against Charles and earn a "get-out-of-jail-free card."

Sharkey also foreshadowed the key elements of the defense about the statute of limitations. She also tried to appeal to the jurors' maturity by reminding them how people change, and suggested that Charles had changed over the years by backing away from an earlier life in which admittedly he had not been an angel. In the end, said Sharkey, when the smoke clears and sensationalism is put aside, the jury would vote not guilty.

Like Seifan, Sharkey's opening remarks were also short, and Judge Weinstein asked Roger Burlingame to call the first group of witnesses. For that, the government called John Carillo. Most of the jurors had seen movies and read books about the Mafia, so they knew generally that it existed, and had a structure to it. But in Mob cases, prosecutors always took the pains to bring in an expert like Carillo to tell the jury in more detail how the crime families were organized, the rules of the Mob, and the reality of life on the street—which could sometimes be very different from what the rules commanded. All rules were made to be broken, and although the penalties for disobedience of the commandments of the Mafia can be severe, it was important for Burlingame and the prosecution team to show how Charles Carneglia broke some of the Mob rules about drug dealing and wearing a beard to prove that he had a special relationship with his Gambino boss, the late John Gotti.

Carillo explained to the jury the general structure of a Mafia family, from the boss whose judgment could never be questioned, all the way down to the lowly associates who sometimes act as freelancers and do illegal business with more than one crime family. Much of what Carillo testified about was stuff that other experts had explained to other juries, so much of it wasn't new or revealing, particularly things about the Mob induction ceremony, which used a gun or knife and the picture saint that was burned in the hands of a new initiate.

"I don't believe they use the gun or the knife anymore for fear of law enforcement detection," explained Carillo. "They've taken other steps to make the ceremony more secure."

Carillo's explanation about Mob life—the rules, how law enforcement conducted surveillance at funerals, weddings, and wakes—was illuminating for a novice Mob buff. But for Judge Weinstein, who had sat through so many Mafia trials, the testimony was getting repetitive and a bit boring. It was nearly an hour before Carillo was asked by Burlingame to identify Charles Carneglia in court.

"The gentleman with the white shirt and beard," said Carillo when asked to point out Charles.

Using enlarged surveillance photographs displayed to the jury, Carillo also identified Charles in the presence of other Gambino family members at funerals, weddings, and hanging around the Bergin Hunt and Fish social club. Carillo's recitation of the mobsters in the photographs was mind-numbing. But in many of them Charles appeared, sometimes in a suit or wearing sunglasses. He appeared rubbing shoulders with the likes of Junior Gotti, his uncle Peter Gotti, the Corozzo brothers, and Leonard DiMaria. Any juror looking at the photo display had to come away with the clear impression that Charles was a member of *La Cosa Nostra*.

The photo review dragged on for hours as prosecutors displayed scores of Gambino mug shots and had Carillo identify each one, including one of a bearded Charles taken the day he was arrested in February 2008. Defense attorney Curtis Farber didn't go over the photographs very much on cross-examination, but instead asked Carillo about a subject that was important to the defense—facial hair. Farber and Sharkey were going to try and show that the Mob frowned on beards and moustaches, and that anyone who had such facial hair was an outcast and not part of the Mafia.

However, Carillo noted that the Mafiosi in the early twentieth century were known as "moustache Petes" because of facial hair, and he personally knew of several mobsters who had beards or moustaches.

"Organized crime frowns upon facial hair, but it is not a rule," said Carillo. "If you have enough clout, you have a certain kind of personality, you're not going to get thrown out of an organized crime family for having facial hair. Any boss, at any particular time, could tell the guy, 'You better shave or else.'"

The defense also wanted to show that drug use and alcohol abuse—things that plagued Charles through much of his adult life—weren't tolerated in Mob life. But again Carillo said the reality of the Mafia was that it had a major substance abuse problem.

"Many drink," said Carillo. "There are many alcoholics and drug addicts."

14

"John Loved Tough Guys."

Michael DiLeonardo wasn't one of those mobsters who had a drug or alcohol problem, even though John Gotti once heard that he used cocaine. Unlike many of the other younger members of the Gambino crime family, he graduated from high school in Brooklyn, spent some time in community college, and had legitimate jobs on the docks. But he was also a product of a long line of Bensonhurst Mafia men. It was natural that he gravitated into the "life."

"Bensonhurst, Brooklyn, you couldn't get more organized crime than Bensonhurst," DiLeonardo would quip.

DiLeonardo traced his Mob roots to his grandfather, who had been a member of the "Black Hand," the early version of the Mafia in the United States. The Black Hand was more of a group of extortionists than anything else, terrorizing the local Italian-American community with threats, bombings, and shootings. Some historians believe that tactics of the Black Hand were copied by other con artists as a way of squeezing money from Italian immigrants, under the guise that there would be retribution if payments weren't made.

DiLeonardo's grandfather eventually became a member of the Gambino crime family and became so respected that when he died, Carlo Gambino decreed that all the other members of the *borgata* must attend the funeral. With that kind of lineage, DiLeonardo was aware of the Mob life as soon as he could walk.

"I lived it on a daily basis," DiLeonardo recalled. "I was enamored with it."

As a child, DiLeonardo would run errands for his grandfather, and the easy money he got in return made him like and respect the men who were part of the crime family.

"My grandfather had fig trees in the yard and other fruits and stuff," DiLeonardo remembered. "As I got older and could cross the street, I was told 'go give Paulie Zac (Zaccaria) and Jimmy Brown (Failla) some figs.' It was a thrill to me because I would go to the club, I would get five dollars, a dollar here, two dollars here, and hang out and watch the videos and whatever they were doing."

Years later, when asked by a prosecutor what Di-Leonardo had wanted to be as a young man in Brooklyn, he answered, "A captain."

"Captain in the army?" he was asked.

"No, a captain in the Mafia," replied DiLeonardo.

Sometimes you should be careful what you wish for. DiLeonardo was inducted into the Gambino crime family on Christmas Eve, 1988, in the same ceremony with John "Junior" Gotti, his close friend. For the next fourteen years, DiLeonardo had a strong run, making money through loan-sharking, construction extortion, and reporting on a daily basis to his captain, Jack D'Amico, one of Senior Gotti's trusted men.

But in June 2002, DiLeonardo was arrested by federal agents for, among other crimes, the murder of Gambino associate Fred Weiss. When he was denied bail, the arrest signaled the end of DiLeonardo's romantic notion of the Mob and his delusions of loyalty to it. For barely five months after his arrest, DiLeonardo learned that he was being "broken," stripped of his power and rackets by the Gambino family's ruling administration, Senior Gotti's brother Peter Gotti and ranking captains Joseph Corozzo and Arnold "Squiggy" Squitieri.

The charges against DiLeonardo were that he had been stealing money from the crime family to line his own pockets, things he said later were completely false. He had invested almost all of his adult life in the Mob, and the act of being stripped down devastated him. He had loved the gangster life; it was in his blood. He loved the loyalty, the camaraderie he knew from his grandfather's generation of Mafiosi. But now he was faced with what he saw as the naked avarice of his so-called superiors. Faced with a murder case and abandoned by the Gambino family, DiLeonardo made the decision to become a cooperating witness for the federal government. The date was October 2002.

Five years after he decided to throw in his lot with the government, on January 29, 2009, it was a fifty-three-year-old Michael DiLeonardo who took the witness stand in Judge Weinstein's court in the trial of Charles Carneglia. A lot had gone on in DiLeonardo's life in that time period, and not all of it was good. He had tried to kill himself one night shortly after becoming a cooperator. Thinking about a way to go out with honor, and not defiling his grandfather's Mafia legacy, Di-Leonardo attempted to overdose on pills, hoping as he gulped down the medicine at the kitchen sink that his friend Junior Gotti would appreciate what he was trying to do. On top of that, his wife discovered by chance that he had a child with another woman. A divorce followed, and DiLeonardo became estranged from his first son, also named Michael.

The suicide bid failed, and DiLeonardo ironically found himself the star witness against Junior Gotti in three trials between 2005 and 2006, which ended in mistrials. By then, DiLeonardo had come to terms with his new life. He was the first cooperating witness to be called in the case against Charles Carneglia. By the time he walked into Judge Weinstein's courtroom on January 29, 2009, DiLeonardo had already testified in nearly a dozen trials. In his debriefings with the FBI, DiLeonardo had given agents information about two hundred dead and living Mafia members.

DiLeonardo didn't know Charles closely, but he did know enough that when Roger Burlingame asked him what the defendant's reputation was on the street, and his value to the Mob, he had a direct response.

"He was a valuable member of the Gambino family," said DiLeonardo in a response that drew an immediate, but futile, objection from defense attorney Curtis Farber.

"He was part of the inner circle. He was [a] guy who did work, did murders," continued the witness.

The inner circle of the Gambino family, explained DiLeonardo, was composed of people that the boss John Gotti could rely on and pick to do murders.

Burlingame asked if he knew of any murders done by the defendant, and DiLeonardo said he did.

"Don't use the word 'murder.' That is to be decided by the jury," cautioned Judge Weinstein.

Questioned about the killings Charles had done, DiLeonardo said yes, he knew of one, the killing of Louis DiBono. At this point, the testimony diverted to DiLeonardo's rapid rise through the crime family. Burlingame then came back with more questions for DiLeonardo about how he came to learn about the way DiBono died in the fall of 1990.

DiLeonardo's source of information was Sammy Gravano, one of Gotti's trusted aides, and the late Bobby Boriello—he wasn't certain who told him first. But sometime in 1991, Boriello confided in him, as he had often done. Normally, made men aren't supposed to talk about hits, but the reality was many did. Boriello was no different.

"My relationship was such that he just shared it with me, that him and Charles did the work," said DiLeonardo, referring to the killing.

But when Burlingame asked DiLeonardo what Borriello had told about the DiBono homicide, and the witness answered, "that Charles and him did it," Weinstein sustained a defense objection and ordered the remark struck from the record. Try as he might, Burlingame couldn't get Weinstein to allow him to ask DiLeonardo to repeat what he had said about Charles's connection to the DiBono killing. It seemed at first that the problem was that Borriello was dead, having been assassinated in April 1991, and couldn't be called to testify. Any statement about what he told DiLeonardo was hearsay and couldn't be admitted.

Testimony about the DiBono murder was crucial to

both the government and Charles. So when Burlingame started asking DiLeonardo about what Gravano had told him about the killing, Judge Weinstein told the prosecutor that he wanted a lot of specifics. Even when DiLeonardo said Gravano talked to him in his office on Stillwell Avenue, that wasn't enough for Weinstein. He prodded Burlingame to ask the witness if both he and Charles were under the same underboss, Gravano. But even then, Weinstein said the conversation, held nineteen years earlier, was too thin and hearsay. He didn't want to let it in as evidence.

This was a shaky point in the trial for the government. A witness, a former member of the Gambino family, was prepared to testify about one of the charged murders, but there was a big legal problem over hearsay. It was clear at this point that Weinstein, the guru of evidence law, wouldn't allow in any reference Gravano had made about Charles doing the DiBono hit. He believed such talk was idle banter among mobsters. (Eventually Judge Weinstein did let DiLeonardo testify about Borriello admitting he took part in the DiBono hit. Charles's name wasn't to be mentioned.)

Blocked by Weinstein, Burlingame then asked DiLeonardo about what other mobsters had said about Charles and his brother, John. He was more successful this time. It seemed that when Gotti took over the family in 1986 that the name Carneglia was heard more and more in Mob circles, said DiLeonardo. "Tough guys" was what he had heard about the brothers. Charles, in particular, he said, was a "loyal worker" who did "murders."

"John loved tough guys. He based your worth on how tough you were. John didn't like meek people, but he took money from them," said DiLeonardo.

The late Paul Castellano respected tough men also.

But Castellano was a leader who valued businessmen and liked to travel in the company of millionaires, not the blue-collar crowd, observed DiLeonardo.

One little known fact that came out as DiLeonardo testified was that after panic set in when Gravano became a cooperator in 1991, the Gambino family considered killing three made members who had visited him while he was in jail. The feeling was that the trio must have known that Gravano was going over to the government's side and didn't report it, so they should be killed to set an example. Some of the big captains in the crime family—including Junior Gotti, James Failla, Daniel Marino, and Nicholas Corozzo—wanted those Gravano visitors to be killed, DiLeonardo testified. Cooler heads prevailed, and it seemed that no one died.

Gravano had been a major loan shark, with $2 million on the street with borrowers. When he did become a witness, DiLeonardo said, Junior Gotti ordered him to collect his payments. Some people balked at paying on a "rat's" money, but many did, he said. As compensation for doing the collection, DiLeonardo testified, he received $500 a week, and Junior Gotti also gave his crew members, including Charles, $500 a week. Guys like Charles weren't big earners, so Junior Gotti spread the money around to keep them loyal and available, in case they were needed to kill, said DiLeonardo. Essentially, it was easy money for doing nothing.

Yet, there was a time between 1992 and 1993, said DiLeonardo, when Junior Gotti had to rely on Charles to be available and kill if necessary. The potentially deadly dispute involved construction industry money and Junior Gotti planned to have Charles and fellow mobster Tommy Sneakers Cacciapoli carry out the hits on captain Daniel Marino and John Gammarano, DiLeonardo told the jury. Gotti had asked that he find a place for the meeting, DiLeonardo added.

"He [Junior Gotti] reiterated, it went bad, we were going to kill these two guys," DiLeonardo testified. "We brought some body bags."

Gammarano and Marino arrived in a limo, along with powerful Gambino family associate Joseph Watts. Driving up in a hired car was a smart move to DiLeonardo because that created another witness if something went wrong. During the meeting, Watts took the offensive and told Junior Gotti that his father had given him carte blanche to handle construction industry funds, which were being used to fund a war chest to pay for the lawyers of all the people indicted after Gravano turned witness, said DiLeonardo. Because Watts was so respected, Junior Gotti was satisfied that he wasn't being cheated out of money, he said.

As a professional witness, DiLeonardo had done modestly well financially, but he was clearly knocked down many financial pegs from what he had been making on the street as the Gambino crime family's key man in the construction rackets. The federal government paid him a $2,500 stipend, as well as medical expenses, as well as $8,000 for furniture—if he and his family relocated—plus $10,000 for a car. But the stress and strain of living as a protected witness had become too much for his new wife, Madeline. So at some point, DiLeonardo said, he dropped out of the witness protection program, although he still got the monthly stipend.

DiLeonardo was the first mobster to take the stand against Charles and had helped the government make some points. Based on DiLeonardo's testimony, Charles was clearly a valued member of the Gambino family, especially under the Gotti family. He also had a reputation for being a killer. But when it came to the DiBono homicide, DiLeonardo was blocked from testifying about what he had heard about Charles in connection with the slaying. It was a major frustration for the prosecution team. The government lawyers hoped to do much better with their next star.

15

Wanting Hunk

When fifty-three-year-old Peter "Bud" Zuccaro came into the courtroom, he had known Charles Carneglia for over forty years. He was the one person called to testify who knew the defendant longer than anyone who was to take the stand.

"He was the best man at my wedding. He has been my friend my whole life," Zuccaro said, when asked by prosecutor Evan Norris how close he was to Charles.

From the moment he opened his mouth, it was evident that Zuccaro was pure gangster. He had a Brooklyn accent as rough as sandpaper, and when he could, he gave terse one-word answers that were as cold as ice, like something he would say just before he pulled the trigger.

Like Michael DiLeonardo, Zuccaro was born and bred to a life of organized crime, and he, too, loved it from his earliest days. He loved the power, the money, everything about the lifestyle. Having left school in tenth grade, Zuccaro earned a rap sheet that spanned years, and was arrested so many times he couldn't remember each and every instance. First under the thumb of the Bonanno crime family, Zuccaro was switched over by Mob dictate in 1986 to the Gambino family and put under the wing of Charles's brother, John.

Zuccaro said he never committed any murders with Charles, but he said his old friend had one special job in the Gambino family: hit man.

"He killed good," said Zuccaro.

"Did the defendant tell you about people he had a role in killing?" Norris asked.

"Yes," said Zuccaro.

"How many people?"

"Three."

Although Kelley Sharkey objected, Judge Weinstein allowed Zuccaro to continue to name the victims he was told about by Charles.

"Albert Gelb, Salvatore Puma, and Louis DiBono," said Zuccaro.

Zuccaro was the first witness who not only knew Charles but was in a position to testify about what he had told him directly about some of the murders charged in the indictment. Unlike DiLeonardo, who could only talk about what others had said to him about the DiBono murder, Zuccaro was recounting what Charles had said. There was no hearsay problem with that.

DiBono's murder was the first one Zuccaro explored under questioning. It had been Charles, Zuccaro testified, who told him he had killed DiBono. The main reason why DiBono died was because John Gotti wanted him killed, said Zuccaro.

As it turned out, Gotti was the main reason Zuccaro soured on life with the Mob. The flamboyant Dapper Don, who relished the limelight, was contrary to everything Zuccaro had expected from gangsters.

"He ruined everything," a disappointed Zuccaro told the jury. "Just the flamboyant nature, he ran around. Always in the newspapers. Nothing was conducted correctly. Everything was John's way, you know. Just everything that I was led to believe—that this is a secret society, and it's the underworld, was exposed."

Zuccaro's contacts with Charles stretched all the way back from when the Carneglia brothers ran a gas station in East New York at the corner of Crescent and Sutter avenues. Charles Carneglia and Zuccaro not only committed crimes together but also did a lot of drugs. When both of them weren't grabbing a bite at the Lindenwood Diner, they were hitting steak houses, like Smith & Wollensky or Peter Luger.

But crime was the focus of Zuccaro and Charles's relationship. Zuccaro testified that from the 1970s he was continually dropping off stolen cars at the Carneglia junkyard on Fountain Avenue, a motor yard on Pine Street, and even at the home of Charles's mother on Hemlock Street. Depending on the type of car that was involved, Charles would either change the vehicle identification number or chop up the auto for parts, said Zuccaro.

But chopping up cars wasn't the only disposal method Charles used, noted Zuccaro. Under some careful questioning by Norris (who had to avoid any mention of acid), Zuccaro testified that Charles had told him he had "disposed" of more than one body at the old "Barn" on the property at Pine Street. Zuccaro admitted he never saw any of the corpses but said that Charles pointed out some jewelry hanging from the building rafters that belonged to his victims. This was the first reference in the trial to body disposal, and the jurors' interest had to be piqued at this point. It was something that wasn't gone into in any depth by Zuccaro, but it would be revisited later by other witnesses.

John Gotti might have been dead seven years, but anything that dealt with him, his wife, or his children became part of an endless soap opera. The Gotti spectacle was revisited when Zuccaro related the now-infamous story of how Carmine Agnello, the future son-in-law of Gotti, was run down, beaten, and shot.

The trouble for Agnello was wrapped up in an impulsive act he took one day by breaking some windows at the Lindenwood Diner, the eatery that John and Charles Carneglia frequented and whose owner was under the protection of the brothers, Zuccaro told the jury. On top of that, Agnello supposedly beat up Victoria Gotti, the crime boss's pretty blond daughter, said Zuccaro. Victoria Gotti would later deny that Agnello ever hit her, and pointed out that she wasn't even dating Agnello at the time of the diner incident.

Since Agnello, who was allied with the Gambino crew of Joseph Corozzo, wanted to disrespect John Carneglia by trashing the diner, it was Senior Gotti who ordered his Bergin crew to "slaughter" Agnello, said Zuccaro.

"Go find Carmine, slaughter him, don't kill him," Gotti ordered, Zuccaro explained.

With Gotti's orders, Zuccaro joined a group that included the Carneglia brothers, which went out and stalked Agnello through Ozone Park. They were armed with guns, blackjacks, knives, and ax handles. After driving around, the group finally came across Agnello as he was driving his tow truck on Liberty Avenue. Zuccaro steered his car into a head-on collision with Agnello, who then jumped out of his truck and fled on foot. He didn't get very far.

"He was shot in the buttocks. He went down on the floor. We all run up on him and beat him down with ax handles," said Zuccaro.

Zuccaro seemed ready to take a shot at Agnello, but he was restrained by John Carneglia, who pointed his own gun at him and said, "Don't do that."

On the stand, Zuccaro spelled out more of his extensive criminal past. He admitted taking part in two Mob murders: John Gebert and Setimo Favia. Gebert was ordered killed by the Albanian gangster John Alite, while Favia had to to die because he had cursed out a Bonanno crime family captain named Frank Bonomo, who just so happened to be his mentor, said Zuccaro. Gebert was killed because he had a habit of chasing mobsters with a machine gun and shooting up bars as he tried to control drug trafficking, explained Zuccaro. Curiously, Zuccaro, who said he took charge of the Gebert hit, said it was Alite's idea to have the murder committed. No mention was made by Zuccaro about Junior Gotti being involved, something that would later contradict Alite's testimony.

Zuccaro admitted committing a lot of mayhem, agreeing to take part in other Mob hits, such as the time Vincent Gotti, the brother of the crime boss, wanted a local baker killed because he was under the apparently false impression that the intended victim was sleeping with his wife. Zuccaro said he wanted to take part in the murder but balked at doing it near St. Helen's Church, the local Howard Beach parish.

"Everybody's family went to that church in the neighborhood," said Zuccaro.

The baker Angelo was ultimately shot in 2000 but survived, and Vincent Gotti was put "on the shelf," or deactivated, as a mobster after that, according to Zuccaro.

There were other Zuccaro stabbings, beatings, and attempted murders. He also admitted slugging and shoving a few women, including his ex-wife, Gina LoFreddo, who went after him after she discovered he had been cheating on her. But the prosecution didn't bring in Zuccaro to talk about his criminal life, although that was unavoidable in a trial like this. Zuccaro was a crucial stepping-stone to building the case against Charles on four of the five murders charged in the indictment.

Norris brought Zuccaro back in his questioning to the night court officer Albert Gelb, who had the fight with Charles at the Esquire in 1975. Zuccaro said that when a dressed-up Charles entered the diner and leaned over the table to talk, he noticed his friend had two handguns.

"I said, 'Hide the guns. Those guns are showing,'" said Zuccaro.

Charles adjusted his coat and then walked down the stairs to the bathroom area, from where, Zuccaro said, he heard a loud argument as Gelb and Charles came to blows just outside the men's room. Zuccaro pulled Gelb off Charles and gave the court officer a few kicks and punches. Although Charles was told to leave before the cops arrived, Zuccaro said, Charles didn't, and as a result got arrested.

After the diner incident, Zuccaro said, Charles told him he was trying to get someone to intervene and get Gelb to back off and not testify in the gun case. The next time Zuccaro heard about Gelb was when he read the newspaper accounts about his killing. It was then he again spoke with Charles.

"He told me the guy couldn't be reached and that he wouldn't back up, and that he had to go, and nobody fucks with us," said Zuccaro.

"It was either him or Charles, so it turned out to be Albert Gelb," added Zuccaro.

The "us" in the conversation, Zuccaro explained, referred to the Bergin crew run by John Gotti.

But as suspicious as those remarks by Charles sounded about Gelb's demise, Zuccaro said his friend never told him who killed the court officer.

Zuccaro remembered more incriminating statements by Charles, and his testimony was damaging to the defense. One day while he and Charles sat alone in a car near some co-op apartments in the Lindenwood section, Zuccaro said his Gambino associate told him how he killed Puma.

"He told me he stabbed him in the chest with a knife, right there," Zuccaro testified, pointing to his right, the same direction Charles did in their conversation. "I looked over there. . . . He told me he wiggled the knife in him, small knife."

"Did he say why he stabbed him?" asked Norris.

"'Cause he kept the commissary money that he was supposed to be sending to Andrew Curro," answered Zuccaro.

Curro was in jail and was supposed to be getting money placed in his commissary account for the purchase of sundry items and snacks. Charles tried to use Puma as a conduit for the money because he feared his own fingerprints could be lifted from the cash at a time when there was a lot of FBI activity, said Zuccaro.

By this point in his testimony, Zuccaro had tied
Charles to two acts of homicide through the defendant's own statements to him. The Gelb connection was
weak, because it was ambiguous talk about reprisal
against the court officer. The Puma statements were
more incriminating because they amounted to admis-
sions by Charles about his direct participation in the
slaying.

Moving ahead, Norris delved into the DiBono killing
in October 1990 in the indoor parking garage at the
World Trade Center. This was a case in which Zuccaro
had evidence that cut very close to Charles, beginning
with a conversation he had with him at his mother's
house before the hit occurred. Charles needed Zuccaro's help.

"He needed to whack out Louie DiBono, and he
needed me to be on call," recalled Zuccaro.

Zuccaro agreed to be part of the hit team, noting that
Charles asked for his help because another mobster,
Bobby Boriello, wasn't being "responsible," and wasn't
showing up when needed.

"Did the defendant tell you why Louie DiBono had
to get whacked?" asked Norris.

"He told me he didn't come in when John sent for
him, and John wanted it taken care of right away. It was
taking too long," said Zuccaro, referring to the Gambino boss.

As it turned out, Zuccaro waited for a call but never
got one. He later learned that DiBono had been killed,
and he spoke with Charles a month later in the backyard of his mother Jennie's house in Howard Beach.
This was a crucial bit of testimony, and Norris had to

get very specific responses about exactly what was said about DiBono's death.

"What exactly did the defendant tell you?" the prosecutor asked.

"That they shot the guy in the head and he was laying down, like three feet off the ground," Zuccaro replied. The height description referred to the fact that DiBono, who was known as Jelly Belly, was so corpulent that his body lay high off the ground.

Under prompting by Norris, Zuccaro described how Charles said that they used a small-caliber handgun— either a .25 caliber or a .22 caliber—to finish off DiBono and left his body on the front seat. When Charles finished telling the story of the shooting, Zuccaro said he told his friend "congratulations." Everybody knew at that point that Charles would be inducted into the Mob because he had carried out the hit, said Zuccaro.

While Zuccaro was testifying, a nasty snowfall was developing around the New York City area. Concerned about the ability of the jurors to get home, Weinstein called a recess in the trial until the next day. But the day had ended with Zuccaro implicating Charles in at least two murders—DiBono and Puma—and casting suspicion about him on the Gelb killing. It had not been a good day for the defense.

The next day, March 4, the snow had abated enough for the trial to continue, and Peter Zuccaro again was on the stand, testifying about his long history of armored-car robberies and how, after he had finished a stint in prison for those crimes, he was solicited to do another by Kevin McMahon. Zuccaro generally liked McMahon, although he found him a bit compulsive and impulsive.

McMahon had a tendency to run off at the mouth and blab too much, something that Zuccaro said caused trouble between him and Charles. But intrigued with the idea of ripping off a cash-filled armored car at John F. Kennedy Airport, Zuccaro met with McMahon and his brother-in-law, Michael Finnerty.

An experienced armored-car robber, Zuccaro opted to go on a surveillance of the target facility, an American Airlines hangar, with McMahon, Finnerty, and Charles. The group followed the truck after it made its early-morning cash drop to LaGuardia Airport, taking note of police presence and anything else that was important for a future heist. But McMahon's impulsive rushing made Zuccaro angry, and the tension caused Finnerty to drop out of the plan.

Zuccaro said the remaining group carried out more surveillance and that he favored doing the robbery at LaGuardia. But then things fell apart. During another surveillance run, Charles drove around drunk, and Zuccaro then said he didn't want to have anything more to do with the plan. But sometime later, Zuccaro said, he saw on a news report that an armored-car driver had been killed during a stickup at JFK, outside the American Airlines hangar. He was not happy to hear about somebody dying.

"I was upset and sick about it," said Zuccaro. "I didn't like the outcome of the situation. I don't do things like that."

Zuccaro didn't have to go very far to find out what had happened. He met a nervous McMahon in Howard Beach, who said that the heist was pulled off by himself, Charles, and Bobby Boriello. It was Boriello, McMahon indicated, who shot the guard, said Zuccaro.

The robbery netted the crew $60,000 in cash, and the guard shouldn't have been killed, according to Zuccaro.

"The guy was a working stiff," explained Zuccaro. "If you got the drop on the guy right away, he wouldn't stop you from robbing him. He would do what he had to do. The FBI would handle it after that."

Nicholas Corozzo and Lenny DiMaria wanted hunk.

As Peter Zuccaro remembered things, both men were angry over another stabbing Charles had been involved in, which led to the death of Michael Cotillo on the steps of the Blue Fountain diner. For hunk, as they say on the street, they wanted revenge against Charles. This wasn't revenge for the sake of revenge, but rather because Cotillo happened to be the nephew of DiMaria, said Zuccaro.

What made the situation very touchy was that Charles was aligned with the Bergin crew of John Gotti, while DiMaria was with Corozzo. Both groups were Gambino crime family, but they represented different cliques that didn't have much love for each other. Word got out quickly that revenge was in the wind, so it was Charles's brother, John, who called for a sit-down to hash things out, and hopefully spare his sibling the *Cosa Nostra* death penalty.

Zuccaro wasn't anywhere near the meeting, but he got his information from Andrew Curro, a close friend of Charles's. From Curro, Zuccaro learned that the sit-down arrayed some powerful mobsters on both sides of the table: John and Gene Gotti, along with Angelo Ruggiero, defended Charles; Nicholas Corozzo and Lenny DiMaria took the opposition. The mediator presiding over the meeting was Aniello Dellacroce, the underboss of the crime family.

Being an associate, Zuccaro didn't attend the meeting, but the decision by Dellacroce became quickly known: DiMaria and Corozzo couldn't retaliate; they had to leave Charles alone. Law enforcement sources said Charles was seen as too valuable an associate by Gotti, who had a natural ally in Dellacroce.

While Zuccaro didn't see the stabbing, which caused the tension in the crime family, he testified that an eyewitness, Phil Brown, told him that during a fight between two groups of young men, Charles stabbed someone. Charles had actually been driving down Cross Bay Boulevard when he noticed that the altercation involved friends of his, a group known on the street as "Charlie's Angels," said Brown.

"Charles pulled over and he went to get involved," Zuccaro recalled Brown telling him. "A kid went to swing at him (Charles). . . . As they pushed him away, Charles stabbed the kid."

At best, Zuccaro's evidence was circumstantial—he didn't see firsthand what had happened during the stabbing at the Blue Fountain. But by relating to the jury what his other Gambino family associates told him, it was one piece of the puzzle about who did what to cause the death of Michael Cotillo. Later, prosecutors would fit it together with other evidence in the hopes of proving that Charles was the culprit. All in all, Zuccaro had implicated Charles in varying degrees to all of the five murders charged against him. He would be followed by others to the witness stand.

* * *

Peter Zuccaro testified about more than murders. He had been one of the Gambino family's premier producers of hydroponic marijuana and trafficked in as much of the stuff as he could get his hands on. After he got out of jail in 1988, Zuccaro went straight to John Carneglia, with whom he had marijuana dealings as far back as the 1970s. According to Zuccaro, John Carneglia gave him a crucial introduction to a businessman in Manhattan who had connections with a major marijuana trafficker in Texas. John also fronted him $10,000 for the first shipment, Zuccaro recalled.

"He just put the connection together and lent me the ten thousand," said Zuccaro. "I was with John. He was overseeing it."

The marijuana operation found lots of willing buyers and made handsome profits, said Zuccaro. He let the money build up, and after paying part of the profits to John Carneglia, he went back down to Texas to drive up more loads. The revenue remained the same at about $300 a pound, while the loads increased to as much as 250 pounds. A load could bring in a total profit of at least $75,000.

But not long after Zuccaro got back into the marijuana business, John Carneglia got convicted of peddling heroin and found himself sentenced in July 1989 to fifty years in prison. It then fell to Charles, said Zuccaro, to step into his brother's shoes and run the pot trade. Charles had been in and out of New York in this period, as he went on the lam in an earlier federal racketeering indictment. But after federal prosecutors dropped the charges, Charles felt comfortable staying around, and his brother told Zuccaro how things would continue with the business.

"I was to report to Charles and keep him abreast and give his end (profit) to Charles," said Zuccaro.

Things continued on the same path with the drug business, and profits kept piling up, said Zuccaro. But then, about two months after Charles took over for his brother, the largest load ever attempted in the operation—about five hundred to six hundred pounds—was seized in Texas. Charles wasn't happy and even thought about killing some of the Texas people, although he was talked out of it, said Zuccaro.

Both Charles and his brother, John, who was then in prison wanted to get the marijuana racket back on track, said Zuccaro. But things became very rocky between them, particularly after Zuccaro couldn't scrape up $30,000, an amount he said represented John Carneglia's share of profits. Zuccaro then started hearing from other Gambino associates that Charles was so angry over the money that he threatened to put Zuccaro in a Dumpster, meaning have him killed. Zuccaro finally robbed a cocaine dealer of a shipment and generated enough money to pay Charles what was owed.

But the relationship between Charles and Zuccaro would never be the same after the marijuana fiasco. Charles continued in the company of Kevin McMahon, a person whose presence aggravated Zuccaro more and more. Finally things came to a head on Charles's birthday, sometime in the late 1990s. Zuccaro was in Michael's, another popular Cross Bay Boulevard restaurant, when Charles entered with McMahon and another hanger-on named Alan. McMahon aggressively approached Zuccaro, who had been enjoying the evening with some friends, and berated him for not acknowledging Charles.

"Who the fuck do you think you are? He is the wiseguy," said McMahon. "You're supposed to be going over there and saying hello to him."

Zuccaro said he tried to brush things off, telling McMahon, "I'll say hello to Charles when I get the chance, when he is not with everybody. Mind your own business."

After Michael's closed, both groups took their business outside, and McMahon began to agitate for trouble, yelling out, "Get the guns! Shoot them."

Zuccaro tried to get Charles to calm things down, particularly since they all might be under surveillance by the FBI. McMahon and his friend Alan were getting more aggressive. Then Alan jumped out of a car and went to the trunk.

Armed with a fourteen-shot .357-caliber SIG Sauer handgun, which he carried concealed in his crotch, Zuccaro went for his weapon, thinking Alan was going to come up with his own gun. Instead, he pulled a golf club out of the trunk.

Zuccaro laughed. *He's coming to a gun battle with a golf club,* Zuccaro thought.

At that point, Peter Zuccaro and his group left. That was, he told the jury, the last time he ever saw Charles Carneglia, until he walked into Judge Weinstein's courtroom.

16

"Worm" Gets Ripped

Unlike his Pop Warner Football League buddy John "Junior" Gotti, Vincent Paul Rossetti Jr., of Howard Beach, wasn't born with blood ties to a Mob family. However, he lived much of his adult life like he had been.

Rossetti and his wife, Yvonne, were married in 1979 and had a sumptuous wedding reception at the popular El Caribe Country Club in Mill Basin, Brooklyn. The catering hall had tables filled to overflowing with so many lobsters that had vegetarians known, they might have picketed the place. Yvonne's wedding party consisted of about a half-dozen pretty Italian girls from the neighborhood. A lithe woman, Yvonne looked electric, long locks of dark hair framing her face. Vincent, a beefy, dark-haired athletic guy, was a hunk. His best man was Joseph, his younger brother.

They were starting their version of an American dream, which would include a nice home, cars, and four children, all girls. However, their life together would become a nightmare. The jurors in the case of Charles Carneglia heard for themselves the price the Rossettis, a seemingly average middle-class couple, paid for playing games with the Mob.

Vincent Rossetti didn't really know Charles much from the days in Howard Beach. They both traveled in different circles. But as a young man growing up in the neighborhood, Vincent knew some of the young people who were part of Charles's crew, notably Sal Puma. He also spotted Charles driving around or stopping in at the Lindenwood Diner. When Charles was in the diner, Vincent Rossetti said, he knew to be on his best behavior.

"Growing up in Howard Beach, that's just what you did, you respected organized crime figures."

Vincent Rossetti went off the tracks early and began using cocaine and marijuana as a teenager. As an adult, he gravitated to painkillers. He became a federal witness in 2006, after getting indicted by a federal grand jury in Brooklyn for securities fraud and extortion. He took the plunge into the witness protection program to save himself from the prospect of a long jail sentence and to protect his wife from retaliation because of her own crimes. Rossetti wasn't a member of any Mob family but, nevertheless, was an associate of the Bonanno *borgata*.

When prosecutors brought Vincent Rossetti into Judge Weinstein's courtroom to testify, they had to quickly air all of the witness's dirty laundry. There was plenty of it. Questioned by Roger Burlingame, Vincent Rossetti said his securities fraud business began back in 1993 when he began deceiving investors into buying worthless stocks in typical pump-and-dump schemes. Rossetti took the proceeds of the stock deals, he said, and put them into legitimate investments as a way of laundering his ill-gotten gains. Yet, like any con artist, Rossetti wasn't above getting ripped off; when that happened, he played the tough-guy routine. When two of his brokers got cash advances worth $30,000 and left the company, he said he went after them.

"I told them they were going to have to pay back the money, or they were going to get a beating," said Rossetti, an idea that he also said came from reputed Bonanno crime family soldier Ronald Giallanzo and Ronald Lashcek, an associate of the Colombo family.

Vincent told Giallanzo, with whom he was on record with in the crime family, where the brokers were working on Staten Island. It was then, he said, Giallanzo went there and, with an associate, beat the two men with anything they could get their hands on. The brokers repaid the money, recalled Rossetti.

Mobsters were typically into Wall Street scams when Vincent Rossetti was in the securities business, and federal prosecutors made headlines with a number of prosecutions. But Rossetti's Mob dealings went beyond securities fraud. Gambling was a constant Mob money-making business, and Rossetti said that he teamed up with Giallanzo in a betting operation. Rossetti played the role of leg breaker, collecting bets and paying out winnings, as well as threatening bettors who didn't want to pay. When he totaled it all up, Vincent said, he made roughly $1.5 million through his various scams.

Rossetti was more than an extortionist and had a restaurant on Cross Bay Boulevard that seemed to be legitimate. However, his family situation appeared to be pushing him and his wife further along the road to committing crimes. The couple had a daughter who was born with Dandy-Walker malformation, a congenital neurological condition that left the child in a wheelchair and in need of constant nursing. The medical bills were huge, and to generate money, Rossetti said, he and Yvonne cooked up a Medicaid fraud scheme in which the couple allowed their daughter's nurses to bill for more hours than they actually worked. The false billing netted about $500,000, of which the Rossettis kept only $10,000, grateful that they were able to bribe the nurses to keep them on the job.

"It was very hard to find capable nurses at that time," Rossetti told the jurors. "These two were very good at what they did—so to keep them coming back and happy, we let them keep the bulk of the money."

Mortgage fraud was also part of Rossetti's résumé. Seeing what later surfaced in the housing-bubble burst in the post-2008 financial meltdown, he was in some good company. He admitted on the witness stand to several instances of mortgage scamming, lying on his own refinance applications, and then using inflated appraisals at a mortgage company he worked for in Mineola, Long Island. Vincent said that he and his wife netted about $150,000 from their personal mortgage frauds.

Meanwhile, Yvonne was using her friends and neighbors in the Howard Beach area as her own group of victims. She embarked on a real estate investment program and promised high returns. But the investors lost close to a million dollars, and Yvonne would later admit in court that what she did was a scam. A number of relatives would complain openly to the news media and prosecutors that she had borrowed money, usually for the expressed purpose of taking care of her daughter or her husband's legal bills, but she never made repayments.

Federal court records also described how Yvonne had the temerity at the height of her real estate scam to take money from investor Agostino Accardo, who had borrowed $100,000 from a reputed Bonanno crime family loan shark named Michael Virtuoso. In 2006, Accardo pleaded with Yvonne for a return of the money, which had been invested with her, but he got nothing back. Then, according to papers filed in court by federal prosecutors, Yvonne was threatened by Virtuoso that if she didn't return the money, she would be killed. Her husband, Vincent, already under his own federal indictment, decided to cooperate with prosecutors in part to save his wife's skin. Vincent Rossetti wore a wire in August 2006 and the recordings he made ultimately led to several indictments in early 2007 of some reputed Bonanno crime family members, including Virtuoso, for allegedly extorting Yvonne. (The cases were settled with plea bargains with no one admitting to extorting Yvonne, except for Accardo.)

While she was well known for her money issues in Howard Beach, the extortion arrests catapulted Yvonne and her husband into the limelight. She became known as the housewife who ripped off the Mob. An attractive woman, Yvonne drew a fair amount of gossip in Howard Beach. She dressed fashionably and a bit provocatively. At one point, rumors started to fly that she had been caught having a tryst in a car with brother-in-law Joseph. Upon hearing that, her husband testified that he slapped her and then pounded his brother over the head with a nightstick. That story was retold around Howard Beach kitchen tables for years.

The couple's soap opera lifestyle, while amusing to some, wasn't the reason the government called Vincent Rossetti to the stand against Charles Carneglia. Vincent

Rossetti knew Sal Puma, a young man who once dated Kim Albanese, the future wife of Junior Gotti, and also knew how he died, something crucial to the prosecution case. Rossetti knew Puma well. They played ball together and went out drinking. Because he was lean and tall, Puma was known as "the Worm." Although Puma stole cars and dealt drugs, Rossetti and he didn't commit any crimes together. For his Gambino crime family associations, Puma had the likes of Peter Zuccaro and Andrew Curro, testified Rossetti.

It was the summer of 1983, a time Vincent remembered because he was out of high school about a year. St. Helen's Church was having its annual Our Lady of Grace summer feast and he had gone there with two friends, Jules Rosen and Lee Gold. The trio left the feast sometime before midnight and drove a few blocks away, to 156th Avenue and Seventy-ninth Street, a popular intersection where young people hung out.

Rossetti's group parked the car and walked over to a small crowd congregating by a driveway near some garden apartments. It was then, recalled Vincent, that he looked across the street and spotted his friend Sal Puma talking with someone whose face he couldn't see. From the look of things, the conversation was pretty heated. Sal was leaning against a car, facing Rossetti. The other person had his back to Rossetti.

After spotting Puma in an argument, Rossetti began to walk away when he ran into a friend, Kurt Russo, who told him what was going on in the altercation.

"Kurt told me Worm was getting his—he was getting ripped," Rossetti said haltingly, not wanting to use profanity.

"You can use the exact words," prompted Burlingame.

"He was getting his ass reamed by 'Charlie Canigs,'" responded Rossetti, using Charles's street name.

Rossetti then said he took a few steps toward the area where Puma was and noticed him and Charles in a side view. They were about fifty to seventy-five yards away, a distance Rossetti was pretty sure about because he played a lot of football. The place where both men were arguing was also lit well, with a streetlamp, added Rossetti. Fearful about being seen as nosy and perhaps getting a beating, Rossetti then walked back to his other friends.

About five minutes later, Rossetti and his group came back around. It was then Rossetti noticed Puma walking diagonally across the intersection of 156th Avenue and Seventy-ninth Street. He was moving slowly and clutching his chest. Then Puma fell down; his hand fell away from his chest, revealing a bloody spot on his shirt.

Russo pulled up his car, and the group, including Rossetti, placed Puma in the vehicle. They then drove quickly to Interboro Hospital, rushing Puma into the emergency room. Word spread quickly and other young people from Howard Beach, including a number of women, gathered outside the hospital's ER, some in tears.

At first, one of Puma's friends said he had heard that the wound wasn't that bad. Rossetti remembered peeking into the ER window and seeing Puma, his shirt off and the stab wound exposed, lying unconscious on a hospital gurney. With nothing else to do, the group returned to the church feast.

The next day, Rossetti said, he learned that Puma had died. The news rocked Howard Beach, and a lot of Puma's friends, particularly old girlfriend Kim Albanese, were particularly upset at what had happened, said Rossetti. After the funeral, there was no police investigation.

The way things were on the street, cops wouldn't have had much luck taking Vincent Rossetti's statement.

"The Gambinos held a lot of weight at that time, and we knew our place in that neighborhood—keep your mouth shut," explained Rossetti.

Again, the evidence was circumstantial. However, Rossetti had done some damage to Charles Carneglia by recounting for the jury the events that immediately led up to Puma's stabbing and death. He had seen Puma argue with Charles, and the next thing he knew, the young man collapsed from a stab wound. Meanwhile, Charles was nowhere to be seen. The circumstances just didn't look good for the defense. The next major witness on deck for the government wouldn't be helping Charles, either.

17

The "Body Shop"

Kevin McMahon was a homeless Howard Beach urchin approaching puberty when John and Charles Carneglia took him under their wing, gave him a home and a purpose in life—albeit criminal. Like some modern-day Dickensian Fagin characters, the Carneglias schooled the young boy to a life of service to *La Cosa Nostra*.

When he walked into Judge Weinstein's courtroom, McMahon was forty-two years old and beholden to a different master: the U.S. government. In the witness security program, McMahon was now part of the prosecution's plan to give Charles a new place for him to live: a maximum-security prison cell.

Charles had not laid eyes upon McMahon since they had a near-violent confrontation in 2001 in the Cherry Video extortion case. Charles thought McMahon was a rat then, which wasn't much of a surprise because Charles thought there were informers and snitches all around him. It was part of his street philosophy that law enforcement was constantly looking for a way of sneaking into his life, putting him in a jail cell, effectively killing his mother.

As McMahon entered the courtroom, there wasn't much of a discernible reaction from Charles. He sat back and focused his eyes on McMahon as he slid his short frame into the witness chair and took the oath to tell the truth, the whole truth. If that was what McMahon did, then Charles knew he had a lot of trouble. McMahon had been his frenetic aide-de-camp, his Sancho Panza, for years during the glory days of the Bergin crew and the volatile 1990s, when the Gambino family was in the midst of power struggles. Charles had confided in McMahon about a great deal, and McMahon himself took part in crimes that the government was trying to pin on his old mentor.

It fell to Roger Burlingame to begin the long march of Keven McMahon through his résumé of Gambino ties and crimes. In doing so, McMahon said that in the eleven years he was under Charles, beginning in 1989—when John Carneglia went away to prison—he knew that the defendant had a very special role in the Gambino family. If murders had to be done, if there was "cleaning up" of bodies to be done, said McMahon, Charles was the person with the specialty. McMahon said he knew that because it was Charles whom he saw shoot Louis DiBono in the World Trade Center parking lot, and it was Charles who was involved in the armored-car robbery, which took the life of guard Jose Delgado Rivera.

The DiBono and Delgado Rivera killings were the only two homicides McMahon said he knew about first-hand by being on the scene. But there were other murders that Charles later admitted taking part in, he said.

"Who else did he tell you he killed?" asked Burlingame.

"Sal Puma, a court officer, and a guy at a diner," McMahon replied.

The court officer—McMahon didn't mention Albert Gelb's name—was somebody Charles shot; Puma, he stabbed; the guy at the diner was also stabbed, McMahon told the jury.

What about bodies? Did Charles say he disposed of bodies? Burlingame asked. Yes, there were many bodies, answered McMahon.

It was back in January, just before the trial started, that the prosecution team revealed in its motion papers that there was going to be evidence about Charles disposing of corpses. Burlingame had hoped to have his witnesses use the word "acid" in talking about Charles's body disposal business, but Judge Weinstein wouldn't have it. It was a loaded word that Weinstein found too prejudicial. So, under some careful, preliminary questioning, McMahon began to hint about the fateful day when his neighborhood acquaintance Frankie Gotti was killed, more specifically about what had happened to John Favara, the driver who accidentally drove over Frankie. After Favara was killed—McMahon didn't know how that happened—it was the late Angelo Ruggiero who gave Charles the body for disposal, the witness said.

The first mention of John Favara was one of those tantalizing trial moments, a hint of things to come. There would be plenty of time to explore that killing and other murders. But first the prosecution went on a detour, showing some photos that looked like they were taken at any opulent Howard Beach wedding. This time, the subject was McMahon himself during his wedding reception at the El Caribe. Though his wife's face was purposely concealed by the prosecution, the color picture showed McMahon in all his sartorial grace, surrounded by the Carneglia clan. On the left, smiling a bit devilishly, was Charles, who, with his brother, John, in prison, was functioning as the family patriarch. Jennie was seated in front and arrayed around the bride and groom were Charles's sister-in-law Helene and her three children: Christopher, Justine, and John Jr. Helene's mother was seated next to Jennie.

Other photos showed McMahon visiting John Carneglia in prison, sometimes with Charles and his mother, as well as Gambino captain Salvatore Scala. Everybody seemed in some strange way to be very cheery. McMahon said he finally got wind of the fact that Charles and John were mobsters in the early 1980s, when he was about fifteen years old. Until then, McMahon believed they were just genial junkyard owners. The inevitable recitation of McMahon's own criminal career covered everything from his taking part in jury tampering during the Gotti and Carneglia trials of the 1980s to his role in the DiBono and Delgado Rivera killings.

McMahon's role in the Louis DiBono slaying was at first to run around in a car with a walkie-talkie as Charles and Bobby Borriello looked all over for the intended victim in Oceanside, a town on Long Island. But as happened on previous forays, DiBono was not to be found. However, one day while the group was at Jennie's house, a call came in that DiBono was at the World Trade Center. It was around noon when the group got into two cars: Charles, a fellow known only as Harpo, because he looked like one of the Marx Brothers, and McMahon got into a gray Cadillac Deville. Borriello drove a van by himself. The two groups both had a police scanner, some plastic ties used for fastening, and walkie-talkies so they could communicate with each other. They also had guns.

The Cadillac, with Charles, McMahon, and Harpo, entered the parking lot and drove down a few levels. Borriello stayed some distance away but remained in radio contact. He then spotted DiBono driving into the garage and radioed an alert.

"Everybody tensed up, and then Louis DiBono pulled up" in another, smaller Cadillac, said McMahon. DiBono nosed in and parked about four spaces away from Charles's car. It was then, recalled McMahon, that Charles made his move. Stepping out of his car, Charles walked toward DiBono's vehicle and hid behind a concrete column, said McMahon.

Because he was so obese, DiBono had to get out of the car in a two-step process. He first opened the door and then swung his legs around so that he could plant his feet firmly on the ground. McMahon said he was watching this process when he suddenly saw Charles get on top of DiBono and start pummeling him.

"I heard . . . I thought it was hitting in the head, but it was popping sounds like you would hit somebody in the head," said McMahon.

The next thing McMahon noticed, DiBono fell back into the front seat of the car, with his legs still dangling out of the vehicle. Charles couldn't get those legs back in, so McMahon said he rushed over, rolled up his sleeves, and pushed DiBono's legs, bending them at the knees so that his feet were behind him. Charles then closed the door, he added.

Back in his Cadillac, Charles pushed the gun under the front seat, McMahon noticed. Borriello then radioed to say he wanted them to take the body out of the car and drive away with it. But with such a large corpse awkwardly arranged on the front seat, McMahon said, there was no way DiBono could be removed from the car. So Charles and his crew drove away, leaving DiBono's body to be found by the police.

"I'm dead," said Charles, which, McMahon testified, sounded like an admission that Charles had screwed up the way the hit had occurred.

Back in Howard Beach, the four men went to Jennie's house, where Borriello pulled McMahon aside and gave him a warning.

"Don't tell anybody. You will end up like Louis DiBono, just forget about it. Don't tell nobody you were there," Borriello said.

McMahon wasn't going to advertise that he was in on the DiBono killing. He was angry that Charles had put him in that position, angry that he was on the scene and implicated. But there wasn't anything he was going to do about it, and he certainly wasn't going to berate Charles. If he did, he might truly end up like DiBono.

If Charles believed Gotti might be mad at him for the way things happened with DiBono, McMahon said, those fears were quickly dispelled the first time the crime boss ran into Charles after the murder. Gotti didn't seem displeased.

"He gave him a big hello and kiss and everything," remembered McMahon.

While the original plan was to kidnap DiBono, McMahon said, he got the sense in the World Trade Center parking lot that the game plan had changed. The tip-off was that nobody grabbed the plastic ties, which would have been used to tie up DiBono. He also remembered that there was no conversation as the group waited for the victim to arrive, no discussion of who would do what to restrain DiBono.

About two weeks after the slaying, the small-caliber gun—it might have been a .22- or .25-caliber firearm—was taken over to the Fountain Avenue junkyard and melted down with an acetylene torch, which got the weapon red-hot. Once torched, the gun was deformed by striking it with a hammer, said McMahon.

The DiBono killing was Charles's entrée to the status of made man in the Gambino family, said McMahon. That was something, he said, that Charles himself told him. Being made, and being made a mobster for an act of homicide, had a special cachet, said McMahon. Some men would become members of the Mob by making a good plate of spaghetti or a good drink, said McMahon. Because of his drunken days and unreliability, Charles would counter critics of his messy work habits by saying he made his rank the old-fashioned way, by a hit, said McMahon.

However, Mob murders didn't often bring in the money. What did supply cash were armored-car robberies, which McMahon took part in, sometimes with Charles, he said. The stickups netted each participant about $30,000 a shot. But the score that McMahon remembered the most was the one at JFK Airport, the one Peter Zuccaro decided to stay away from, and which ended so badly.

McMahon admitted that he drove the car containing Charles and Bobby Boriello to the airport early the morning of December 14, at around five o'clock. He remembered the date because it was the same week that Gambino boss John Gotti had been arrested at the Ravenite in Manhattan. But boss or no boss, money still had to be made, and the stickup team went to the airport, stopping the car a short distance away from the armored car. Borriello had a shotgun and Charles had a pistol, remembered McMahon.

When the driver exited the truck, he walked to the front of the vehicle and then was lost from McMahon's view. At that point, Charles and Borriello got out of their car and walked to the front of the armored car and also disappeared from view. Although he couldn't see anything, McMahon had no doubt about what he heard.

"I heard a lot of shots fired and noises, and firecracker noises," he told the jury.

McMahon wasn't sure if all of the shots sounded the same, but in a moment, he saw Borriello coming back to his car, carrying two bags of cash. However, Charles was nowhere in sight. McMahon said he ran over to the armored car and then saw his old friend pistol-whipping the driver, who at that point was on his knees and facing away from Charles.

Fearful that they would be discovered if they hung around any longer, McMahon testified, he pulled Charles away from the driver, saying, "Let's go." Charles complied, letting go of the driver who then fell facedown. Glancing at the truck, McMahon noticed the guard hiding under the vehicle.

McMahon drove away from the scene quickly, too fast for the liking of Charles, who, he said, told him to slow down, apparently out of fear they might get stopped by a cop. The trio drove back to McMahon's apartment, where Charles said he didn't know what had happened, an apparent reference to the shooting. He then took all of the hats the trio wore—they had donned American Airlines headgear—put them in a bag and left, said McMahon.

Recalling the chance meeting he had with Peter Zuccaro in the street, McMahon said, he denied losing a hat at the crime scene, which Zuccaro said police had found. This clearly rattled McMahon, who denied taking part in any airport robbery. He knew that the hat could provide clues to police, especially if any piece of hair or other matter containing DNA was on it. It was a week later that Charles stopped by and gave him $20,000, his take, and told him to keep denying that he was involved, said McMahon.

Charles was angered and hurt by McMahon. Kevin had turned on him and implicated him directly through eyewitness accounts in two of the five homicides charged in the indictment. At times, listening to McMahon's testimony, Charles made scoffing and grunting sounds, which irritated Judge Weinstein.

"I don't want the witness making noise when the defendant is speaking. He just did that repeatedly," said Weinstein. "He communicated loudly enough by grunts so that I was annoyed."

If the first part of Kevin McMahon's testimony prompted grunting from Charles Carneglia, the next phase made him want to scream. The rest of the day McMahon was asked by Roger Burlingame to recall conversations the witness had with the defendant about not only the other killings but also about the sensational and macabre body disposal and torture claims the prosecutors had brought up in earlier court filings.

Charles was such a drinker that McMahon was his minder, his nursemaid, to make sure he didn't do anything embarrassing or say stupid things at weddings and other festivities. But that didn't stop the Gambino soldier from having loose lips around McMahon. There were times when Charles said things that were contradictory. For instance, McMahon said that when Charles once talked about the murder of court officer Albert Gelb, he said "some asshole did it" and went on to explain that the killing was done by "someone who thought they were doing him a favor." But years later, at the Fountain Avenue junkyard, Charles was glancing at a photo and item on the Internet about Gelb, pointed to himself, and made a hand gesture to show a gun to the head, said McMahon. That was an indication that Charles had killed Gelb, said McMahon.

Vincent Rossetti was the person who was the closest thing to an eyewitness to the stabbing of Sal Puma, although he didn't actually see who did the deed. McMahon learned about the stabbing from his street sources, and it was Charles's reaction when McMahon told him what had happened that sounded suspicious, indifferent, and coldhearted. Once Charles even mocked him for showing sadness over Puma's death, relating how the dead man had been stealing commissary money, said McMahon.

Charles also told of a jocular conversation he had with Junior Gotti about stabbings, a discussion during a wedding in which Sal Puma's name came up, said McMahon. When Junior Gotti began bragging about his stabbings and Puma's name was mentioned, Charles said he interjected a sarcastic comment to Gotti: "If you would have did him right the first time, I wouldn't have had to do it," remembered McMahon.

"They were kind of making fun of John Junior that he couldn't stab the guy right," said McMahon, who admitted that he didn't know if Gotti had ever stabbed Puma.

But it was Charles, not Junior Gotti, who was on trial for the Puma killing. Every little bit of testimony from McMahon about Charles's reaction to Puma's death, or any suggestion he did the stabbing, was being used by the prosecution as a critical mass of evidence. Burlingame and the rest of the government team hoped that enough circumstantial evidence would convince the jurors that Charles had committed the homicide.

The disappearance of John Favara after the accidental death of twelve-year-old Frankie Gotti was so a part of the folklore of the Mob that it was almost certain that the jurors had heard of it before. But, barring a sneak look at newspaper articles, it is highly unlikely that they had heard of the acid bath Charles allegedly used to dispose of Favara's body. That had come from government court filings, and while it was easy pickings for news reporters, it was a different matter to hear anything about that from a live witness.

Because of Weinstein's ruling prohibiting the word "acid" from use in this trial, Burlingame had to walk McMahon carefully through the story of what had happened to John Favara after the young Gotti's death. Under closely phrased questions, McMahon said he first learned that Charles had a role in the body disposal when they were discussing minibikes—McMahon had actually been using the bike minutes before Frankie rode it to his death. The corpse was given to Charles by the now-deceased Angelo Ruggiero Sr., one of Senior Gotti's close friends and a captain in the Gambino family, said McMahon. But, according to Charles, there was a problem in getting rid of the body, McMahon said.

"What was the problem?" asked Burlingame.

"It wasn't dissolving as quickly as they liked it to," McMahon replied.

Charles was getting criticism from his Mob cronies for the problem; they thought he was incompetent and drunk, said McMahon. So, when the job was finished, he took some of the bones and threw them into the soup dish of Ruggiero as he noshed, said McMahon.

The word "acid" wasn't mentioned by McMahon. But the jurors must have been able to put things together when they heard the word "dissolve." Judge Weinstein sensed a problem and immediately cautioned the jury, saying the panel wasn't to decide about issues that weren't charged in the indictment or whether Charles was a good person. He also told the jurors to strike the word "dissolve" from their minds. Yet, it is very hard to *un*ring the bell, once words are said. Human nature must have led the individual jurors to speculate about what they had just heard, particularly about the bones in the soup. McMahon obviously wasn't talking about chicken bones.

Even with the court's caution, the testimony continued about the macabre. McMahon said that Charles referred to an abandoned house as the "body shop," a place where he disposed of bodies. McMahon said that one day he did find something in the basement of the old house, but Judge Weinstein wouldn't let him say what was found. Had McMahon continued, he would have mentioned some barrels of acid, which had been stored in the basement.

McMahon did say that Charles quipped about the place, saying that if the walls could talk, he and others would be in big trouble. There was also jewelry fastened to the walls and rafters of the building, stuff that Charles said he had taken from victims, McMahon stated. The items brought bad luck, though. One of Charles's associates, Andrew Curro, had been given a piece of jewelry from the collection and wound up getting a prison term, said McMahon. (Curro was sentenced to twenty-five years to life on state homicide charges in 1991. He was paroled in 2009.)

Acid did get into the testimony when McMahon was asked to recount the incident where two or three young men, including David D'Arpino, were allegedly abducted and taken to Charles's junkyard in an effort to find out who had fired a gun outside the home of John Carneglia during a teenage party. Charles had called to tell him to come to the junkyard and to bring a video camera, remembered McMahon. When he got there, Charles wasn't in a good state of mind.

"He was drinking or doing something, and he was sweating and screaming and yelling, and he said, 'I am going to get to the bottom of this,'" McMahon said. "He told three kids or two kids that if they didn't come willingly, and he had to go get them, they'd have a problem."

A car then pulled up to the Fountain Avenue yard, and McMahon saw two or three people, all with white translucent garbage bags over their heads and their hands tied, get out. The restrained people were then lined up, side by side. It was then Charles began his interrogation, asking each of them if they knew who did the shooting, said McMahon. All of them denied knowing, and it was then that their shoes and socks were removed. After another round of denials, Charles took out a turkey baster and began dropping acid onto the feet of the victims, according to McMahon.

The pain of the acid was excruciating. McMahon was recording the scene and between screams he noticed the victims tried rubbing the acid off their feet, succeeding only to slough off the red "bubbly" skin. But even then, the young men denied knowing who had fired the shots. Finally Charles pulled down their trousers and announced that he was going to stick the baster up their rectums, said McMahon. Well, that was enough. The youngsters cried out, "Chris did it!" and the torture session stopped, according to McMahon. It wasn't clear whom McMahon was referring to, although John Carneglia did have a son named Christopher. Both McMahon and Charles viewed the video, which was later destroyed because it was potentially evidence of a crime. Charles seemed amused by the images, said McMahon.

Although none of the acid torture or body disposal testimony related to crimes in the indictment, its effect on the jury must have been sobering. It all painted a picture of a disturbed, sadistic person. It seemed that there was no way the jurors could erase its impression.

Throughout the rest of his time on the witness stand, McMahon recounted vignettes that illuminated Charles's strange personality. His paranoia led him to put red pepper out to deter police dogs from sniffing around his car and to run the water faucet inside an apartment he lived at, apparently to defeat surveillance devices. Charles also had a fondness for guns and knives and even fabricated a silencer out of a plastic soda bottle, said McMahon.

McMahon also testified about the $500 weekly pay-offs Charles got from securities fraud specialist Hunter Adams. There were also robberies committed at the Papavero Funeral Home in Maspeth—the place where John Gotti's wake took place—and at a Sears store in New Jersey, all of which McMahon said Charles had played a role in.

When defense attorney Kelley Sharkey got a chance to cross-examine Kevin McMahon, the witness had covered a lot of territory.

McMahon got combative under Sharkey's questioning. He hectored her and tried to belittle her command of the facts. Finally, Judge Weinstein had had enough.

"Don't snap back at the cross-examiner, just answer," said Weinstein.

Sharkey brought out a few subtleties about McMahon. He had written prosecutors once to say his memory of the Sears and armed-car robberies were blurry and that he was afraid during his debriefings with the FBI that he might be confusing things he had seen in newspapers, on television, or read in the column "Gang Land News."

McMahon also admitted lying to the FBI in order to make Charles look better and to undercut the notion that there was a Mob, an admittedly foolish tactic. McMahon also admitted that most of the incriminating conversations he had with Charles took place when no one else was present to corroborate his account. McMahon also said that if government notes of his interviews and debriefings contradicted with his recollection, it was because the FBI and prosecutors took things down incorrectly.

While Sharkey didn't appear to shake the main points of McMahon's testimony, the defense did show that as a witness he had problems with recollection and clearly wanted to stay out of jail for the rest of his life. It was the Holy Grail of everyone who was testifying to get a government letter that might keep them out of prison—especially the next big gun in the prosecution arsenal: John Alite.

18

"I'm Honest."

The real threat the ethnic Albanian gangster John Alite posed wasn't just to Charles Carneglia as he sat on trial in Brooklyn federal court. Alite also was a very big problem to John "Junior" Gotti, the son of the late Gambino boss. In fact, he was a very, very big problem.

Gotti had been arrested, again, in the summer of 2008 on racketeering charges out of Tampa, Florida. The choice of venue for the case came as a surprise to some. But seeing that the FBI had developed Alite and McMahon as cooperating witnesses because of the Trucchio indictment, it made sense at first blush.

The case against the forty-six-year-old Mob scion was an extension of the older racketeering charges that had led to three mistrials in New York. But now, federal prosecutor Jay Trezevant, whose disability from an accident in his youth kept him in a wheelchair, structured the indictment differently, adding two homicide charges against Gotti. There was no secret where the counts about the Bruce Gotterup and George Grosso murders came from. Those were killings Alite played a role in; now he was claiming that Gotti ordered the homicides.

Early in the case, Gotti, who was held without bail in Florida, won a tactical victory when a Tampa federal judge saw through the government's attempt to have the trial there as nothing more than forum shopping and ordered it back to Manhattan. The new indictment, the judge said, really was just a dressed-up version of the earlier case, with most of the crimes having occurred in New York State. But once the case was transferred back to Manhattan, Judge Kevin Castel, in a blow to Gotti, refused to grant him bail. Junior Gotti had been granted bail in the previous federal cases and had never missed a court date or caused any problems. But what apparently made a difference to Castel was the addition of homicide charges.

Alite's appearance in Charles's case was a curtain-raiser on the things he was expected to testify about in Gotti's upcoming trial. Seth Ginsberg, one of Gotti's defense attorneys, sat in the courtroom and took copious notes and made the observation to reporters outside the courtroom that Alite was "giving the prosecutors what they want to hear about John to save himself."

The tabloids referred to Alite as Gotti's "worst nightmare"; from the beginning of his testimony against Charles, that certainly seemed true. Alite was assigned to Charles's crew in the Gambino family after he had a falling-out with Gotti and knew all of the younger Gotti's dark secrets—so he claimed. Altogether, from the time he first met Junior Gotti at a bar in Queens until he decided to cooperate in the spring of 2007, Alite had twenty-five years of experience with the Gambino crime family.

Under questioning by Roger Burlingame, Alite said he knew Charles to be "an enforcer" and a "killer." Alite said he knew that because in 1990 he worked with Charles to carry out the DiBono murder, a slaying Alite said he pleaded guilty to as part of his cooperation deal. He had also heard from Charles, as well as Junior Gotti, that three other murders were part of Charles's crime family résumé: "Sal Puma, an armored-car guard, and a court officer."

Aside from the DiBono murder, Alite didn't have direct knowledge of the Puma, Gelb, and Delgado Rivera killings. But he did know what happened during two armed robberies attributed to Charles. The Papavero Funeral Home heist and the robbery of the Sears in Vineland, New Jersey, were things Charles played a role in planning, said Alite. He also told the jury that Charles had told him he had disposed of bodies, something that bolstered what Kevin McMahon had talked about in his testimony.

John Alite's evidence against Charles Carneglia was an important piece of the case. But it was Gotti's alleged connections with the Albanian mobster that served as the subject of a trial-within-a-trial scenario, pushing Charles into the background. Gotti had somewhat rehabilitated his image with three mistrials and his claims that he had left the Mob as far back as 2000. But Alite claimed that Gotti was not only involved in the murders but had been partners with him in one of the biggest cocaine rings operating in the Forest Park area of Queens, one that made millions of dollars.

Alite said that in his late teens he began moving small amounts of cocaine in Queens. Soon after, his friend Kevin Bonner said that if he was going to push drugs, he had to give an envelope with cash to Junior Gotti, just like all the other dealers and criminals did.

"I started paying John Gotti Junior a small amount of money, like everybody else," Alite testified, adding that Gotti put him in contact through a cousin, Johnny Boy Ruggiero, with a new supplier. Alite said he wasn't moving large loads of cocaine, maybe two pounds a month, when he decided in 1984 to give Junior Gotti a third of his profits.

Protection of turf is part of the drug trade. After John Gebert, Gotti's partner in the marijuana business, got robbed by some Jamaican dealers, Alite said, he teamed up with Gotti and his crew to seek revenge. The group drove around until they spotted the Jamaicans and Gebert fired at them, wounding them, according to Alite. The shooting incident solidified Alite's ties with Gotti, and both men became close personal friends. Gotti was even Alite's best man in 1989.

On the witness stand, Alite recounted what he had told investigators about the size of the drug operation, claiming that he pocketed $100,000 a month and that the 150 or so men working for him pulled in from $5,000 to $40,000 monthly. The profits easily came to $1 million a month, and some of that was also split with Junior Gotti, who, Alite testified, was giving some to his father. Had Senior Gotti known where the money was coming from, it would have put him in direct violation of the Mafia rule—routinely ignored—against dealing in drugs. According to Alite, Senior Gotti was turning a blind eye to his drug dealing, but he said that if Alite got caught, he would have to be killed.

"John Gotti Senior is telling me, *I know what you are doing, but I don't know what you are doing, and if you get caught, you are dead,*" Alite testified.

* * *

John Alite admitted to playing roles in five murders. In one of them, the killing of George Grosso, he actually was intimately involved in the slayings. He said he did it on the younger Gotti's orders.

"Were you ordered to kill him?" asked Burlingame.

"Yes," answered Alite.

"By who?"

"John Gotti Junior."

Grosso died because he had been running around town saying he had been dealing cocaine for the Gottis, and was warned to stop saying such a thing, said Alite. He explained that while he was dealing drugs, he never invoked the Gotti name in his business—even though the Gottis were "standing in the closet" and not out front. Another thing that made Alite want revenge was that Grosso and his brother-in-law John Gebert actually took a shot at him and tried to kill him. With that, Alite said, he sought and obtained Junior Gotti's permission for killing both Grosso and Gebert.

Grosso was about twenty-four years old when he was shot twice in the head by Alite in December 1988 after a night of drinking that led the victim into a false sense of security. Grosso was seated in the front seat of a car when, Alite said, he shot him and dumped his body on the Grand Central Parkway. (On cross-examination, Alite added that one of the other men in the car was Nick Tobia, an old friend who went on to become a Suffolk County police officer.)

Bruce Gotterup had been foolhardy to try and shake down some Mob-connected bars in Queens, doing it with a machine gun and demanding $500 a week. Alite testified that he sought Junior Gotti's permission to kill

Gotterup and then passed along the order to Johnny
Burke. Gotterup was dispatched after he, too, was lulled
into a false sense of security during a night of drinking.
Alite testified that he told Burke to take Gotterup out
and then, on a pretext, drive down to a beach area and
kill him. Gotterup was found shot dead.

Frank "Geeky" Boccia's great sin in the world of the
Mob was to punch out Francine Ruggiano, the daughter of the elderly and respected Gambino captain
Albert Ruggiano. Not only did Boccia strike Francine,
but when her mother tried to step in, she got struck as
well, said Alite. Angered by the disrespect Boccia had
shown, Alite said, he asked Junior Gotti's permission to
retaliate. In 1988, Boccia was killed in a Mob social club
on Liberty Avenue. Gambino soldier Dominick Pizzonia and Anthony Ruggiano committed the murder, said
Alite. (Pizzonia was convicted of federal rackcteering in
2007 for being involved in the Boccia slaying. Ruggiano
admitted his role when he pleaded guilty and became
a cooperating witness.)

John Gebert, the relative of Grosso and the man who
as a teenager introduced Alite to Junior Gotti, was slain
in 1996. Alite, who earlier said Gotti gave the approval
for the murder, testified that he farmed out the hit contract to Peter Zuccaro, and the actual killing was done
by two Gambino associates, Patsy Adriano and David
D'Arpino, the same man whom Charles Carneglia once
tortured with acid.

So when he was done going through the litany of
murders, Alite had testified that Gotti played a role in
approving or orchestrating five Mob hits: Louis DiBono,
George Grosso, Bruce Gotterup, Frank Boccia, and
John Gebert. If Alite was to be believed, Junior Gotti
took the bloody job of acting Gambino boss and crime

captain very seriously. For added measure, Alite also linked Junior Gotti in his testimony to a 1983 fatal stabbing of a young man in the Silver Fox bar, testifying that Gotti admitted doing so. Alite also said he took part in jury tampering with the younger Gotti during federal court trials of various Gambino family members in the 1980s.

Alite's claims about Gotti being so intimately tied to Gambino family murders and other crimes generated lots of headlines. But the most salacious bits of testimony related not to Gotti but rather to his sister Victoria. For years, Gotti family members said that John Alite had a crush on Victoria, the parochial school–educated daughter of the late crime boss. Alite would visit the Gotti home on Eighty-fifth Street and tell Victoria's parents that he was in love with her. This didn't sit well with her family. As a teenager, Victoria was kept on a short leash by her father when it came to dating and seeing boys. Sex in a traditional Italian-American household was meant for marriage and not before—although in her autobiography, Victoria said she became pregnant by Agnello while they were engaged.

It was around 1993, said Alite, that his relationship with Junior Gotti became fractured. He didn't like the way the young Gambino captain was treating some of his associates, particularly those like Mark Reiter who went to prison for life and never turned on Gotti's father. His view of Mob life was getting more jaded.

"It was kind of like looking at a brochure when you are a kid," said Alite, "here everything looks nice. You are going to Paradise Island. You forget to read the small print, fine print."

But what also caused problems for Alite was, as he

claimed, that he was "fooling around with sister Vicky Gotti, on the sneak," which was taken to mean that he was having a sexual relationship with Gotti's married sister Victoria. The spark for the relationship, and why Victoria turned to him, said Alite, was that her husband, Carmine Agnello, beat her up.

"That turned into me [and] Vicky fooling around a lot, seeing each other on the sneak." Angered by stories of his wife turning to Alite, Agnello and five guys came looking for the Albanian gangster. But none of Agnello's crew had the nerve to shoot him, said Alite. Of course, Alite wanted to retaliate, but he said Junior Gotti wouldn't give him permission, something that made him fear for his safety.

Alite's claim about a relationship with Victoria, star of the A&E reality show *Growing Up Gotti,* exploded in the press. The very next day, Victoria's sixty-six-year-old mother stormed into court. Charles had never really met the late crime boss's wife but recognized her right away, nodding in recognition as she took her seat. Victoria acknowledged Charles and then took a front-row position in the spectator gallery, her lips pressed tight together as if she was trying to stop herself from an explosion of anger.

After she had two strokes and underwent the stress of her son's three federal mistrials, Victoria was begged by her family to stay away from court. But with her daughter's morals impugned by the likes of Alite, there was no keeping the Gotti matriarch away from the Brooklyn courthouse. Her graying hair pulled back in a ponytail, Victoria wasn't recognizable to many in court, including some of the FBI agents who thought she was just another curiosity seeker. She glared at

Alite as he continued his testimony, ready to defend her family honor, and gave an earful to any reporter ready to listen.

"He's an insect," she said. "He would hump a cockroach."

"In Mr. Alite's dreams, would someone like me even give him a second glance," said the younger, maligned Victoria as she disavowed any extramarital relationship.

To defend herself, Victoria took a two-hour lie detector test for which she paid $1,300 and was asked pointed questions such as "Did you ever have sexual intercourse with John Alite?" Judd Bank, the polygrapher, said in a report that the *subject was being truthful regarding to pertinent questions asked.*

"I did this for my kids," she told the *Daily News.* "While they always believe me and have stood behind me, I never wanted there to be an ounce of doubt in their minds."

While the Gotti element of John Alite's testimony provided a sensational angle to the trial, a great deal of what he told the jury also had to do with Charles Carneglia—the guy who was really on trial. The most critical aspect for the prosecution's case was what Alite remembered about the Louis DiBono hit. Alite said that Gotti first talked with him about the need to locate DiBono during a walk-and-talk conversation in the fall of 1990 outside the younger Gotti's social club by 101st Avenue and 105th Street in Ozone Park, not far from Bergin Hunt and Fish. Gotti, Bobby Borriello, and Alite walked together, and it was Gotti who said that the Louis DiBono hit was his first big assignment as a captain, according to Alite.

"First job as a captain to kill somebody, to follow orders," said Alite.

The reason Gotti spoke with Borriello and Alite about the need to get DiBono was because it was difficult to locate the intended victim, who was proving elusive, said Alite. Gotti wanted Alite, who lived in Cherry Hill, New Jersey, to try and find DiBono in Atlantic City, where he had been spotted, said the witness. The hit team included Charles Carneglia, Borriello, and himself, Alite recalled.

Borriello voiced some concern about running around to plan a hit because he believed he was being targeted himself. Alite didn't explain what Borriello's fears stemmed from, but he was most likely referring to a fight he had with the volatile Genovese associate Preston Geritano in Brooklyn. However, Gotti wouldn't delay the hunt for DiBono, recalled Alite.

After a two- or three-week search of the casinos in Atlantic City, Alite and Borriello didn't find DiBono. Meanwhile, Gotti had learned that DiBono would be at the World Trade Center; as a result, he reconstituted the hit team. According to Alite, he was taken off because of his unfamiliarity with New York City roads and was replaced by Kevin McMahon.

"Kevin is good with surveillance and a car thief, and he is good with driving—that's his thing. I'm not. I'm from Jersey," explained Alite.

As Gotti spelled things out, said Alite, Charles was to do the shooting, McMahon was doing surveillance and driving, while Borriello was to be a backup. The hit was to go down in the underground garage and the body was just to be left there. After the killing took place, an elated Gotti said that the operation had been a success, with Charles doing the shooting, said Alite.

There were other crimes, Alite said, that he had committed with Charles, particularly after he was placed under his wing around 1993 following his break with Junior Gotti. Extortion, drug dealing, bookmaking, murder conspiracy, police corruption, were all things Alite said he did with Charles. One intended murder victim, remembered Alite, happened to be Peter Zuccaro, who, Charles said, owed him and his brother money for marijuana deals. Though Charles wanted Alite to lure Zuccaro into an ambush, the Albanian mobster secretly warned Zuccaro.

Alite also shed some light on Charles's paranoia about the police and FBI. Charles wouldn't sit at the same restaurant booth, out of fear that it would be too easy for the cops to place a bugging device at the table, said Alite. Charles would cover his mouth when he talked and mumble. He even had McMahon pick up some electronic equipment to debug his house, recalled Alite.

Paranoia wasn't just a trait of Charles's. Alite said that at one point he refused to enter Charles's apartment one day because he feared that Carmine Agnello was trying to get him. What made Alite suspicious was that after he knocked on the door, Charles didn't open up but instead told him to come in, something he never used to do. Fearing that someone might be lurking behind the door, Alite bluffed and said he couldn't visit because he had two people waiting for him in the car. It was then that two Gambino gangsters came out from behind the door, as if they were joking. But Alite didn't think it was a gag. He noticed the bathroom door in the apartment was closed and suspected there might be a tarp in the bathtub for disposing of his body.

* * *

Despite his problems with some in the Gambino hierarchy, John Alite's criminal life treated him well. He said he made millions of dollars as a loan shark and laundered his money through legitimate companies. He did home invasion robberies, made payoffs to get business contracts, cheated on his taxes, and committed mortgage fraud. When necessary, Alite kidnapped people, breaking the victim's bones in the process. He said he bribed cops, judges, and jurors. Alite even recalled running an escort service, which wasn't as profitable as it could be because he sometimes didn't charge his friends. Though he was a big ladies' man, Alite admitted to being abusive to women, smacking his wife around, even knocking out a lady friend of Charles's outside a bar.

Alite thought about settling a lot of scores and said he had a wish list of hits that numbered around fifteen, with Junior Gotti and his brother-in-law high on the list. But he was also a target of the Gambino family. At one point, an FBI agent told Alite that he was being set up for a hit because he wouldn't come to meetings. Charles Carneglia also tipped him off about trouble, which had its roots in a deep-seated mistrust between John Carneglia and Junior Gotti.

Although he was in prison, John Carneglia was supposed to keep getting his cut of his old rackets. But when Junior Gotti was in charge, he appeared to be pulling back from John Carneglia and bad-mouthing him by calling him a "junkie," said Alite. Angered over the way Gotti was treating his brother, Charles not only told Alite he was in danger but also gave him a machine gun to use on the crime boss's son. Charles called Junior Gotti, "the half Jew," in reference to his mother Victoria's part Jewish heritage on her mother's side.

Alite also stepped into more trouble with the Gambino hierarchy when, during a stint in prison, he berated and threatened Gene Gotti for pushing around another Gambino family inmate in front of other prisoners. As a result, Gene Gotti wanted him killed, said Alite.

The mistrust, double crossing, and disloyalty Alite saw in the Mob life started to gnaw at him. By the mid-1990s, he was becoming disillusioned. The fantasy life he envisoned as a young man was fast evaporating.

"I see that everything is not about loyalty, friendship, the group," mused Alite. "It is about greed, lies, manipulation. Machiavelli shit."

His real problem revolved around Junior Gotti, whom he no longer trusted.

"I didn't trust his leadership. I thought he was weak, soft, [a]conniver, jealous, envious. Those things started to turn me away from him," explained Alite.

The defense had a crack at John Alite and brought out more about his relationship with Nick Tobia, who later went on to become a Long Island cop. In desperation, Alite testified, he wrote to Tobia while he was in custody in Brazil, asking his old friend to reach out to some other people so he could get money from them. If some $400,000 didn't materialize, then Alite was prepared to reveal crimes they had committed, according to the letter introduced into evidence.

Alite wasn't ashamed about talking about his crimes and admitted he wrote the letter to shake down people.

He admitted lying during his days as a criminal on the street, since that was the way to survive. But now that he was a cooperating witness and his future depended on it, he was bound to tell the truth, Alite said.

Curtis Farber and Alite sparred and became combative throughout the cross-examination. Alite couldn't be shaken on any major point, and Judge Weinstein saw the futility of some of the questioning. He told Farber at one point, "Move to something else, please. You are not getting anyplace."

Farber eventually finished up with a series of pointed questions about Alite's history of lies and deceit. The defense attorney asked Alite if he agreed that honesty wasn't a trait he possessed.

"No," Alite responded. "It would be right if you said that to me a while ago. Now, no, I'm honest."

19

"He's the Same Criminal."

The trial of Charles Carneglia went on for over a month. It generated a transcript of well over five thousand pages. The government called forty witnesses and put in enough photographs from police surveillances, mug shots, and crime scenes to fill an encyclopedia about the Mob. With its final witness, who authenticated some prison tape records, the government rested on March 3. Roger Burlingame and company felt certain that they had presented a compelling case.

Unlike most organized crime defendants, Charles actually presented a defense. His main contention was that he had left the life of the Mob far behind a long time ago, at least five years before his 2008 indictment. That was a statute of limitations defense that had worked, to some degree, with Junior Gotti and, in 1975, with old Bonanno boss Joseph Massino during one of his earlier racketeering defenses.

Charles used his hirsute looks to buttress the point

that he was no longer in the Mob life. Since the Mob
didn't favor beards or moustaches, anyone who wore
one couldn't be a made member. Judge Weinstein
trashed that argument at one point, without the jury
present, calling it "absurd." He also said that if Charles
took the stand, he personally wouldn't believe a word
he said. Charles wasn't going to testify, anyway, a strate-
gic decision that some of his friends said angered him.
So to prove he had turned his back on the Mob,
Charles called a number of old friends to the witness
stand. It would be his only shot at convincing the jury
on that point.

John White was a twenty-five-year-old man who grew
up in the Lancaster, Pennsylvania, area. That is an unlikely place for a bank robber to come from. But at the
age of nineteen, White had fallen in love with an
eighteen-year-old woman named Savannah who happened to be a bank teller and who wasn't happy with
her job. One thing led to another and White schemed
with Savannah to rob the bank. The plan was simple.
White would come in with a pellet gun and stick up Savannah at her workstation. The two would then run
away and live on the money. Sometimes love really
blinds.

White told the jury in Charles's case that he netted
$77,000 from the stickup. He and Savannah also got
caught. Both were indicted. White took a plea and
wound up getting a sentence of fifty-one months in a
federal correctional institution. He was sent in 2004 to
Fort Dix, which just so happened to be where Charles
was serving his time for the Cherry Video extortion
conviction.

White noticed that the inmate population at Fort Dix was divided ethnically. He said there seemed to be an Italian clique of guys who were organized crime–related. They played bocci ball and had elaborate parties whenever an inmate was going home. There were also sexual predators among the inmates and a guy named Moe seemed to have his eye on him, recalled White. It was a very uncomfortable situation for White to find himself in prison and being selected as a "bitch" by another male inmate. White had a similar experience in a different facility and said he got no help from the Federal Bureau of Prisons personnel. So, when the same thing happened in Fort Dix, White said he got referred by one of the Italian inmates to Charles Carneglia.

White said that when Charles took him under his wing, the inmate Moe kept his distance and never bothered him again. In the meantime, White struck up a friendship with Charles, who became something of a mentor. The two men became gin rummy players, and Charles would make the younger inmate sandwiches, said White.

One thing that White said he noticed about Charles was that he stayed away from the Italian clique, the Mob group, preferring to walk around the prison compound with him, a younger Irish inmate. That began to anger some of the Italians, whom Charles argued with, said White. From that point on, Charles avoided the Italian crowd, he said.

White also recalled that when Charles received a copy of the *New York Post,* he pointed out a story about the trial of Junior Gotti, telling White that the death of Gotti's father spelled the death of an old way of Mob life.

"He said [Junior's] father, John Gotti, you know, he

died a man and he died in prison, and when he died, the old Mob died, and he was part of the old Mob. It's dead now, he was no longer part of the new Mob," said White, paraphrasing Charles.

When he got out of prison, Charles said, he was going back to the Fountain Avenue junkyard and would also take care of his mother before she died, added White.

The defense had called White to show that Charles was through with the Mob life back in 2004, a period that was still within the statute of limitations. But the defense hoped that White's recollections, combined with other witnesses, would help show that Charles had separated himself from the Mob.

Another defense witness was Mark Gioia, an old friend of Charles's who had helped make arrangements for the care of Jennie Carneglia when her son was going to jail in 2001. Gioia said that the period just before Charles surrendered to begin his sentence was an emotional time for him, particularly because of concern for Jennie. Both men talked about the Mob life Charles had once known.

"He would sit with us for hours, sometimes at Carosello's, and tell me and Alan (Mershanski) he was done, he was finished with things," said Gioia, who had admitted to numerous run-ins of his own with the law. "He was disgusted with the—I guess, new generation of the Mob."

Charles called the new Mob guys who got arrested the inmates of the "new millennium" who would turn cooperating witness to save themselves, said Gioia.

"You could see Charles was done. He was exhausted, physically exhausted, and he just didn't want to be bothered anymore with anything," noted Gioia.

The picture Gioia painted was of Charles as a Mob romantic, an anachronism, whose whole reason for being had disappeared. There seemed to be no place for him in a world that had changed too much for him to bear. He couldn't care less about the new Mob. Instead, Charles sought refuge, Gioia said, in some old friends and, of course, in caring for his mother, Jennie.

Jodi Ryan met Charles around 1998 when her common-law spouse, Allen Mershanski, got a job working at the plate-glass section of the Fountain Avenue junkyard. Mershanski had a spinal condition that deteriorated over time, but he managed to keep his junkyard job. Charles actually lived for a time across from the couple and their five children at the Greentree Condominiums complex and became like a father-in-law, said Ryan. Despite Charles's various arrests and his stint in prison, Ryan said, she and Mershanski remained close with him. During the time Charles was incarcerated, it was Ryan and Mershanski who took care of Jennie and looked after her.

The main point of Ryan's testimony was to explain to the jury her attempt to find an unsigned letter Kevin McMahon had sent to Charles after getting arrested in the Florida case. Ryan said she had glanced at the letter and remembered McMahon stating that the FBI wanted him to incriminate Charles and his brother. The letter also stated that McMahon wanted $10,000 for expenses related to his Florida trial, Ryan recalled.

Charles believed the letter was a shakedown attempt and wanted Ryan to retrieve it from his attic, being sure to use gloves and a plastic bag to prevent contamination of the paper by too many fingerprints, she said. If the letter was found, it would have been ammunition for the defense to discredit McMahon. But try as she might, Ryan said, she could never find the document.

"Ms. Ryan, do you love Charles Carneglia?" asked defense attorney Kelley Sharkey.

"Yes, I do, dearly."

On March 9, 2009, after the trial of Charles Carneglia opened, prosecutor Evan Norris gave the government's summation, or closing statement. With a case that spanned events over thirty years, and an intricate indictment that had numerous allegations, Norris would deliver a summation that went on for over five hours. Judge Weinstein let the jurors take notes because nothing the prosecutor or defense attorneys said at the conclusion of the case would be read back to them.

Norris showed the jurors a flurry of surveillance photographs to remind them of the connection Charles had with the varied Gambino mobsters who showed up at funerals, diners, and street meetings. It was a photo review of criminals that would make even the most attentive bleary-eyed. But that kind of evidence showed Charles was in the Mob, specifically the Gambino crime family, and conspired with others to further its aims, said Norris.

The prosecutor had fourteen acts of racketeering to remind the jury of. The murders of Gelb, DiBono, Delgado Rivera, Cotillo, and Puma were the most graphically described during the trial. However, to connect Charles to each, Norris summarized the evidence. Charles didn't survive by blood alone, though, the prosecutor argued. There was enough evidence, Norris maintained, to show that Charles made his money over the years through marijuana dealing with Peter

Zuccaro and taking a cut of the proceeds from the robbery of a New Jersey Sears store and the Papavero Funeral Home. Charles also made hundreds of thousands of dollars through the extortion of Hunter Adams, the adept securities fraud artist and drug dealer, who, nevertheless, felt compelled out of fear to fork over money to Charles, said Norris.

Charles even turned to shaking down Zuccaro, who feared becoming a hit target, and his friend Bobby Schiavo, argued the prosecutor. On top of that, Charles was involved in securities fraud because he took part in Mob sit-downs to settle disputes and tried to extort condominium owners of Greentree through exorbitant overcharges and other forms of coercion, said Norris.

Charles's march through the world of crime spanned the time from when he was a young man of twenty-nine, who murdered Albert Gelb, until he was past sixty years old and still taking "Christmas money"—which meant extortion payments—from old friends, Norris said.

"Ladies and gentlemen, Charles Carneglia was no choirboy as a young man, and he's no choirboy today. He is the same man. He's the same criminal. He's the same killer," argued Norris. "We end where we started—Albert Gelb, Michael Cotillo, Salvatore Puma, Louis DiBono, Jose Delgado Rivera. The defendant ended all of their lives. He took all of them away from their families. They are never going home again."

The message now was clear: Charles should never go home again—and wouldn't—if the jury convicted him.

Curtis Farber knew he had an uphill fight in the case and would take nearly four hours for his summation. He focused immediately on the character of the main prosecution witnesses, all of whom had signed cooperation agreements with the government. Each of them hoped to get a letter from the prosecution that would allow a federal judge to consider giving them reduced prison terms, instead of the life terms most of them faced.

"In a nutshell, you have liars working off life sentences," said Farber. "Liars—corroborating liars—does not rise to the level of proof beyond a reasonable doubt as required in our system of justice."

Each of the cooperating witnesses knew the value of the so-called 5K1.1 letter to a sentencing judge. They only had to look back at what had happened to Sammy Gravano after he testified against the late John Gotti, said Farber. Gravano got a five-year term, even though he had committed nineteen murders, less than four months per murder, argued Farber. Take out these witnesses and the case against Charles failed, he said.

On each of the five homicides, Farber noted, Charles had never been charged over the years. There was no direct evidence then, nor was there any now, which proved he committed those murders, argued Farber. One of the most important arguments Farber made related to the Gelb case. He reminded the jury that the only eyewitness, the now-deceased Charles Ball, had described the shooter as being nearly six feet tall, with Afro-style hair, a moustache, and being in his late twenties. Charles was five-six and never had an Afro, said Farber. Although Gelb's car was dusted for fingerprints, none from Charles were found on the vehicle, he noted.

"The shooter was not Charles," the attorney said.

Since the main point of the defense was that Charles had withdrawn from the Gambino crime family more than five years before he was indicted, Farber attacked the prosecution's evidence. Charles admittedly had

stayed in touch with some reputed Gambino crime figures, and there were prison telephone records that
showed that, including some calls connected to his
brother, John, who quizzed him about what some old
gangsters were doing. In another call, Charles, who was
in jail, was discussing the large Gambino case that had
led to his trial.

"What do these calls show? It showed a conversation between two men who had known each other
almost their entire lives discussing the status of a multidefendant prosecution, a sixty-two-defendant indictment of which Charles was originally a part. This
case," said Farber.

"A conversation with an old friend is not furthering
the object of the conspiracy," the attorney argued. "A
conversation with an old friend about the charges
against him and his codefendants is not participation in
the conspiracy."

The prosecution drained the sewers of New York to
bring in despicable witnesses to try and convict Charles,
said Farber. But the truth was, he said, that Charles
dropped out of the Mob life because it had changed
too much for him. He just wanted to live quietly, at
home, with Jennie.

The jury deliberated over a five-day period. On
March 17, 2009, the panel came back with a verdict that
convicted Charles Carneglia of everything—with three
exceptions. The jurors couldn't come to a unanimous
decision on racketeering act one, the murder of Albert
Gelb, and two extortion charges. It was a result that
stunned not only the prosecutors but the legion of

court officers who crowded the spectator seats to listen to the verdict.

Charles showed no emotion as the verdict was read. He had been convicted of the main racketeering charge and more than a dozen acts of racketeering. As Charles was convicted of gunning down armored-car driver Jose Delgado Rivera, the victim's twin daughters wept in relief.

"He has no remorse," said one of the daughters, Mildred Delgado-Jimenez, as she watched Charles. Her mother, Anna Alejandro, a former New York City police detective, said her heart dropped as the moment she had waited for so many years had arrived. Someone had been brought to justice for her husband's murder.

U.S. Attorney Benton Campbell, of the Eastern District-Brooklyn, put out a statement saying he hoped the verdict brought a measure of closure to the families of Charles's victims. But while Delgado's kin were happy, the court officers were disappointed. Dennis Quirk, the union leader of the officers, found the result mind-boggling.

"We're somewhat disappointed," Quirk told reporters outside the courtroom. "Indirectly, we got what we wanted. We got him caged.

"He is going to spend the rest of his days living like an animal, because he is an animal," said Quirk.

While the anonymous jurors gave no statements or interviews to the news media, it is likely that the Gelb charge failed to win them over completely because, unlike the other murders, there was no strong circumstantial or direct evidence tying Charles to the actual shooting. It is also likely that the difference between Charles's height and haircut and that of the shooter as described by eyewitness Charles Ball gave some jurors reasonable doubt.

Emily Gelb lives over two hours outside of New York City and there was no way she could have made it to court in time to hear the verdict or to watch Charles's reaction. It was up to Dennis Quirk to call her and relay the disappointing news. When she heard the result—that her brother's murder wasn't avenged—Emily was devastated. She cried out in pain. Why did she have to relive this terrible part of her life again, only to have no closure? The question would swirl through Emily's confused and tormented mind for weeks.

For days, Emily was inconsolable. She couldn't speak. Her husband, David, had to handle all of the news media telephone calls. The one ray of hope was that she might get a chance to speak when the killer was sentenced.

Epilogue

The sentencing of Charles Carneglia wasn't the only big Mob story in New York on September 17, 2009. Across the East River in Manhattan federal court, John A. Gotti, who for years had been Charles's overseer in the Gambino crime family, was on trial for the fourth time as the FBI tried to nail him for racketeering. Some of the same witnesses who had been arrayed against Charles—Michael DiLeonardo and John Alite in particular—were also being used in the effort to put Junior Gotti away for life.

But in Brooklyn federal court, on this particular day, the families of Charles's murder victims weren't interested in Gotti's travails. They were lined up and waiting for their chance finally to tell Charles what they thought of him. Judge Weinstein had allowed relatives of those who were found by the verdict to have died at Charles's hand to talk about the impact of the deaths. This would include Emily Gelb, even though the jury had not found Charles guilty of her brother Albert's death. This would be her moment, as it was for the other family members, to get solace and continue the healing process caused by the senseless killings so long ago.

There wasn't going to be any mincing of words by Weinstein. Under federal sentencing guidelines, Charles Carneglia was facing life in prison without parole. He would remain defiant to the last. Defense attorneys Curtis Farber and Kelley Sharkey had filed papers saying he was a changed man and should only get a fifteen-year sentence.

As is customary in such situations, prosecutor Roger Burlingame spoke first, saying that Charles had led a profane life, with his only role in the Gambino crime family being to kill and dispose of bodies. While evidentiary rulings had hamstrung the prosecution's effort to bring up reference to acid baths in body disposal, such wasn't the case now.

"He relished the job," said Burlingame. "He desecrated the bodies of Gambino family victims by melting them in acid."

In so many ways, the day was for the families of the dead. The four daughters of slain armored-car driver Jose Delgado Rivera wanted the maximum sentence, and it fell to Mildred Delgado-Jimenez to address the court. She didn't hide her loathing of Charles Carneglia.

"I hate you with everything I have," she said, glancing at Charles.

For Emily Gelb, the day turned out to be one of healing. The jury deadlock over the death of her brother, Albert, had wounded her terribly. But now, standing in court with Evelyn Colon, another of Delgado Rivera's daughters, she felt a great strength. Behind Emily, packing the public gallery, were a mass of court officers who had steadfastly carried the torch for justice, as well as Emily's family and friends. Holding a framed photo of her brother, Emily then underwent the cathartic experience of speaking directly to Charles.

"Charles Carneglia, you have no soul. There is a darkness that surrounds you every day," said Emily. "My brother would ask to show you mercy, but I am not my brother. I ask that they lock you up in a cage fitting for the animal you are."

Relieved by her words, Emily and the rest of the courtroom spectators waited to see if Charles would say anything. Most Mob defendants opt not to speak. But Charles, his beard no longer trimmed but instead unruly like the day he was arrested, grabbed a microphone. As far as anyone could tell, there wasn't a single member of his family in court. True to form, he railed against the "rats," his old friends who had turned on him.

"Liar upon liar testified against me, and they all had cooperation agreements," said Charles. He then bemoaned the fact that the overwhelming body of evidence, and the lack of time given him to prepare, denied him a fair trial. He then sat down.

Judge Weinstein gave him life without parole. No surprise. Although the Gelb homicide didn't result in any verdict, Weinstein said that what the government did prove about that killing at trial was enough for him to consider it for sentencing. He also turned down a defense request that Charles Carneglia be able to spend time in a jail in the New York City area; spectators applauded. With that, Charles was taken by the U.S. Marshals from the courtroom.

* * *

U.S. Marshals had also been bringing Junior Gotti to and from court every day of his latest racketeering trial. Denied bail since his arrest in July 2008, it was a slimmer, paler Gotti who appeared in court each day. Gone was the beefy, menacing physique. His dark hair now flecked with gray, and wearing reading glasses, Gotti seemed like an accountant rather than an aging Mafioso. But after three embarrassing failures to get guilty verdicts earlier, prosecutors were confident they had Junior dead to rights, particularly with the kind of testimony they were getting from John Alite, the man who seemed so effective in helping them win the case against Charles Carneglia just a few months earlier.

From the kind of headlines it generated, the trial of Junior Gotti didn't fail to deliver on sensationalism. Prosecutors portrayed him as a monster who made his money in drugs, extortion, and murder. Defense attorney Charles Carnesi, as he did in previous trials, said Gotti was a changed man who saw the futility of the Mob life as he matured. While once seduced by his father's strong personality to enter *La Cosa Nostra,* Gotti saw that the only thing his father had in the end was a lonely death from cancer in a prison hospital, said Carnesi. This was the long-standing withdrawal defense that had worked so well in previous trials, but which had failed when Charles Carneglia tried it. The defense also denied Gotti's involvement in the murders charged in the new indictment.

The prosecution portrayed Gotti through one of its first witnesses as the callous killer of Danny Silva during a knife-fighting melee in the Silver Fox bar in 1983, something John Alite had talked about earlier with the FBI. Though the Silva killing wasn't part of the indictment, prosecutor Elie Honig brought it up through the

witness, as well as the death of one of the witnesses to
the Silva homicide and the shooting of Louis DiBono.
So by the time Alite took the stand, there were three
killings linked by the prosecution to Junior Gotti.

Alite's appearance as a witness against Gotti was seen
by many lawyers as being pivotal to the case, which had
thrice before frustrated the government. Rehashing
what he had told the jury in Charles's trial, Alite related
his own involvement in the Bruce Gotterup and George
Grosso murders, but saying that in each instance Gotti
had given him the approval. He also linked Gotti to
drug dealing and other crimes.

However, one thing in which Alite appeared to shift
his testimony from the Charles Carneglia trial was in
what he said about Victoria Gotti, the daughter of the
late Mob boss. In Charles's trial, Alite testified in such a
way that it seemed unmistakable that he and Victoria
were regularly winding up in bed together. But in the
Junior Gotti case, Alite said he and Victoria had "feelings" for each other, a sculpted answer that backed away
from any indication of a sexual relationship. Nevertheless, Alite testified consistently about Gotti's alleged involvement in the two charged murders, and some
journalists covering the trial privately thought the
former Gambino captain was in deep trouble.

But you can never tell with juries. When the jurors
started deliberating in Junior Gotti's case, the threat of
another deadlock loomed almost from the start of deliberations. The panel sent out signals that it couldn't
agree on anything, an astonishing development. Finally, on December 1, 2009, the jurors sent out a note
indicating they were hopelessly deadlocked. Judge
Castel declared a mistrial, and under a deal worked out
earlier with the government, Gotti was freed on bail

and allowed to go home to his family in Oyster Bay Cove. He had missed Thanksgiving but would have the chance to celebrate Christmas in his own bed. Gotti quipped with reporters about passing the hat around to get money to replace what had been drained by five years of legal battles.

Anonymous jurors who talked with news media afterward said the government's star witness, John Alite, had been a dud. Alite had too much incentive to lie and to shape the truth for his own purposes, the jurors said. He seemed to try and shift all of the blame to Gotti, who the panel members thought was being unfairly targeted. The basic split among the jurors seemed to be pretty evenly divided, with government faring slightly worse on the murder counts, they said. After four trials and so much money, it was best that the government leave Gotti alone, the jurors believed. Fought to a stalemate four times, the prosecution finally moved to dismiss the Gotti indictment in early 2010.

Both Charles Carneglia and John "Junior" Gotti had in their time played central roles in the waning days of the Gambino crime family. Charles wanted to be a member of the *borgata* as a way of being part of something that seemed to him noble and exciting. Life in the Mob gave him a sense of belonging, validated his worth. Junior Gotti came into the Mob through his father's machinations and with a sense of entitlement. His mother, Victoria, had fought with her spouse about the way her son had been brought into the Mob life. At one point during the marriage, she left, traveling to London. Her husband only discovered that she was gone when he noticed her treasured coffeepot, a fixture on the kitchen counter, was gone. But the older Gotti wanted to project himself through his son, and the problems it caused in the house didn't do much to dissuade him. It seemed, as Charles Carneglia would later remark, to be plain old nepotism.

While Senior Gotti brought a flair to the job as crime boss, history shows that he wasn't a good manager and failed to prepare for contingencies. Gotti failed to appreciate that the government would not only take him out but also those whom he wanted to succeed him. By putting his son in a leadership position, he exposed his own flesh and blood to possible reprisals and the full weight of the FBI. The racketeering laws were such a potent weapon that much of the Mob leadership was at risk whenever a big indictment came down. Charles might have made the elder Gotti dangerous on the street by allowing him to extend his power in deadly ways. But both Charles and Gotti were no match for the way law enforcement had evolved. The threat of life sentences, the lack of allegiance to their fellow criminals, the shredding of the Old World Mafia code of silence, meant that modern-day Mafiosi would easily become government witnesses. Charles could cry as much as he wanted to outside Carosello's about the good old days of the Mob, but those days were gone.

It is ironic. Charles was the willing Mob acolyte who, as the evidence showed, killed and eradicated his victims as if it was his special calling. He winds up spending life in prison. Junior Gotti, the somewhat reluctant prince he once disdained, gets a second chance at life and is free to go where he pleases. Charles toiled in the shadows as the lonely, sadistic, and ghoulish killer. Junior Gotti lived as a mobster in the glow of his father's notoriety. Yet, as the jurors in Gotti's case indicated, the constant publicity about the continuing prosecutions might have given him the image of a man unfairly persecuted. The name Gotti may have actually worked to his advantage through all of this. There is a lesson in that for the government.

Charles was moved to the Canaan federal penitentiary in May 2010, a high-security facility located about 134 miles north of Philadelphia. The one thing he looked forward to each day was a call back home to Howard Beach, usually around 11:00 A.M. if he could manage it, so that he could speak to Jennie.

Where Are They Now?

As of March 1, 2011

John Alite (former Gambino associate): Alite, a key witness against Charles Carneglia and John A. Gotti, has yet to be sentenced for his guilty plea to various federal crimes. He is expected to be a prosecution witness in the case of *United States* v. *Burke, et al*, in Brooklyn federal court.

Roger Burlingame (prosecutor): After serving as lead prosecutor of Charles Carneglia and securing his conviction, Burlingame was promoted in February 2010 to head of the official corruption unit (OCU) in the Brooklyn U.S. Attorney's Office.

Charles Carneglia (Gambino soldier): Following his conviction in March 2009, Charles Carneglia was sentenced to life in prison. He appealed his conviction but the U.S. Court of Appeals for the Second Circuit in New York affirmed the verdict in 2010. He is currently serving his sentence in the United States Penitentiary in Canaan, Pennsylvania. He declined to be interviewed for this book.

Jennie Carneglia (mother): The retired seamstress died on September 26, 2010, at the age of ninety-six.

John Carneglia (brother): A soldier in the Gambino crime family, John Carneglia is serving a fifty-year sentence for heroin trafficking, in Allenwood Federal Correctional Complex in White Deer, Pennsylvania. He is due to be released in August 2018. His wife and family still live in Howard Beach.

Joseph Corozzo Sr. (Gambino *consigliere*): Joseph Corozzo is serving a sentence in Fort Dix, New Jersey, and is scheduled to be released in June 2011.

Nicholas Corozzo (Gambino captain): Nicholas Corozzo is serving an eleven-year sentence in Florence federal penitentiary in Colorado and is set to be released in March 2020.

Michael "Mikey Scars" DiLeonardo (former Gambino captain): After testifying in numerous federal trials against the likes of Charles Carneglia, John A. Gotti, and Dominick Pizzonia, DiLeonardo is no longer in the federal witness protection program.

Curtis Farber (defense attorney): Farber still has an active New York City criminal defense practice and has offices in Lower Manhattan.

Emily Gelb (sister of murder victim): Emily still maintains close ties to the fellow court officers of her slain

brother Albert. Once a year, Emily, who lives outside
the New York City area, makes an appearance at a special day when the court officers association honors em-
ployees. In 2009, she accepted on behalf of her brother
his posthumous award for heroism given by the New
York State Unified Court System.

Eugene Gotti (Gambino soldier): The brother of the late
Gambino boss John Gotti, Gene is serving the same fifty-
year sentence for drug trafficking as John Carneglia, at
the United States Penitentiary in Pollock, Louisiana.
He is scheduled for release in September 2018.

John A. Gotti (former Gambino captain and acting
boss): The son of the late Mob boss, John J. Gotti,
Junior endured four federal racketeering trials in Manhattan between 2005 and 2009. In each case, the jury
couldn't agree on a verdict, resulting in mistrials.
Gotti's defense was that he had withdrawn from Mob
life, a tactic some jurors in his trials said they found convincing. He is living on Long Island with his wife, Kim,
and their six children. Gotti said he wants to move away
from New York. In April 2010, he gave an interview that
appeared on the CBS news program *60 Minutes*. He has
denied allegations by various cooperating witnesses that
he took part in murders or murder conspiracies.

Victoria Gotti (mother of John A. Gotti): Victoria lives
in the same house in Howard Beach she bought with
her husband, the late crime boss John Gotti, in the
1970s. After federal prosecutors dropped the charges
against her son following a fourth mistrial, she began to
tend to her painting, an activity she abandoned while
her son was still under indictment. She continues to

speak out with contempt about the way prosecutors used John Alite as a witness against her son.

Victoria Gotti Agnello (sister of John A. Gotti): The celebrity daughter of the late crime boss, Victoria continues to write, and in 2009 published the book *This Family of Mine: What It Was Like Growing Up Gotti.*

Greg Hagarty (FBI special agent): Hagarty continues to work for the FBI in New York. In 2009, he was assigned to be part of the team investigating historic Ponzi schemer Bernard Madoff. Prior to that, he served about three months as part of an FBI team assigned to Afghanistan, returning in time to testify at the trial of Charles Carneglia.

Steve Kaplan (investigator): After retiring from the NYPD, Kaplan took a position with the Brooklyn U.S. Attorney's Office as an investigator specializing in organized crime cases. He remains extremely busy.

Kevin McMahon (former Gambino associate): After testifying against Charles Carneglia and for the defense in the 2009 trial of John A. Gotti, he was sentenced to time served for various federal crimes to which he pleaded guilty. He is expected to testify as a prosecution witness in the case of *United States* v. *Burke, et al,* in Brooklyn federal court.

Evan Norris (prosecutor): Norris continues to work as a prosecutor with the Brooklyn U.S. Attorney's Office.

Vincent Rossetti (former Bonanno associate): After testifying against Charles Carneglia, Rossetti was sentenced in 2010 in Brooklyn federal court to five years' probation.

Yvonne Rossetti (wife of Vincent): After pleading guilty in 2009 to scamming investors, Yvonne was sentenced to five years' probation by Brooklyn federal judge Raymond Dearie. At sentencing, Dearie took into consideration her cooperation in a Bonanno crime family extortion case and the chronic illness of her daughter Jessica. She no longer lives in Howard Beach.

Anthony Ruggiano (former Gambino associate): Ruggiano remains in the witness security program and has yet to be sentenced for his federal crimes.

Jodi Ryan (friend): Ryan continues to live in the Howard Beach area. She also believes that Charles Carneglia was railroaded.

Marisa Megur Seifan (prosecutor): Seifan remains working as a prosecutor with the Brooklyn U.S. Attorney's Office.

Kelley Sharkey (defense attorney): Sharkey maintains an active criminal law practice in New York City with an office in downtown Brooklyn.

Jack B. Weinstein (federal judge): Weinstein is the oldest senior judge in Brooklyn federal court and has shown no signs of wanting to retire, turning out long, intricate, and often provocative decisions that have been the hallmark of his judicial career. He likes to spend his lunch hours walking around Brooklyn Heights.

Peter Zuccaro (former Gambino associate): Zuccaro has testified numerous times in federal court, including the trials of John A. Gotti and Dominick Pizzonia, as well as Charles Carneglia. He is awaiting sentence for his federal crimes.

Chapter Notes

Introduction: The opening quotation was provided by a confidential news source. Information about Charles Carneglia's early years was taken from the testimony in *United States* v. *Charles Carneglia*, 08-cr-76 (EDNY), as well as the author's visit to the East New York section of Brooklyn. The opinions about Charles's emotional make-up are derived in part from the testimony at his above-cited trial, as were the details of his involvement and initiation into the Mafia. The allegations of criminal conduct such as the murders and disposal of bodies are also derived from the records of *United States* v. *Charles Carneglia*. A number of old friends of Charles's were interviewed who attempted to provide insight into his character and family life to balance the image he had as a result of his criminal history. Charles himself did not consent to be interviewed for this book, telling a friend that such publicity couldn't help him.

1. "What's with the Beard?" Details about the raid on Charles's home were obtained from an interview of Special Agent Greg Hagarty, which was approved by FBI public information officials, as well as the statements of the investigator Steve Kaplan filed in *United States* v. *Charles Carneglia*. Kaplan also testified at Charles's trial about the day he arrested him. Hagarty also testified in *United States* v. *Charles Carneglia* about the 2000 arrest of Charles. Quotes attributed to Charles were taken from Kaplan's statements, as were events during the arrest processing at Federal Plaza in Manhattan. A list of others arrested and charged in the case were obtained from the records of *Unites States* v. *Joseph Agate*, 08-cr-76 (EDNY), the companion case to the one brought against Charles. For clarity, the notes in this section will generally refer to the case file pertaining to Charles and will cite to his name in the case caption.

2. "Alby Is Dead." Quotations attributed to Peter Zuccaro and his life history come from his testimony in *United States* v. *Charles Carneglia*. Details about the events at the Esquire diner come not only from Zuccaro's testimony but also that of Lynn Baranello. Charles's criminal history is contained in federal court records. Dennis Quirk and Queens DA Richard Brown were interviewed by the author about the night Albert Gelb was shot dead. Further details about Gelb's death were obtained from the testimony of David Vartian in *United States* v. *Charles Carneglia*. Emily Gelb, the sister of Albert, was interviewed by the author. The funeral of Albert Gelb was also described in an article in the *New York Times*.

3. The Bergin Crew The author covered the trial of Ronell Wilson and is familiar with the facts and circumstances of the death penalty case. The concern in Ozone Park among friends of Charles over the death of Gelb was indicated by testimony in *United States* v. *Charles Carneglia*. Dennis Quirk gave the author a number of telephone interviews about Gelb's death. Details about John Gotti's early family life were derived from his daughter Victoria's book, *This Family of Mine: What It Was Like Growing Up Gotti*, as well as Selwyn Raab's *Five Families*. The history of Carmine and Daniel Fatico is contained in several articles from the *New York Times*, as well as records in *United States* v. *Carmine Fatico and Daniel Fatico*, 579 F. 2d 707 (1978) and *People* v. *Eddie De Curtis, et al*, 324 N.Y.S. 2d 406 (1971). Details about the 1976 federal hjjacking case are contained in articles of the *Daily News* (NY) and the *New York Times*. The docket of *United States* v. *John Carneglia, et al*, 76-cr-46 (EDNY) provided details of the disposition of the hijack case against Charles and his brother, John. The results of the 1976 gun possession trial of Charles are contained in *People of the State of New York* v. *Charles Carneglia*, 63 A.D. 2d 734 (1978). Retired FBI agent Steve Morrill was interviewed by the author. Details of the Cotillo stabbing come from testimony in *United States* v. *Charles Carneglia* 08-cr-76 (EDNY). The ownership records of the Carneglia family property are contained in the files of the New York City Department of Finance. Information about the drug dealing of earlier Mafia members is found in *New York State Joint Legislative Committee on Crime, Its Causes, Control and Effect on Society, Report for 1970, September 1970*. Details about the suspected drug dealing of members of the Bergin crew, the federal indictments of John Gotti and John Carneglia are contained in articles of the *New York Times*. Kevin McMahon's testimony is found in *United States* v. *Charles*

Carneglia, 08-cr-76 (EDNY). Former FBI supervisory special agent Bruce Mouw was interviewed by the author.

4. Father's Day Details about the summer 1989 gathering of John Carneglia and his friends, as well as the words spoken by the guests, are found in a video recording submitted into evidence in *United States* v. *Charles Carneglia*, 08-cr-76 (EDNY). Details about the illegal dealings of Hunter Adams and Michael Reiter are also found in the testimony and records of the Carneglia case, just cited. A summary of the homicide case against John Gotti for the McBratney killing is found in Raab's *Five Families*, as well as John H. Davis's *Mafia Dynasty: The Rise and Fall of the Gambino Crime Family*. The final surrender in 1989 of John Carneglia and Gene Gotti is found in articles of the *New York Times*.

5. The Albanian Details about the life and times of John Alite, as well as his statements about his relationship with John A. Gotti and the alleged crimes they did together, are found in Alite's testimony in *United States* v. *Charles Carneglia*, 08-cr-76 (EDNY). Alite's description to the FBI of confrontations he had with John J. Gotti are contained in government records. Alite's description to the FBI of confrontations he had with others in the Gambino crime family are also contained in government records.

6. The Weasel Details about the early life and growing up of Kevin McMahon come from his testimony in *United States* v. *Charles Carneglia*, 08-cr-76 (EDNY). The photographs of his wedding were submitted into evidence in the just cited trial. McMahon's testimony about the slaying of Louis DiBono, the armored-car robberies, the stabbing of Sal Puma, and his relationship with Charles all come from his testimony in the Carneglia trial. Zuccaro's recollection of events in the armored-car robberies also comes from his testimony in the Carneglia trial, cited earlier in this note. Events surrounding the death of Frankie Gotti have been widely reported in various books and newspaper articles, but the remarks made by his mother, Victoria, as the child lay dying are contained in the book by her daughter, also named Victoria, *This Family of Mine*. The grief of the Gotti family was reported to the author in interviews with various sources from the Howard Beach community, as well as from *This Family of Mine*. John A. Gotti's comment about his father's probable involvement in the death of John Favara came from his April 11, 2010, interview on *60 Minutes*. McMahon's story about the acid bath disposal of Favara's body came from his testimony in the Carneglia trial, cited in this note. Federal prosecutors also alleged other uses of acid by Charles to dispose of bodies in court filings. Information about the Adolph L. Luetgert trial for killing his wife and disposing of her with acid comes from Internet research, as do details about British killer John George Haigh. The *New York Times* reported a story in 2009 about the use of acid by Mexican drug cartel killers to dispose of bodies, and the development in the funeral industry of the process of alkaline hydrolysis comes from industry Web sites and news reports. McMahon's description of the use of acid by Charles to torture two or three young men also comes from his testimony in *United States* v. *Charles Carneglia*.

7. "A Sad State" The author was present for part of the evening on Mulberry Street the night in December 1990 when John J. Gotti was arrested but didn't actually witness the arrest. A fuller description of events taking place during the arrest is contained in Howard Blum's book *Gangland: How the FBI Broke the Mob.* Bruce Mouw also gave the author an interview about the night of the arrest. The effects of the Gotti arrest within the Gambino crime family have been widely reported in New York City newspapers, as well as in proceedings in *United States* v. *John Gotti, et al,* 90-cr-TK (EDNY). The death of Bobby Borriello was reported in the *New York Times,* while information about the sauce he was carrying came from a person who was with him during the evening. Details about Borriello and Preston Geritano's ties to the Gallo Gang were given to the author by a confidential source who was familiar with the gang's operation. Events in the aftermath of Borriello's death come from the author's personal observation of the funeral.

Kevin McMahon also testified in *United States* v. *Charles Carneglia* about Charles's actions after Borriello was killed. Details about the federal civil lawsuit over the stolen car operation allegedly involving Charles's Fountain Avenue property are contained in the case file of *United States* v. *All Assets of Statewide Auto Parts, Inc., et al,* 91-cv-4494 (EDNY). Information about John A. Gotti's rise to a leadership role in the Gambino crime family was reported in the *New York Times* and other newspapers. Michael DiLeonardo's testimony about events surrounding an alleged murder conspiracy involving Charles and others in Brooklyn comes from his testimony in the Charles Carneglia trial. John Alite's recollection about John A. Gotti accidentally shooting McMahon and the aftermath was given during his interview with the FBI. Alite's description of his falling-out with Gotti came from his testimony in various federal trials. Bruce Mouw's remark about the terrible state of the Gambino family was reported in the *New York Times*. Nicholas Corozzo's arrests were reported in the *New York Times*, as was the arrests and 1999 guilty plea of John A. Gotti.

8. "He's a Rat." Hunter Adams's relationship with Charles is described in the testimony of *United States* v. *Charles Carneglia*, 08-cr-76 (EDNY). Details about the Forbidden Fruit and Cherry Video extortion cases are found in *United States* v. *Charles Carneglia, et al*, 00-cr-638 (EDNY), *United States* v. *Charles Carneglia and Salvatore Scala*, 47 Fed. Appx. 27, United States Court of Appeals for the Second Circuit (2002), *Charles Kline* v. *United States*, 02-cv-6398 (EDNY), and *Charles Carneglia* v. *United States*, 03-cv-6388 (EDNY). Kevin McMahon's recollection of his falling-out with Charles comes from his testimony in one of the Charles Carneglia trials cited earlier in this note. John Alite's fugitive status and capture were reported in the *Daily News* (NY) and the *Sun-Sentinel* (FL). The experience of Alite and McMahon in the Florida indictment are contained in the files of *United States* v. *Ronald Trucchio, et al*, 04-cr-348 (MDFL). The confrontation between Alite and McMahon in prison is found in their testimony in the Carneglia trial previously cited. McMahon's early approaches to the FBI were described by a confidential law enforcement source.

9. Code Name "Zipper" Charles's activities after he was released from prison were the subject of testimony in *United States* v. *Charles Carneglia*, 08-cr-76 (EDNY). The sequence of investigations that ultimately led to the 2008

Gambino crime family indictment was described to the author by Assistant U.S. Attorney Burton Ryan. Details about the charges and guilty pleas involving the Scalamandre brothers come from federal court records in *United States* v. *Joseph and Fred Scalamandre,* 01-cr-1230 (EDNY) and government news releases. Joseph Vollaro's criminal history and his interaction with Gambino crime family members is found in various court filings in *United States* v. *Joseph Agate,* 08-cr-76 (EDNY). A description of the marijuana operation involving Peter Zuccaro and Angelo Ruggiero Jr. is found in *United States* v. *Angelo S. Ruggiero,* 05-cr-196 (EDNY). Lewis Kasman's becoming a cooperating witness was detailed in documents turned over by the FBI during pretrial proceedings in the Charles Carneglia trial cited earlier. Information about John A. Gotti's various mistrials comes from the author's notes and articles in *Newsday.* The February 7, 2008, Gambino crime family arrests were widely reported in all New York City newspapers. See also the case file and filings in *United States* v. *Joseph Agate,* previously cited.

10. The Letter Jodi Ryan's testimony occurred in *United States* v. *Charles Carneglia,* 08-cr-76 (EDNY).

11. Let's Make a Deal. Judge Nicholas Garaufis's handling of the case of Vincent Basciano is found in the author's notes and court filings. The issue surrounding the random assignment of the Gambino family indictment is spelled out in the filings of *United States* v. *Joseph Agate,* 08-cr-76 (EDNY). The author also attended court for the disqualification hearing involving attorney Joseph Corozzo. Details about Judge Jack B. Weinstein's handling of the Gambino case are found in various court filings related to the indictment, especially the Charles Carneglia trial cited earlier.

12. Soup Bones The description of the use of acid by Charles comes from the statements of cooperating witnesses filed in *United States* v. *Charles Carneglia*, 08-cr-76.

13. "His Executioner" The trial of Charles Carneglia is contained in the transcript of *United States* v. *Charles Carneglia*, 08-cr-76 (EDNY) and the author's notes.

14. "John Loved Tough Guys." Michael DiLeonardo's testimony is found in the record of *United States* v. *Charles Carneglia*, 08-cr-76 (EDNY).

15. Wanting Hunk Peter Zuccaro's testimony is found in the record of *United States* v. *Charles Carneglia*, 08-cr-76 (EDNY).

16. "Worm" Gets Ripped Vincent Rossetti's testimony is found in the record of *United States* v. *Charles Carneglia*, 08-cr-76 (EDNY). Details about Yvonne Rossetti's legal troubles can be found in various filings in *United States* v. *Michael Cassese*, 06-cr-800 (EDNY).

17. The "Body Shop" Kevin McMahon's testimony is found in the record of *United States* v. *Charles Carneglia*, 08-cr-76 (EDNY).

18. "I'm Honest." John Alite's testimony is found in the record of *United States* v. *Charles Carneglia*, 08-cr-76 (EDNY). The reaction of Victoria Gotti and her daughter Victoria to Alite's claim of infidelity with the younger woman were reported in the *Daily News* (NY) and the *New York Post*.

19. "He's the Same Criminal." The testimony and closing arguments in the trial of Charles Carneglia can be found in the record of *United States* v. *Charles Carneglia*, 08-cr-76 (EDNY). The reactions to the verdict by Dennis Quirk and the family of Jose Delgado Rivera were reported in the *Daily News* (NY) and the *New York Post*. Emily Gelb's reaction was told to the author by her in a telephone interview and e-mail correspondence.

Epilogue Comments made during the sentencing of Charles Carneglia were reported in the *Daily News* (NY), *Newsday,* and the *New York Post.* The 2009 trial of John A. Gotti was reported in those three daily newspapers. The author also covered the declaration of the mistrial and interviewed some jurors.

Acknowledgments

When writing books about the Mob, an author usually finds that there are people who are happy to be acknowledged in print for their help, while others, for a variety of reasons, prefer to be thanked privately. My experience in writing this book about Charles Carneglia, the man who helped make the late John Gotti dangerous, was no different. There are those I can thank openly, while others will have to remain secret sources. Some still live in Howard Beach and still fear the power of the Mob.

I did ask Charles Carneglia after his federal conviction in 2009 if he would grant me an interview to talk about his life. He declined, and I must admit that I didn't really expect him to say yes. Through an intermediary, he said that talking to the press now wouldn't do him any good. So be it.

Among those I would like to thank is Gary Goldstein, my editor at Kensington. It was Gary who approached me in 2004 with the idea of doing a book about ex–Bonanno boss Joseph Massino, which became, in hardcover, *The Last Godfather*, to be followed by paperback versions entitled *King of the Godfathers*. The Massino book became popular in the Mob true crime genre and raised my profile. After Charles was convicted, something in the story led

Gary to push the idea of a book, and over a number of months the idea finally came together, leading me to tackle a complex subject that spanned decades of Mafia history. (While some purists will say that the term "Mafia" signifies the Italian-based crime syndicates and *"La Cosa Nostra"* refers to the American-grown variation, the terms have acquired meanings that are interchangeable in popular culture, so I often use them that way.)

Among those in law enforcement whom I want to thank are Robert Nardoza, chief spokesman for the Brooklyn U.S. Attorney's Office, and James Margolin, a spokesman for the New York FBI Office. Also to be thanked are Assistant U.S. Attorney Roger Burlingame and paralegal Shernita Moore, of the Brooklyn U.S. Attorney's Office, for helping me get my hands on the voluminous public records filed in the case of *United States* v. *Charles·Carneglia*. Also meriting special thanks is investigator Steve Kaplan and FBI special agent Greg Hagarty.

Defense attorney Curtis Farber and Kelley Sharkey were generous with their time, answering questions during and after Charles's trial, giving tantalizing bits of perspective that have worked their way into this story.

A number of retired law enforcement officials also helped in piecing together the story: John Goode, Steve Morrill, and Bruce Mouw, all ex-FBI, and Joseph Coffey, the former NYPD detective. Over the years, another ex-FBI agent, Phil Scala, who supervised the Gambino squad after Mouw retired from that position, gave critical perspective about the Mob and the crime family.

Defense attorneys are often fonts of information and anecdotes, and for that I would like to thank Frank Bari, Joseph Benfante, Charles Carnesi, Joseph DiBenedetto, James DiPietro, Steven K. Frankel, Susan Kellman, Jeffrey Lichtman, John Meringolo, Murray Richman, Michael Rosen, and Joel Winograd. I also want to thank private investigator Jerry Gardner for his terrific memory about events in the trial of John A. Gotti in 2009.

In writing this book, I relied on the published works of a number of writers and journalists. They are Stewart Ain, Joseph Berger, James Bone (UK), Jimmy Breslin, Leonard Buder, Jerry Capeci, Larry Celona, Katie Cornell, Alison Gendar, Bruce Golding, Charles Grutzner, Tommy Hallissey, Tom Hays, Bill Hutchinson, Marvine Howe, Umberto Lucentini (Italy), John Marzulli, Larry McShane, Thomas Morgan, Alexandra Mosca, Gene Mustain, Selwyn Raab, William K. Rashbaum, John Riley, Max H. Seigel, Pervaiz Shallwani, Don Singleton, and Benjamin Weiser.

I also would like to note an interesting article on forensic anthropology posted on the Internet by Michael Kelleher that included details about the murder case against Adolph Luetgert, who, police said, dissolved his wife in acid in Chicago during the latter part of the nineteenth century. His article led me to others about the fascinating and gruesome process.

During the trials of John A. Gotti, his family members were accessible and courteous. Thanks go to his mother, Victoria, sisters Victoria and Angel, as well as his younger brother, Peter.

I also want to thank my former editor at *Newsday*, John Mancini, for allowing me to do this book, and then-metro editor Rosemary McManus for helping me through the clearance process.

Susan helped me through some computer hurdles, and Mousse, the wandering poodle, gave me enough diversion to help me through the writing process.

Finally I would like to thank my agent, Jill Marsal, for once again helping me through the process of seeing this book wind its way over the long road from an idea to a completed work.

Bibliography

Books:

Blum, Howard. *Gangland: How the FBI Broke the Mob*. New York: Simon & Schuster, 1993.

Blumenthal, Ralph. *Last Days of the Sicilians: The FBI's War Against the Mafia*. New York: Times Books, 1988.

Capeci, Jerry, and Mustain, Gene. *Gotti*. New York: Penguin Books, USA, Inc., 1996.

Davis, John H. *Mafia Dynasty: The Rise and Fall of the Gambino Crime Family*. New York: HarperPaperbacks, 1993.

DeStefano, Anthony M., *King of the Godfathers: "Big Joey" Massino and the Fall of the Bonanno Crime Family*. New York: Citadel Press, 2008.

Gotti, Victoria. *This Family of Mine: What It Was Like Growing Up Gotti*. New York: Pocket Books, 2009.

Jackson, Kenneth T. *The Encyclopedia of New York City*. New Haven, CT: Yale University Press, 1994.

Maas, Peter. *The Valachi Papers*. New York: Bantam Books, 1968.

————. *Underboss: Sammy the Bull Gravano's Story of Life in the Mafia*. New York: HarperCollins Publishers, Inc, 1997.

O'Brien, Joseph F., and Kurins, Andris. *Boss of Bosses: The Fall of the Godfather: The FBI and Paul Castellano*. New York: Simon & Schuster, 1991.

Raab, Selwyn. *Five Families: The Rise, Decline, and Resurgence of America's Most Powerful Mafia Empires*. New York: Thomas Dunne Books, 2005.

Sciacca, Tony. *Luciano: The Man Who Modernized the American Mafia*. New York: Pinnacle, 1975.

Court documents and cases:

Charles Carneglia v. *United States*, 03-cv-6388, United States District Court for the Eastern District of New York.

Charles Kline v. *United States*, 02-cv-6398, United States District Court for the Eastern District of New York.

People of the State of New York v. *Charles Carneglia*, 63 A.D. 2d 734 (1978).

People of the State of New York v. *Eddie DeCurtis, et al.,* 324 N.Y.S. 2d 406 (1971).

United States v. *Joseph Agate, et al.,* 08-cr- 76, United States District Court for the Eastern District of New York.

United States v. *All Assets of Statewide Auto Parts, Inc. et al.,* 971 F. 2d 896, United States Court of Appeals for the Second Circuit. (1992)

United States v. *All Assets of Statewide Auto Parts, Inc., et al.,* 91-cv-4494, United States District Court for the Eastern District of New York.

United States v. *Vincent Basciano,* 05-cr-60, United States District Court for the Eastern District of New York.

United States v. *John A. Burke, et al.,* 09-cr-135, United States District Court for the Eastern District of New York.

United States v. *Charles Carneglia and Salvatore Scala,* 47 Fed. Appx. 27, United States Court of Appeals for the Second Circuit. (2002)

United States v. *Charles Carneglia,* 00-cr-638, United States District Court for the Eastern District of New York.

United States v. *John Carneglia, 70-cr-707,* United States District Court for the Eastern District of New York.

United States v. *John Carneglia, et al.,* 76-cr-46, United States District Court for the Eastern District of New York.

United States v. *Daniel Fatico, et al.,* 579 F2d. 707, United States Court of Appeals for the Second Circuit. (1978)

United States v. *John A. Gotti,* 04-cr-690, United States District Court for the Southern District of New York.

United States v. *John A. Gotti,* 08-cr-1220, United States District Court for the Southern District of New York.

United States v. *John Gotti, et al.,* 85-cr-178, United States District Court for the Eastern District of New York.

United States v. *John Gotti, et al.,* 90-cr-1051. United States District Court for the Eastern District of New York.

United States v. *Joseph Massino,* 02-cr-307, United States District Court for the Eastern District of New York.

United States v. *Angelo S. Ruggiero,* 05-cr-196, United States District Court for the Eastern District of New York.

United States v. *Joseph and Fred Scalamandre,* 01-cr-1230, United States District Court for the Eastern District of New York.

United States v. *Ronald Trucchio, et al.,* 04-cr-348, United States District Court for the Middle District of Florida, Tampa Division.

United States v. *Michael Virtuoso, et al.,* 06-cr-800, United States District Court for the Eastern District of New York.

United States v. *Peter Zuccaro, et al.,* 05-cr-196, United States District Court for the Eastern District of New York.

Government publications:

City of New York, Department of Investigation, "New York Construct Contractors Plead Guilty to Mob Payoffs and Fraud Schemes Totaling 40 Million Dollars," November 14, 2001. (news release)

New York State Joint Legislative Committee on Crime, Its Causes, Control and Effect on Society, Report for 1970, September 1970.

U.S. Department of Transportation, Office of Inspector General, "Guilty Pleas in Multimillion FHWA and FTA Contract Fraud Case," November 14, 2001. (news release)

Newspapers consulted:

Daily News (NY)

La Repubblica (Italy)

Newsday (Long Island)

New York Newsday

New York Post

New York Times

Sun-Sentinel (Florida)

The Chief (New York)

The Times (London)

Web sites consulted:

http://watercourses.typepad.com

www.fbi.gov

www.Lexis.com

www.msnbc.com

www.nycourts.gov

www.Nexis.com

www.Salon.com

www.usdoj.gov/usao.nye (U.S. Attorney's Office, Eastern District of New York)

www.wikipedia.com